No. 1776
$26.95

Programming with
dBASE II®

By Cary N. Prague & James E. Hammitt

TAB BOOKS Inc.
BLUE RIDGE SUMMIT, PA. 17214

FIRST EDITION

FIRST PRINTING

Copyright © 1984 by TAB BOOKS Inc.

Printed in the United States of America

Library of Congress Cataloging in Publication Data

Prague, Cary N.
Programming with dBASE II.

Includes index.
1. dBase II (Computer program)   2. Data base manage-
ment.   I. Hammitt, James E.   II. Title.   III. Title:
Programming with dBASE Two.   IV. Title: Programming with
dBASE 2.
QA76.9.D3P727   1984   001.64'25   84-119
ISBN 0-8306-0776-5
ISBN 0-8306-1776-0 (pbk.)

dBASE II® is a registered trademark of Ashton-Tate.

Contents

Preface   **vi**

Section I   PROGRAMMING FUNDAMENTALS   **1**

1   The Basics of Programming   **2**
Data Versus Information—Data Types—Variables—Literals—Statements—Statement Types

2   Developing Programs   **5**
The Business Problem—Defining the Problem—Defining the Output—Documentation and Design—
Defining the Input—Defining the Process

3   Mapping the Process   **8**
Flowcharting—Pseudocoding

4   Designing Processes   **13**
Designing the Process—Function Charting—Fundamentals of a Good Program—The EZ2s of
Programming—Styles of Programming—Selection Menus—Data Entry Screens—Editing Data—Error
Messages—Some Typical Processes —Summary

5   The Workings of Language   **20**
Types of Statements—Using Logical Constructs in Process Design—Comparisons—Using the DO
WHILE Statement—The CASE Figure—Checking Out Your Pseudocode

6   Coding, Testing, and Debugging   **30**
Documentation—Making Sure the Program Will Work—Designing Data

7 Business Considerations   34

Large Versus Small—Administrative Automation—Interactive Programming

8 Fred's Friendly Fish Market   37

Problem Definition—Defining the Output Data—Two Things at Once—Reexamining the Design—Fred
Divides to Conquer—Designing Screens—A Menu System—The Functions—The Subfunctions

9 Fred Gets Ambitious   53

The Problem Definition—The Output Definition—The Input Definition—A Two File System—The Function
Hierarchy—The Add Order Function—The Change Order Function—The Remove Order Function—The
Display Order Function—The Print Order Form Function—The Print Shipping Label Function—The
Inventory System—Summary

Section II   DATABASE FUNDAMENTALS   83

10 What Is a Database?   84

Database Structures

11 Creating and Using the Database Structure   89

Designing the Database—Creating the Database—Using the Database—Viewing the Database
Structure—Changing the Database

12 Database Records   95

Adding Records—Displaying Records—Changing Records—Deleting Records

13 Sorting the Database   102

A New Order—Sorting the Database—Indexing the Database

14 Searching the Database—A Second Look   106

Compound Expressions—Displaying Selected Records—LOCATE—FIND—REPORT

15 Data Relations   115

Data Redundancy—Multiple Databases—Joining Multiple Databases—The REPORT Command Revisited

16 The Efficient Design and Use of Databases   127

Speed Versus Storage—Designing with Multiple Databases—Maintenance of Databases—Programming
and Databases

17 Fred's Friendly Fish Market Revisited   134

Fred and the Database Design—Fred Defines His Customer Database—Fred Defines His Order
Database—Fred Redesigns the Order Files—Fred Gets the Big Picture—Fred Remembers the Inventory
System—Fred Calculates His Storage Size

Section III   PROGRAMMING USING dBASE II   141

18 Re-examining Fred's Fish Markets Design   143

Creating the Databases—Indexing the Databases—Modifying Databases

19 dBASE II Programming Commands   149

Assignment Statements—Screen and Printer Output Commands—Screen Input Commands—Character,
String, and Numeric Commands—Comparison Operators and Logical Connectors—Logical Constructs
Used in dBase II—Database Commands Used in Programming —Summary

20 Coding Selection Menus   **163**
Setting the Environment—Coding the Selection Menus —Summary

21 Coding Data Entry Screens   **173**
Changing Records—Removing Records—Displaying Records

22 Customizing and Printing Reports   **194**
A Mailing Label Program—A Directory Program —Summary

23 Adding Records in a Two-File System   **205**
The Main Record—The Subsidiary Records

24 Producing Reports in a Multifile System   **216**
Multiple Files—Calculating and Totalling —Summary

Appendix A   The System Design   **224**

Appendix B   The Complete Programs   **250**

Appendix C   dBase II Database Commands Used in this Book   **277**

Appendix D   dBASE II Programming Commands Used in this Book   **278**

Index   **280**

Preface

dBASE II is a very powerful database language. It features user-friendly commands that are used to create database structures and to add, change, and delete data items. dBASE II also allows the operator to search for, select, and display records in the database. Reports can easily be designed and printed. For many users, these commands are sufficient to provide them with simple database queries and reports. Other users, however, would like to unlock the power of dBASE II as a programming language.

In the ever expanding world of microcomputers, dBASE II is quickly gaining popularity as a programming language. For many people it has replaced BASIC or PASCAL. In big business, it is even used as a replacement for COBOL, FORTRAN, and PL/1. dBASE II includes a full programming language that is capable of solving almost any data processing problem. Because of its use of specialized database techniques, dBASE II makes business programming easier than traditional languages do.

All normal programming techniques can be used with dBASE II including decision making, looping, sorting, searching, selecting, displaying, data manipulating, and custom reporting. Full screen selection and data entry menus are simple to design and implement. Many database programming commands can also be integrated into dBASE II programs. The programming environment can be established and housekeeping can be done with very simple commands. If a record description needs to be changed after the program is substantially complete, it is a simple task to change the program. It is not a complicated task as it is with nondatabase languages. Database query commands used to sort, search, and select records are also used as programming commands to replace many programming statements found in traditional languages. dBASE II is truly the fourth generation programming language for the eighties.

This book is written for the computer novice as well as the experienced programmer wishing to add a new language to his or her toolbox. The book will help both the weekend hacker and the businessman. It is expected that the reader is somewhat familiar with dBASE II and has at least created a database and produced simple reports. The novice will find this book a good introduction to programming concepts and database techniques. Experienced programmers will find the book a complete guide that will enable them to make the transition from whatever languages they already know to dBASE II.

The book is organized into three main sections; Programming Fundamentals, Database Fundamentals, and Programming with dBASE II. In each section, you will meet Fred. Fred owns a fish market and will help teach you to program. The Programming Fundamentals section covers a complete introduction to programming along with comparisons showing how dBASE II differs from traditional programming languages. The Database Fundamentals section explains what a database is and how to efficiently and effectively design and use databases. The final section, Programming with dBASE II, is subdivided into several chapters. Each chapter shows how to use dBASE II to perform a specific task. Each chapter presents the topic as a stand-alone subject and also integrates it with the previously discussed topics. This allows the reader to understand the programming topics as individual subjects and also to understand how they come together to form the complete program. After reading this book, both novice and expert will be prepared to design, code, and implement the solution to any problem using the dBASE II system.

Section I
Programming Fundamentals

Chapter 1

The Basics of Programming

Database programming is the use of specialized language statements to manipulate items of information. The purpose of this manipulation is to produce a desired result that is presented in the form of reports, graphs, or tables of information. The name that programmers give to unprocessed information is *data*.

DATA VERSUS INFORMATION

Simply stated, data is the raw form of information; that is, facts and figures that alone have very little or no meaning. The purpose of computer programs is to arrange data into more meaningful and/or useful forms.

For example, if you saw a list of numbers 199462482010454, the numbers appear totally meaningless. The list could be anything. However, when it is broken up slightly, the result is 199462482-010454. The list is still data; that is, no new information has resulted from that division.

If the number is broken into its smallest components, 199-46-2482-01-04-54, it appears, and I mean *appears*, to be a social security number and a date. If the data is now labeled

SNN   DATE
199-46-2482/01-04-54

you know something that was not known before; the meaningless *data* has become *information*. This example explains the difference between data and information.

DATA TYPES

Computer programming is the manipulation of data to form information. The data items that are manipulated can take two basic forms: *character* and *numeric*.

Character data includes things like names, addresses, telephone numbers, and any other items that are later reported in the same form that they are stored in. Character data items can be manipulated in some ways but cannot be used in mathematical calculations. For example, names can be stored in a last, first, middle order, but appear on a report in a "first middle last" format. The manipulation in this case involved the rearrangement of the characters that make up the data item. Any attempt to add, subtract, multiply, divide, or perform any other type of mathematical calculation using the name information would not only be meaningless, but would quite probably cause an error.

Numeric data is stored in a slightly different manner. This type of data can be reported as-is, or can be used in mathematical calculations. Numeric data items include dollar amounts, dates, counts of anything, or any other data item that is to be used in a calculation. Numeric information can be added to totals, averaged, or used in calculations to obtain another data item.

When character or numeric data items appear in computer programs they are called *expressions*, whether they are used alone or in combination with other data items. Expressions contain only one type of data. Using character data in a numeric expression is called *mixing modes* and is illegal in a program.

VARIABLES

Variables are "areas of storage" used in a program to hold data items. The use of variables is what gives the computer program its basic flexibility. Because of variables, computer programs can be written to work for any value that the variable can contain.

Variables can be thought of as buckets that hold the values that the program will use. In this manner, a program might refer to a variable called NAME, which can hold any value. Without knowing the exact contents, the NAME variable can be positioned on an output report, displayed as a title of section, or used for whatever function is needed. If the maximum length of the NAME variable is 25 characters, the program must allow for 25 characters in the *output* (the printed report or screen display in most cases).

As an example a *record* may contain a NAME (25 characters) and a PHONE number (10 characters). The first record on the file may read

CARY PRAGUE   2035557685

The second record may read

JIM HAMMITT   2035556281

Now, if the first record is requested, the value of NAME will be CARY PRAGUE and the value of PHONE will be 2035557685. If the purpose of the program is to print a name and phone number list, the program would first read a record, print the values of the variables NAME and (possibly with some modifications) PHONE, and then loop back to read the next record. By referring to NAME and PHONE, the program becomes general; that is, it works for any record that is set up in the same format with the same variable names (NAME and PHONE).

The ability to work with variables is the most useful feature of computers in general. Computers work with the values, but you, in your programming, do not.

The manipulation of variables is the most important function of computer programs, and the concept of variables is important to understanding the way programs work. When a variable is assigned a certain value, the value stays in that variable until it is either replaced with a new value or the program ends, which ever comes first. The only way to change the value of a variable is to place a new value into it. So, if you create a variable called TITLE to use as the title of your output report and never change it, you may use it throughout your program, and it will retain its value.

LITERALS

Another way a value can be used in a program is by the value itself appearing in the program. This type of value is called a *literal*, and cannot be manipulated by the program. A literal is inserted directly into the expression in which it is to be used.

Let's look at an example of an expression. The calculation that is necessary to convert Fahrenheit temperatures into Celcius temperatures is

$$C = (F - 32)*5/9$$

In this expression, the F and the C are variables; that is, they can have varying values. The 32, 5, and 9 are literals, because their values never change. In a mathematical expression like the one just used, the equal sign ($=$) is used to show equality between the left and right halves of the equation. In a computer language, such an equation is called an assignment statement and does not express equality. It tells the computer to take the value expressed on the right side of the statement and *place* it into the variable on the left side.

STATEMENTS

Computer languages are comprised of *statements* like the one mentioned in the previous paragraph. That statement is an assignment statement, because it assigns a new value to the variable C. No matter what value F has when that particular statement is executed, the calculation is performed using that value and the literal values. The result, the Celcius temperature, is placed into the variable

C. This procedure does not change the value of F, nor are the literals changed. Only the variable that is on the left side of the equals sign is changed. Most of the statements in a computer program are assignment statements.

The assignment statement in dBASE II assignment statement is

STORE [expression] TO variablename

The computation of Celcius temperature would then appear as:

STORE (F-32)*(5/9) TO CELCIUS

This form of the assignment is probably more readable than the traditional format shown in the previous paragraphs. It shows action occurring left-to-right: STORE value TO variable.

STATEMENT TYPES

There are generally four types of statements in a computer language. Apart from the assignment statement, there are decision statements, loop control statements, and input/output statements.

Computer language statements are used to cause action. Assignment statements cause new values to be assigned to variables: those new values can be the result of calculations. *Decision statements* can cause a section of statements to be executed or skipped over depending on the value of variables. *Loop statements* can cause a series of statements to be executed over and over until some condition occurs, such as a count exceeding a target value. *Input/output statements* cause the computer to copy information to or from some external device. Computer language statements always cause action of some type.

Chapter 2

Developing Programs

The result of all the actions taken in a computer program is the output. It was the need for the output that caused the program to be written in the first place. To assure that a computer program is written properly, every item of information that is required from that program must be defined before the program can be written. As with all problem solving methods, including the scientific method, the first step in finding the solution is to have an accurate definition of the problem. This is the first step in the seven-step problem solving method that will be used in creating a computer program. The seven steps are

1. Define the problem.
2. Define the output.
3. Define the input.
4. Determine the process.
5. Code the program.
6. Test the program.
7. Evaluate the program.

THE BUSINESS PROBLEM

A business problem occurs when the current way of performing some business-oriented activity can no longer produce acceptable results. This can happen for a variety of reasons: a reduction in manpower (personpower?), an increase in the workload, a need for instantaneous retrieval of information, or a need for a change in the way of doing things. In a company where the entire payroll is four persons, including the president, there is probably no need for a computer program to handle the payroll. If, however, that company expands to four hundred people, whatever method is used to process the payroll for the smaller group would probably be a seven-day-a-week job when performed for the larger group.

Another example of a problem that would make a small company need a computer: what if that company with four people on the payroll handles sales to two hundred companies with an inventory that runs into hundreds of thousands of dollars? Unless all four people are doing nothing but inventory control seven days a week, nothing could be shipped! Now, this example might be a little exaggerated, but it illustrates the point at which an automated method of handling the business could be necessary. Then, once the computer was installed and set up for inventory control, the payroll could be computerized if time and resources permit.

DEFINING THE PROBLEM

Whatever the business need, the correct first step in finding a solution to it is defining just what has to be done, when it has to be done, how much is to be done, etc. This overall statement of objective is necessary to keep the process of finding the solution on course, without troublesome wrong turns and side issues.

A problem definition should state why action is necessary, and just what is expected from any solution. A problem definition should also avoid precluding a solution by placing restrictions on how it is to be achieved. This means you should not include any mention of what tools are to be used to construct the final solution, whether computer-based or not.

It is also important to include a description of the expected results in the problem definition. The description should not be vague and should be as complete as possible. This description will help determine just what information is needed to produce the desired results. If a computer solution is to be implemented, extensive data entry work may be necessary to make the required information available to the computer system. Data entry time must also be taken into account when creating cost estimates of the new system.

A well-written problem definition will reduce the time spent on speculation; this will make the solution available faster.

DEFINING THE OUTPUT

The next step after completing the problem definition is to define the exact content of what the solution is to produce, in short, "define the output." Output is any product that is essential to solving the business problem. The output in a payroll system is the checks, reports to management about the hours worked, vacation and sick time reports, reports to the IRS, and the pay stubs. These are varied in form, and some, at least from an employee's point of view, seem irrelevant. However, each output form helps to solve a part of the total business problem. There might also be files to be kept for year-end reporting; these are also output.

A complete output definition would include a description of each data item to appear in the output. A proper description should include the data type (character or numeric), a name for each variable to be used, the length of the item, and its source, whether from an already existing file or through calculation. the necessity of this step should be apparent: without knowing the exact output specifications, it would be impossible to determine what input is needed. It is unlikely that all the input that a new computer system must use would be available in usable form. Problems of data entry must therefore also be considered. If existing files are to be used, are they available for use, and what format are they in? Consideration of these key points at this time can save time and sweat later.

DOCUMENTATION AND DESIGN

Once there is a complete, clearly-written definition of the problem, coupled with a complete, clearly-written set of specifications for the output, these two documents will be used as the basis for the rest of the problem solution. Any such important documents should be finished prior to coding any computer programs, the textbook writers will tell you. So why do most companies spend less time at these activities than at program coding?

The answer is obvious. The time spent up-front in designing a program is inversely proportional to the time that will be spent coding. In simpler terms, when the design of a program is complete and well-documented, the programs almost code themselves! When the necessary designing is skipped over in the name of productivity, coding takes many times longer, because mistakes that should have been eliminated in the design phase did not surface until program coding phase.

DEFINING THE INPUT

The next step in the design phase is defining the input necessary to produce the output that was just defined. Since, in the output definition, care was taken to note the source of all items, the input definition should be the process describing these data items and in what form they are available. They may need to be entered by hand, in which case this is probably a good time to find out who will do the work. In new systems, probably all the input data items needed will be entered by hand. Fortunately, with dBASE II, this is a task that is performed more easily than with most other languages. With dBASE II, when you define what your

data files/data bases will look like, dBASE will allow you to start entering data immediately. dBASE II generates input screens that allow easy entry of the items to be stored. This may be an answer to management's productivity obsession, because the data entry can start while the next step of the design process is going on. If management wants to see production, you can show them the data entry effort and give yourself some additional design time.

DEFINING THE PROCESS

Now the problem has been defined, the output specifications have been written, and the input has been determined. With these documents firmly in hand, you are ready to define the actual process of turning the input data items into the output information.

The overall functions of the system, as set out in the problem definition, must each be divided into their component functions. This is when the actual process of programming takes place. The problem, output, and input definitions were the beginning of this process, but only now is the actual process defined. This can be done using many different methods.

Chapter 3

Mapping the Process

The methods used by professional programmers to define processes most often are flowcharting and pseudocoding. These are representative of the two categories of process mapping: *charting* a process involves drawing a pictorial representation of the flow of control using symbols that depict the functions; *pseudocoding* means to define the process in terms of its functions using a structured style that mirrors the workings of computer programs.

Breaking down a process into its component functions makes the program coding phase go faster. This is because each piece of the solution is easier to master than the entire solution all at once. By dividing the functions during the design stage coding becomes faster and more controlled.

FLOWCHARTING

Flowcharting has been used since the inception of computers in the business environment. There are some advantages and disadvantages that you should be aware of before choosing the use of flowcharts as the standard for your business.

First, the pictorial representation of the logic of a program is very readable; that is, it can be understood easily and by anyone. Unfortunately, they are hard to draw. They are difficult to envision and cumbersome to change, and because of this, they are usually not finished before coding starts. A system design should be living and evolving as new, efficient paths are discovered. Flowcharts have to be redrawn each time a change is made.

Flowchart Examples

By using the flowchart symbols shown in Fig. 3-1, a programmer or process designer can show the flow of paperwork through a department. Think of the rectangles as desks. The paperwork moves from desk to desk along the lines of control (Fig. 3-2). If there is a decision, a choice between desks, the decision point is denoted by a diamond.

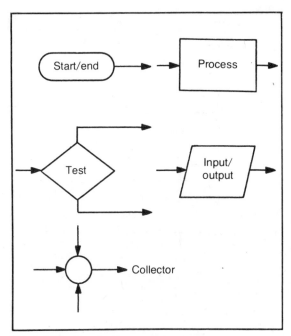

Fig. 3-1. The flowcharting symbols.

Any process, whether a computer process or not, can be depicted with a flowchart. For example, Fig. 3-3 shows a flowchart of boiling water for tea.

In many programming classes, this type of flowchart is used to drill future programmers in breaking a process down into its simplest components. If you want to practice flowcharting, try making flowcharts of answering the phone, or choosing a television show. As you find simpler and simpler steps to break the process into, you will find yourself drawing and redrawing your flowchart.

Note that the following examples use *logical constructs* which demonstrate how both flowcharts and pseudocodes are developed. These constructs are explained in detail in Chapter 5 and are used here only to help clarify the initial mapping process.

Let's look at another example of a flowchart. In this process, a company is looking through its employee records, and they are choosing records that meet certain criteria. The employees that meet

the qualifications are going to be asked if they would like to transfer to a foreign branch office. The process could be defined (flowcharted) as shown in Fig. 3-4.

The flowchart in Fig. 3-4 actually works; that is to say, it will perform the requested process. However, it is not very consistent or readable. Notice that all of the diamond blocks have NO legs on the left, except the last one, which has a YES. This flowchart falls short on readability and consistency.

A better way of depicting the process can be accomplished by using the logical construct flowchart shown in Fig. 3-5. Notice that every diamond block has the YES leg out to the right side. The

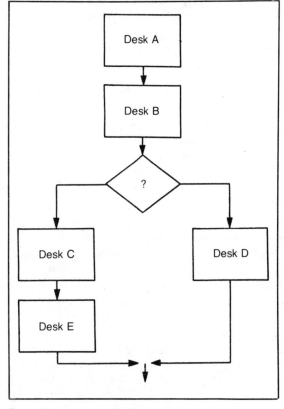

Fig. 3-2. An example of a flowchart.

entire process is contained in a *READ LOOP*, in which the records are read. After each read operation, a question is asked; "are there any more records to read?" This determines whether or not the last record has been processed.

Another thing you might notice is that the flowchart could define the logical structure of a program or could show the flow of paperwork in the office! If the records were sheets of paper in a file cabinet and all the questions were answered by human examination of the document, this flowchart would still be valid. A process definition does not have to be computer-based.

On first sight, the second flowchart seems to be larger and more complicated than the first. However, each logical construct is apparent, and the resulting chart is much more readable.

You can see the problems with trying to modify flowcharts. Usually the whole chart must be redrawn. In a growing, evolving system design this can be a drawback.

PSEUDOCODING

In recent years, pseudocoding has become the backbone of the programmer's toolchest. It reduces programming into the coding of the simplest relationships. Pseudocoding uses *logical constructs* that appear in some form in most computer languages.

With logical constructs, processes may be mapped out in very general terms, and slowly be made more detailed, until the final solution has evolved. Each subfunction may be concentrated on until it is solved and eventually becomes a part of the system. This divide and conquer method of problem solving is the answer to the problem of complexity. Functions are reduced to subfunctions of less complexity until a detailed, accurate map of the process has been obtained. Coding is now just a matter of translating the *pseudo* code into a real computer language. Coding takes less time, and

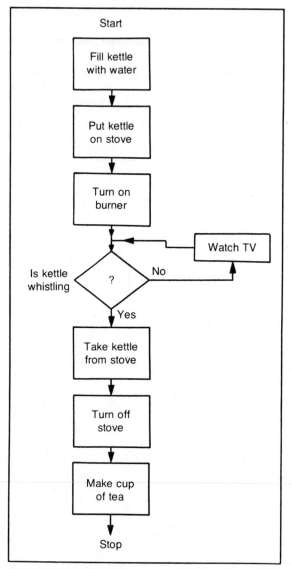

Fig. 3-3. A flowchart for making a cup of tea.

testing can be started at the same time coding commences.

Pseudocode Examples

Pseudocode is a representation of a logic flow,

10

but unlike the pictorial flowchart, pseudocode is written in plain language. This fact makes pseudocode easier to change and/or rewrite than a flowchart. Figure 3-2 showed the flow of paperwork from desk to desk in an office. That same process, shown as pseudocode, would look like this:

```
DESK A
DESK B
IF   X
```

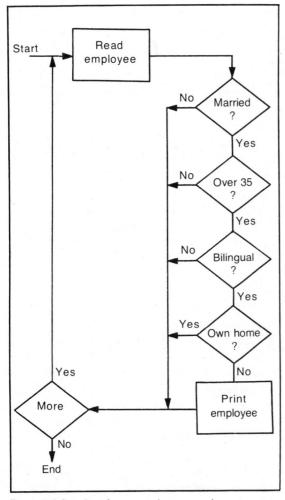

Fig. 3-4. A flowchart for an employee search.

```
THEN
     DESK C
     DESK E
ELSE
     DESK D
ENDIF
   . . .
```

The diamond block, with its YES and NO legs, becomes an IF-THEN-ELSE logical construct. The THEN part is done if condition X is true; the ELSE part if condition X is false.

The "waiting for the tea kettle" process shown in Fig. 3-3 would look like this in pseudocode:

```
PLACE KETTLE ON BURNER
TURN ON BURNER KETTLE IS ON
DO WHILE KETTLE NOT WHISTLING
     WATCH TV
ENDDO
REMOVE KETTLE FROM HEAT
TURN OFF BURNER
MAKE TEA!
```

The DO WHILE construct is a loop that is performed over and over again while the condition "kettle not whistling" is true.

For a final example of pseudocode, let's look at the process flowchart in Fig. 3-5.

```
READ EMPLOYEE
DO WHILE MORE RECORDS
    IF MARRIED
       THEN
          IF OVER 35
             THEN
                IF BILINGUAL
                   THEN
                      IF OWNS HOME
                         THEN NOTHING
                         ELSE PRINT EMPLOYEE
                      ENDIF
                ENDIF
          ENDIF
    ENDIF
    READ NEXT EMPLOYEE
ENDDO
```

First, notice the IF OWNS HOME construct. The THEN leg of the flow has no process associated with it. That construct could be changed to a negative comparison by the addition of NOT:

```
. . .
IF DOES NOT OWN HOME
   THEN PRINT EMPLOYEE
ENDIF
. . .
```

Also notice that there is a series of IF-THEN-IF-THEN... . These constructs could be replaced by a single IF if you make the condition complex. This is accomplished by connecting the conditions with AND. The final version of the pseudocode would look like this:

```
READ EMPLOYEE
DO WHILE MORE EMPLOYEES
   IF MARRIED AND OVER 35 AND
      BILINGUAL THEN
      IF DOES NOT OWN HOME
         THEN
            PRINT EMPLOYEE
      ENDIF
   ENDIF
   READ MORE RECORDS
ENDDO
```

The pseudocode has become simpler than the flowchart by use of a complex condition. It is much easier to combine expressions in pseudocode than to type all those conditions in a little diamond block! Since pseudocode is so easily changed, it is much more desirable than a flowchart for a *design* tool. Flowcharts are excellent *documentation* tools; they should be drawn after the design is complete.

SUMMARY

In the first pages of this book you have seen the initial stages of the development of a computer software system. This is the design phase, when the whole shape of the system is determined. After the design is completed, the actual process must be constructed. In the cases that are addressed by this book, that means that it is time to code the programs in a computer language—dBASE II. The steps taken so far have been

1. Define the problem.
2. Define the output.
3. Define the input.
4. Define the process.

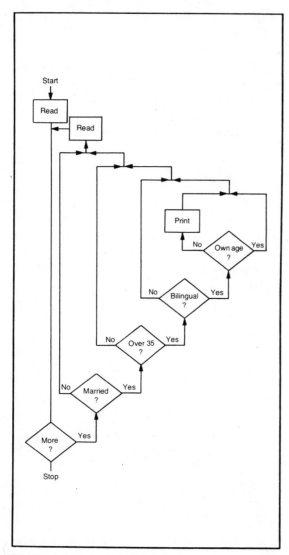

Fig. 3-5. A logical construct flowchart.

Chapter 4

Designing Processes

The design phase of a project should be completed prior to program coding. To make use of the design techniques advocated by this book, the completion of the design should be a hard-and-fast rule: be alert to and suspicious of any other course of action. An incomplete design will guarantee a late and unproductive solution.

Another obstacle that faces the programmer is alteration of the design during the coding phase. By changing the system requirements during coding, more time must be spent adding "bells and whistles" and not enough time can be given to the construction of the required solution.

The new business computer programmer and those others who find programming tedious, time consuming, and frustrating should consider these rules:

Always complete the design phase prior to program coding.

Freeze the design until coding and testing are complete.

Once coding and testing are done in a structured manner, enhancing the system or program is merely a problem of adding or changing already existing functions. A *plug-in* sort of structure can be changed with very little trouble.

DESIGNING THE PROCESS

Up to this point, you have been introduced to the system (or program) development process. The next step is to design the process. This step depends on understanding the three fundamental concepts involved in a good program (or system). They are generality, modularity, and hierarchy. Also, it is important to keep in mind the "EZ2s" of development: easy to write, easy to read, easy to test.

FUNCTION CHARTING

The first step in system/program development is to chart the major functions of the system.

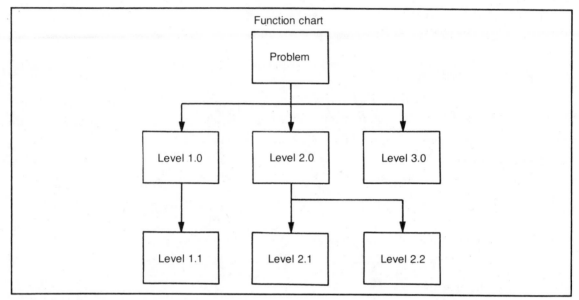

Fig. 4-1. Function Hierarchy Chart.

These should be listed in the problem definition that was developed earlier. Each of the major functions should be written in a box on a blank sheet of paper, one function to a sheet. These sheets of paper will become the function hierarchy charts for the system. Figure 4-1 shows a sample function hierarchy chart.

FUNDAMENTALS OF A GOOD PROGRAM

The first fundamental of a good program, generality, means that the system will work for all input received by the system. In effect, this means that a program should check each input variable for validity and show error messages for any invalid data. This is done by making sure that numeric fields have numeric data in them, and checking numeric data items for a proper range of values. Character data may have to be checked for specific values or formats. When one of the criteria is not met, an error message must be displayed (somehow).

Modularity describes the result of breaking individual functions into separate programming problems. This approach means easier programming, because only one function need be addressed at one time. With large systems, this is particularly necessary, because quite often, one person could not conceive and design the entire system. By making the system modular, this problem is eliminated.

This method of system design also results in a hierarchy of functions. The top-level boxes that you have drawn on the otherwise blank sheets of paper become the top of the functional hierarchy of the system. Then, as each major function is divided into still smaller functions, you can add interconnecting boxes that describe the hierarchical relationship between the functions. In programming terms, each function becomes a *module* or *subroutine*, each of which calls still other modules until the lowest level of function is reached. By using this top-down hierarchical approach, lowest level functions that are not unique can be seen readily. They can then be shared between modules as needed, without repeating the work.

THE EZ2s OF PROGRAMMING

If you follow this type of approach to program design, the EZ2s take care of themselves. Once the functional hierarchy is determined, the first step is designing the logic for the top-level functions/modules. When the design of the major functions is complete, they can be coded and, using a programming trick called *program stubs*, can be tested for logical correctness. Since the major functions will become the most-used code in the program, they can also be the most-tested. As each lower level function is designed and coded, it can be inserted into its stub and tested. When the lowest-level functions have been tested and the output approved, the system will be ready for implementation, with the program logic completely tested out.

Keep the fundamentals of a good program in mind as you step into the world of process design. They are (once again)

generality
modularity
hierarchy

STYLES OF PROGRAMMING

There are two major styles of programming, interactive and passive. Passive programs are processes that can run from start to finish with no interruption by the operator. Sometimes misnamed *batch* programs by professional programmers, passive programs make up most of the work cycle at large installations. Huge number of transactions are accumulated during normal business hours and then processed during the second and third shifts. The series of passive programs process these transactions, update files, create reports, print bills, and so forth. All this happens with little or no direct input from the computer operators; the operations staff has enough to do! They place the media containing transactions records, cards, tapes, or disks, into the proper units, put paper in the printers, align the bill forms, and determine the order that the programs are to be run in.

Interactive programming, on the other hand, requires extensive communication with the operator. This type of program would not be welcome in a batch environment, since in big shops there are large numbers of programs running at any given time; the operations staff cannot (and will not!) devote a lot of attention to an individual program. Microcomputers, however are ideal for interactive programming. They are usually run as dedicated systems, which means that only one program can be running at a time.

Interactive programs usually handle just one transaction at a time. The operator requests a function, enters the data, and a file is updated. He then requests another function, and a report is produced. The interactive quality of the program lets the operator control which functions are performed and in what order. Interactive programming also helps alleviate operator boredom by showing the operator that the system is working and by allowing him control over the outcome.

SELECTION MENUS

One method of creating an interactive program is to design use of a selection menu as shown in Fig. 4-2. The program displays a list of the functions available on the computer monitor. The operator then chooses an option and enters data, and the file is updated. He can choose another function, and a report is produced. In this manner, the operator can choose the functions and the order the functions are to be performed in.

Usually, the function selections are displayed with an option number for the operator to select. In some limited instances, the operator may have to

```
----------------------------------------
:                                        :
:           MAIN MENU SCREEN             :
:                                        :
:       ENTER SELECTION ==>  __          :
:                                        :
:                                        :
:                                        :
:       1 -   ADD  RECORD                :
:       2 -   CHANGE  RECORD             :
:       3 -   REMOVE  RECORD             :
:       4 -   DISPLAY  RECORD            :
:                                        :
:       P -  PRINT  RECORD               :
:                                        :
:       X -  EXIT  SYSTEM                :
:                                        :
:                                        :
:                                        :
:                                        :
----------------------------------------
```

Fig. 4-2. An example of a Menu Screen.

type the first letter of the function name or the entire function name. Since the design and creation of the menus is up to you (the programmer), you may design your menus in a manner comfortable to you and/or your operator (probably you, also). There are, however, two guidelines you should observe:

Don't make the operator enter too many characters, because it's easy to make typing errors. Make the option choice easy to read and understand.

When considering interactive programming, remember that people make mistakes, and people will be interacting with your programs. Just as it is important for you to design the screens and menus for human understanding, it is important for the program to double-check input typed by a human. People make mistakes because of fatigue or misunderstanding, a trait that computers (fortunately) lack. Even a simple mistake such as typing with the shift-lock key engaged can cause endless havoc with your data.

So is that the computer program must judge the input data for itself. Each piece of input, including a menu selection, must be examined for validity before a function can be performed. If there is a list of functions and selection codes on the menu screen, the program must match the input from the operator against a list of the valid selections. If the code is typed wrong, an error message should be displayed. An error message of this type should be readable, and list the valid choices for the operator.

DATA ENTRY SCREENS

Interactive programs can use screens for the entry of data. A sample screen is shown in Fig. 4-3. These screens are forms for the data, just like any paper form that you fill out with a pencil. The data entry screen is filled out by using the keyboard to enter information into each area on the screen. This information is then stored into variables by the program. The program can then examine each entry for validity.

Data entry screens should be designed for ease of use. The operator must be able to read the screen and understand the placement of data on the form.

Sometimes, when a shop is first automating, the input screens are designed directly from the paper form being replaced. This helps to add a sense of continuity to the system, but a better practice is to ask the people who fill out and/or read those forms for their suggestions. They can tell you what they would like to see changed and how to best design the screens for ease of data entry. This is most important in companies where a large number of transactions are entered daily, but it can help to cut down needless work and increase productivity even in small shops.

EDITING DATA

Once the operator has entered the data on the screen, the program must examine it for validity. This means that the input data should meet certain predetermined criteria.

First, the data must conform to the required data type. If the input data is numeric, that is, to be used in calculations, the program must be sure that the input contains only numbers. This is called a *class* edit. Database managers like dBASE II do not allow characters in a field defined as numeric data.

The keyboard locks-up or an audible alarm is sounded when the attempt is made. Most character data items are not checked, since any character is valid. In some cases, however, you might want to check for improper data, such as numbers in a name field.

Second, if the input is numeric, the contents of the field may have to fall within a certain range of values. If, for instance, a field called month is created, the value probably has to be between 1 and 12 inclusive. This is called a *range* edit.

Third, the data should conform to data already in the file. This is called a *correctness* edit. For example, in a payroll system, a transaction can be entered to pay an employee for overtime hours worked. If the employee is not eligible to receive overtime pay, the transaction is in error (or someone is trying to put one over on you).

Programs should check data for all possible violations. Any input presented to the program, even if *you* plan to be doing the data entry, should be edited for class, range, and correctness. Remember that anyone can make mistakes, and you want your data to be as error-free as humanly possible.

Fig. 4-3. An example of a Data Entry Screen.

```
-------------------------------------------------
:                                                 :
:            DATA ENTRY SCREEN                    :
:                                                 :
:                                                 :
:                                                 :
:                                                 :
:    Name:        :                   :           :
:                                                 :
:    Address: :                      :            :
:    City:        :                  :            :
:    State:       :   :   Zip:  :        :         :
:                                                 :
:    Date of Birth: :  /  /  :                    :
:                                                 :
:    Credit Limit: :              :               :
:                                                 :
:                                                 :
:                                                 :
-------------------------------------------------
```

ERROR MESSAGES

When errors are detected in input data, it is necessary to notify the operator. In passive-style programming, this usually means producing an error report for the data entry staff to use the next day in correcting the input transactions. In interactive programming, it means telling the operator immediately that there is something wrong.

One means of accomplishing this is the use of an audible alarm signal. Most microcomputers have a beep or bell character that sounds an alarm. Usually, the sound is used in conjunction with a message describing the error. When the alarm is used alone, the operator might not easily see the problem.

Error messages are displayed on the monitor screen. When used with the audible alarm, they alert the operator to the fact that a problem has occurred. The message should explain the problem and offer suggestions for correction. These are messages to be read by people; they should be easily understandable.

An example of a good error message from a menu selection screen would be

```
    *** INVALID SELECTION ***
  VALID OPTIONS ARE 1,2,3,4,AND X
        REENTER SELECTION
```

The error is described in the first line, the correct choices are listed in the second line, and the next course of action is indicated in the third line. These are the three elements of a good error message. This is not to say that you must use three lines; there are also good one liners, and there are other enhancements to make the message stand out more. Error messages should always appear on the same part of the screen, preferably near the top, so that the operator will know where to focus his attention. When the alarm sounds, the operator will be trained to look at that certain place for the error message. Displaying the message in color or in high intensity characters will also draw attention to it.

You should not use blinking text, however, as it can be quite annoying. Another method is called *flower-boxing*. Using this technique, the message is surrounded by astericks to make it very apparent, as shown below.

```
****************************************
*          INVALID SELECTION           *
* VALID OPTIONS ARE 1,2,3,4 AND X *
*          REENTER SELECTION            *
****************************************
```

SOME TYPICAL PROCESSES

One type of typical process has been discussed in detail: the edit or *data validation* process. This unit will show you some other frequently-used data processes you will need in your programs.

The first process that will be discussed is the data search. Usually, a file of records is searched for individual records that meet certain conditions, called the *search criteria*. In the simplest cases, this means comparing a field in each record to a value, and listing the records in which the field contains the value. For example, you may be searching an employee file for a particular social security number. When the record with that number is found, you may want to perform some process using it; you may change or delete the record or just display its contents. This kind of search is called a *unique* search, because only one record will be retrieved.

A search could be used as a correctness edit for input data. If you are adding a new employee to the payroll file, you could first search the file for the social security number of the new employee. If a match is found it may mean that (1) something strange is going on, (2) you entered the wrong social security number (possibly), or (3) the employee has already been added to the file (most likely). In any case, if unique data is found in the file when it should not be there, something is wrong; the transaction should fail with an appropriate error message. Pseudocode for a unique search could look like this:

```
DISPLAY "SSN TO BE SEARCHED FOR"
GET ANSWER
READ A RECORD
DO WHILE MORE RECORDS
   AND SSN NOT FOUND
 READ NEXT RECORD
ENDDO
DISPLAY RECORD IF FOUND
```

A *generic* search occurs when there are more than one record meeting the search criteria. For example, you may want to list all employees with the last name of Smith. This could result in several records being listed or processed in some other way.

One way of using a generic search is to use it to display fields for use in another process. In the payroll system example, you may need the social security number to change an employee record. However, if all you know is the employee's name, you could use a generic search to display all the employees with that particular last name, along with their social security numbers. You could then choose the proper social security number to use for the change transaction. Pseudocode for a generic search could look like this:

```
DISPLAY "NAME TO BE SEARCHED FOR"
GET ANSWER
READ A RECORD
DO WHILE MORE RECORDS
   IF NAME FOUND
     THEN PRINT NAME AND SSN
   ENDIF
   READ NEXT RECORD
ENDDO
```

Another frequently-used process is totaling. When billing a customer, the total of the bill is printed somewhere on the form that is sent to the customer. Administrative reports have totals of dollar amounts, employees, quantities etc.

Totals are said to be accumulated in computer programs. That is, each required total is defined as a field in the program. Each time a record is read or an amount is calculated, that amount is added to the accumulated total. Using the payroll system example, an employee record might include regular hours worked and overtime hours worked. An administrative report generated by this system would include a total for regular hours, a total for overtime hours, and a total for the total of all hours worked. Each time a record is read, the "regular hours" and "overtime hours" are added to their respective totals. Then, after calculating the total hours worked for that employee (regular + overtime), that sum is added to the "total hours" total field. When the report is examined, the "total hours" should match the sum of the total regular hours plus the total overtime hours. This is called *cross footing* in the business vernacular and is another method of checking the correctness of the process.

SUMMARY

This chapter has discussed the basis for designing computer processes. Keep in mind the fundamentals of a good program: generality, modularity, and hierarchy. These should be used in conjunction with the EZ2s of programming: easy to read, easy to write, and easy to change.

This chapter also discussed the styles of interactive, and passive programming, including the use of screens and menus as tools for data entry and process control. You also saw some typical processes found in computer programs: checking input data, searching files, and totaling amounts. These are not all of the possible processes—just a sample of those most frequently used.

In later chapters, you will see how the logical constructs work and how to examine your design for errors. You will also see some systems designed from start to finish.

Chapter 5

The Workings of Language

The design of a process is hierarchical in nature, proceeding from the major functions at the top of the function chart through the lowest functions at the bottom. The problem most new or nonprogrammers have is "how low to go?" To understand this, it is important to understand how a computer language is put together.

TYPES OF STATEMENTS

The concept of statements in computer programs was discussed earlier. Each statement accomplishes some purpose within the program. The general types of statements are

```
Assignment Statements
Decision Statements
Input-Output Statements
Control Statements
    (Loops and Branches)
```

Assignment Statements

The assignment statement is used to assign a value to a variable. It is the most common program statement at the lowest levels of the function hierarchy. They become scarcer as you rise through the chart. However, you will be traversing the chart top-down. The first modules to be designed will be the major functions and will have few if any assignment statements.

Here are some examples of assignment statements in various languages. Each statement assigns the value of 3 + 4 to the variable A:

Language	Statement
BASIC	LET A = 3 + 4
dBase II	STORE 3 + 4 TO A
COBOL	MOVE 3 + 4 TO A
PL/1	A = 3 + 4;
Pascal	COMPUTE A = 3 + 4

In pseudocode, you can make up your own version of the assignment. Be sure that it can be easily understood by others. Most programmers tend to use the syntax (computer grammar) of the language that they are familiar with.

Calling Subroutines

The second-most common statement, and the most common at the top level, is the *subroutine call*. It is a control statement that causes a subroutine or subfunction to be performed. When the function is complete, control returns to the statement following the call. Subroutine calls are used to establish the hierarchy of functions. Each major function module calls the functions listed in the second level in the function chart, and they in turn, call the next level. A chart illustrating the flow of control that occurs when subroutines are used is shown in Fig. 5-1.

The program stubs that were mentioned earlier are empty lower-level modules that have not been coded yet. Since, the function chart will tell you what subfunctions there will be, it is possible to set up stubs for them. As each subfunction is coded, it can be placed in the stub, and lower level stubs added. This way, the most used program logic will be the most tested.

USING LOGICAL CONSTRUCTS IN PROCESS DESIGN

Keeping this idea of modularity in mind, let's discuss the actual form of the process design. As described before, process logic can be depicted in two ways: charting and pseudocoding. They can both be accomplished using a few logical constructs, which will be discussed next. Charting methods are good ways of documenting a complete design, because they are pictorial in nature. How-

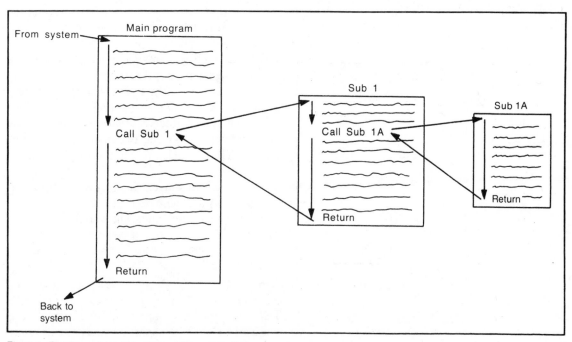

Fig. 5-1. The flow of control when calling subroutines.

ever, they are difficult to change as the process evolves, so the recommended procedure is to design with pseudocode and document afterwards with a chart.

As you remember, pseudocode is a language-based way of designing processes. You can design your system by using the simple logical constructs combined with plainly written "human-language" statements that describe the logic that the process will follow.

The logical constructs are

```
SEQUENCE
IF-THEN-ELSE
DO WHILE
CASE
```

The SEQUENCE logical construct is just that—one statement following another. This is the simplest form of construct, and simply depicts one action following another. A SEQUENCE flowchart and an example of SEQUENCE pseudocode are shown in Fig. 5-2.

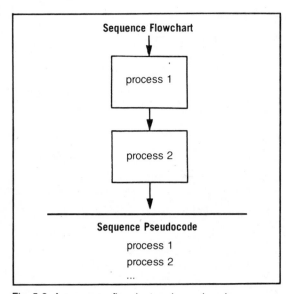

Fig. 5-2. A sequence flowchart and pseudocode.

The others, IF-THEN-ELSE, DO WHILE, and CASE are decision statements, and most languages have them in one form or another. It may be necessary in some languages to use the statements available to create the construct. In dBASE II they exist in these forms.

Notice that there are no input/output type statements used in pseudocode. That is because the design process should not be tied down to the exact form to be used. This type of design allows flexibility, so that a change of computers or software does not affect the design. The only necessary references to input and output might be statements such as

GET A RECORD
GET NEXT RECORD
WRITE A LINE

IF-THEN-ELSE

The IF-THEN-ELSE logical construct is the simplest form of decision statement. It asks a question in the form of a comparison. For example, IF PAYROLL CODE IS 2. There are two possible results from a comparison of this type: true or false. If the comparison in the IF is true, then whatever processing is invoked in the THEN part of the statement is performed, and when completed, the next statement following the IF construct is performed. If the result is FALSE, the ELSE section is performed.

Some IF statements have only a THEN following them: if the comparison is false, the THEN unit is not performed, and control falls to the next statement. A flowchart and pseudocode for an IF-THEN-ELSE construct is shown in Fig. 5-3.

IF-THEN-ELSE statements, and for that matter all the logical constructs, are or can be considered individual statements. Therefore, the THEN unit of an IF-THEN-ELSE construct can also have an IF statement in it. This is called *nesting* by programmers and is quite valid. Care should be

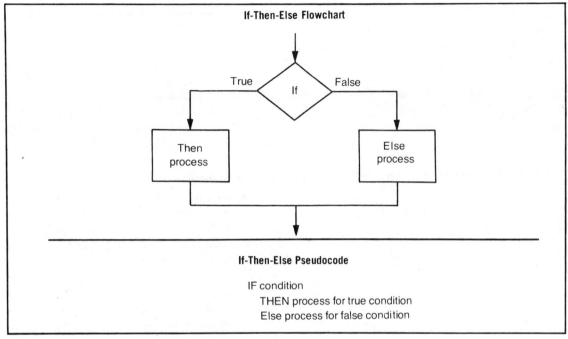

Fig. 5-3. An If-Then-Else flowchart and pseudocode.

taken, however, that IFs and THENs match up with the proper ELSEs. This can be done through the use of indentation to indicate which statements are on the same nesting level. It is not wise to nest too deeply, as this can become unwieldy and unreadable. If necessary, another function should be created.

In dBASE II, the IF statement looks like this:

```
IF conditional expression
   statements to be performed
       if TRUE
       ELSE
   statements to be performed
       if FALSE
       ENDIF
```

Notice that there is no word THEN in the statement. dBASE II takes the statements after the IF as the THEN part of the construct. If the expression is

FALSE, dBASE II looks for an ELSE in the code and if ELSE is present, performs the statements following it. If there is no ELSE, the ENDIF is reached, and the next statement is executed. Indentation is important in IF-THEN-ELSE constructs to make the code easier to read and understand. In dBASE II the end of an IF statement is marked by an ENDIF.

Let's look at some examples of conditions in the IF-THEN-ELSE construct format. For example, if the program needs to perform some special processing when a date is in November the pseudocode would look like this.

```
IF MONTH = 11
   THEN
       perform "November processing"
   ELSE
       perform "normal processing"
ENDIF
```

23

In this example, the conditional expression is month = 11 on the line starting with IF. The expression asks a question to which there can be only two possible answers. "Is month equal to 11? Yes or no?" When the system sees an expression like this, it examines the value of the variable MONTH and compares it to the literal value 11. If they are equal, the system signals a true or yes answer for the question, and the process contained in the THEN unit of the construct is performed. If the value of MONTH is not equal to "11", the ELSE unit gets control, and that processing is performed.

Here are other examples:

```
IF STATE = "CT"
   THEN ...

IF ZIP = 06040
   THEN ...

IF DATE = EXPIRE:DATE
   THEN ...
```

In the third example above, the contents of the variable DATE are compared against the contents of the variable EXPIRE:DATE. Again there are only two possibilities: the contents are either equal or not equal, so the expression is either true or false. There is no other answer to a conditional expression.

COMPARISONS

The comparisons that can be made in a decision statement such as IF-THEN-ELSE can be simple or complex. The simplest form involves testing one variable against another or against a literal value.

The comparisons that can be made are:

```
EQUALS (=)
NOT EQUALS (#)
```

```
GREATER THAN (>)
LESS THAN (<)
GREATER THAN OR EQUAL TO (>=)
LESS THAN OR EQUAL TO (<=)
```

Some languages have two more, NOT GREATER THAN and NOT LESS THAN. These should be used with caution and replaced with GREATER THAN OR EQUAL TO and LESS THAN OR EQUAL TO when possible.

Complex Comparisons

Simple comparison expressions have two possible results true or false. Comparison expressions can be combined to form complex expressions when they are connected with the *Boolean* operators AND and OR. A complex expression is evaluated by the AND and OR rules.

The AND rule. For an AND expression to be true, both sides of the expression must be true. If one of the expressions is false, the AND expression is false.

The OR rule. For an OR expression to be true, ONE side of the expression must be true. If both sides are false, the OR expression is false.

ANDs and ORs can be used within complex expressions; for instance, two OR expressions could be connected by an AND, or the expression could be even more complex. The best rule to follow is the KISS rule: Keep It Simple, Stupid! Use complex expressions only where necessary.

Let's look at some examples of complex conditional expressions. In complex expressions, each conditional expression is evaluated separately, and then the results of the ANDs and ORs are evaluated according to the AND and OR rules. For example

```
IF STATE = "CT" AND ZIP = 06040
   THEN ....
```

In this example, the value of the variable "STATE" is compared against the literal CT. Likewise, the value of the variable ZIP is compared to 06040.

Only if both of these conditions are true is the entire expression true. If either is false, the entire condition is false.

In the following example, the two simple conditions are made into a complex expression by joining them with an OR:

```
IF STATE = "CT" OR STATE = "MA"
   THEN ...
```

It is obvious that at least one of these conditions must be false; STATE cannot have two different values! However, the OR rule states that only one of the joined expressions need be true for the entire condition to be true. In this case, if the value of STATE is CT, the condition is true. The condition is also true if the value is MA. If anything other than these two values is in STATE, the condition is false.

In more complicated conditional expressions, two expressions connected with an AND can be connected to still other expressions:

```
IF (STATE="CT" OR STATE="MA")
   AND NAME="SMITH"
   THEN ...
```

In this example, the condition inside the parentheses is evaluated first and then ANDed with the evaluation of the third expression. If the variable STATE contains either CT or MA, the condition in the parentheses is evaluated as true using the OR rule. Then the value of the variable NAME is compared with the literal value SMITH. Therefore, this complex condition is true if NAME is equal to SMITH, and if the STATE is either CT or MA.

When evaluating complex conditional expressions, it is important to evaluate the expressions inside parentheses first and to remember the AND and OR rules. Also, don't make conditions too complex, for readability's sake; the KISS ("Keep It Simple, Stupid") method is the best compromise.

In dBASE II the symbols for AND and OR are .AND. and .OR., respectively. The above example would look like this:

```
IF (STATE="CT" .OR. STATE="MA")
   .AND. NAME="SMITH"
ENDIF
   THEN ...
```

USING THE DO WHILE STATEMENT

DO WHILE is another type of conditional statement. A DO WHILE is a series of statements that is performed over and over WHILE the condition remains true. Each time the loop of statements is performed, the condition is reevaluated and if it is still true, the process in the loop is performed again. A flowchart and pseudocode for a DO WHILE process is shown in Fig. 5-4.

Programmers us DO WHILE loops to perform a series of statements as long as some condition is

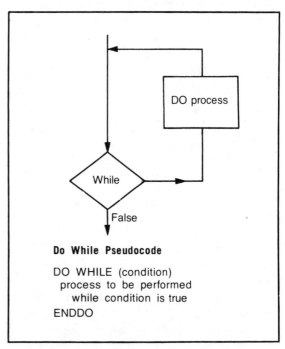

Do While Pseudocode

```
DO WHILE (condition)
   process to be performed
      while condition is true
ENDDO
```

Fig. 5-4. A DO WHILE flowchart and pseudocode.

true. This condition can be internal to the program; for example:

```
SET COUNTER TO 1
DOWHILE COUNTER <= 15
    ...
    statements
    ...
    add 1 to counter
ENDDO
```

The DO WHILE loop will be performed 15 times; each time through the loop, the counter is incremented by one. The condition in the DO WHILE statement (COUNTER<=15) is tested immediately after each time the counter is incremented. When the value of COUNTER exceeds 15, the loop is ended, and control passes to the statement following the ENDDO.

Another way that DO WHILE is used is to test for a condition external to the program. One such condition is end-of-file, which answers the question "Are there any more records to read?". Using a DO WHILE loop will be performed once for each record in the file, regardless of the number of records. Most major function routines are based on this type of loop:

```
read a record
DOWHILE more records
    ...
    statements
    ...
    read next record
ENDDO
```

The condition is external to the program; the loop will be performed once for each record in the file. If records are added to the file in the future, the program will still work because the condition determines when the end-of-file is reached regardless of the number of records in the file.

Notice also that the condition is tested after both READ statements. The condition is tested at the start of the loop, as well as after each subsequent READ. While the condition remains true, the loop is executed. When the condition becomes false, the statement after the ENDDO is executed, and the program continues from there.

The DO WHILE logical construct takes the following form in dBASE II:

```
DO WHILE conditional expression
    statements to be performed as
    long as the condition is TRUE
ENDDO
```

The loop continues to be executed as long as the conditional expression tests true; it is tested each time the ENDDO is encountered. The end of the DO WHILE loop is always marked by an ENDDO in dBASE II.

THE CASE FIGURE

The last logical construct to learn is the CASE figure. A CASE is a decision point that allows more than two processes to be performed for various values of a variable. For instance, the variable SEX appears to have only two possible values. However, there are three: male, female, and invalid (not valid). Here the CASE condition has three possible processes to perform: one for MALE, one for FEMALE, and one for invalid data. The CASE figure would look like this:

```
CASE SEX
    WHEN MALE
        male processing
    WHEN FEMALE
        female processing
    OTHERWISE invalid sex code
    processing
ENDCASE
```

In dBASE II, there can be any number of WHEN conditions in a CASE figure, and each of them can head a process that can contain any nested

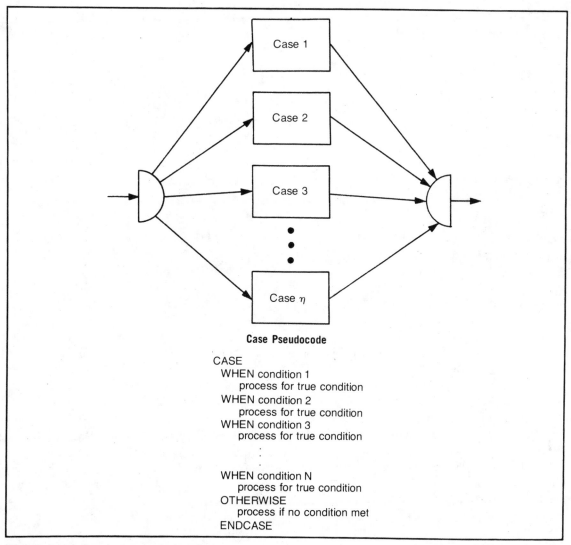

Case Pseudocode

```
CASE
   WHEN condition 1
      process for true condition
   WHEN condition 2
      process for true condition
   WHEN condition 3
      process for true condition
          .
          .
          .
   WHEN condition N
      process for true condition
   OTHERWISE
      process if no condition met
ENDCASE
```

Fig. 5-5. A case flowchart and pseudocode.

logical constructs except other CASE figures. Some other languages do permit nested CASE statements. Figure 5-5 shows a flowchart and pseudocode for a case figure.

The CASE figure in dBASE II is a form of the DO command. The format looks like this:

```
DO CASE
   CASE expression 1
      commands to be performed if
         condition 1 is TRUE
   CASE expression 2
      commands to be performed if
         condition 2 is TRUE
```

```
CASE expression 3
  commands to be performed if
  condition 3 is TRUE
...
OTHERWISE
  commands to be  performed if
  all  previous conditions
  are FALSE
ENDCASE
```

Each condition is evaluated and if true, the commands are performed until the next CASE, the OTHERWISE, or the ENDCASE is reached. Then the next statement following the ENDCASE is performed, and the program continues from there. If no condition in a CASE is true, the OTHERWISE unit, if present, is executed until the ENDCASE is reached.

CHECKING OUT YOUR PSEUDOCODE

When you have finished your pseudocode for a function, it is necessary to test it out, that is, to examine it for logical correctness and to make sure it does what you want it to!

To check out your pseudocode, read each statement one at a time. This is the way the computer will execute your statements when you translate your pseudocode into dBASE II code. Point a pencil to each line as you read it.

When you execute conditional statements, examine the flow of control for both true and false conditions. In CASE figures, test the flow for every WHEN condition.

Tracing the Flow in IF-THEN-ELSE Constructs

In an IF-THEN-ELSE logical construct, when the IF condition is true, the statements in the THEN unit are executed, and control passes to the statement following the ENDIF. For example:

1.   IF MONTH = 2
2.   THEN MONTH NAME is "February"
3.   ENDIF
4.   ...

If MONTH does equal 2, the flow of control, in terms of the line numbers, would be 1,2,3,4. On the other hand, if MONTH was anything other than 2, the flow would be "1,3,4". With no ELSE unit for a false condition, control passes out of the IF-THEN construct to the next statement (line 4).

If the IF construct includes an ELSE unit, slightly different processing occurs

1.   IF STATE = "CT"
2.   THEN perform in-state process
3.   ELSE perform out-of-state process
4.   ENDIF
5.   ...

A true condition in the example above (STATE equal to CT) would result in the execution of statements 1,2,4,5. The ELSE unit is skipped over when the condition is true. A false condition in the above example would result in the execution of statements 1,3,4,5; the THEN unit is skipped over.

Tracing the Flow in CASE Constructs

In a CASE construct, control is passed to the statements in the WHEN unit when the condition tests true and then jumps to the statement following the ENDCASE. If no WHEN condition tests true, control jumps to the OTHERWISE unit, if it exists. For example

```
1. CASE
2.    WHEN state="CT"
3.       perform "in Connecticut"
4.    WHEN state="MA"
5.       perform "in Massachusetts"
6.    WHEN state="NY"
7.       perform "in New York"
```

```
  8.     OTHERWISE
  9.         perform "other state"
 10. ENDCASE
 11. ...
```

When this construct is executed, and the value of state is CT, the statements will be performed 1,2,3,10,11. If state is MA, the flow of processing would be 1,4,5,10,11; for state of NY, the flow would be 1,6,7,10,11. If the state was anything other than CT, MA, or NY, the flow would be 1,8,9,10,11.

Tracing the Flow in DO WHILE Constructs

In a DO WHILE construct, a loop of statements is performed as long as a condition is true. In the following example, a counter is incremented and then tested by the DO WHILE statement.

```
  1.  set counter to 1
  2.  DO WHILE counter <= 3
  3.      add counter to total
  4.      add 1 to counter
  5.  ENDDO
  6.  ...
```

First, the variable COUNTER is set to one. The DO WHILE then tests the variable COUNTER against a literal (3). While COUNTER remains at three or below, this loop is executed. The flow of processing would be 1,2,3,4 (COUNTER now 2),5,2,3,4 (COUNTER now 3),5,2,3,4 (COUNTER now 4), 5,2 (condition now false), 5,6.

The variable TOTAL would now contain 6 (1+2+3), while COUNTER would be set to 4. Notice that the loop was performed three times; while COUNTER was 1, 2, and finally 3. The incrementation to 4 made the condition false and the statements inside the loop were not performed after counter became 4.

Tracing the Values of Variables

Another aid in testing your pseudocode is to write any variable names down on a separate sheet of paper and write in the values you wish to test. As the values change, cross out the old values and write in the new ones. This will show the exact values of the variables at each statement in the code.

This type of careful examination of the process design is called a *walk-thru* and is invaluable as a testing tool. By getting the design right before the actual computer program is written, you can save yourself a lot of aggravation caused by having missed problems in your design. Your program may even work the first time, if you take the time to design it properly and test the design.

Chapter 6

Coding, Testing, and Debugging

Now for the second phase of the project, the coding phase. In the design phase you defined the problem, the output, the input, and the process. Now it is time to code and test the new system.

DOCUMENTATION

The reference materials you will need during your coding phase are the manuals for whatever software you are using, the problem definition, the output definition, the input definition, and the process definition. These materials, aside from the reference manual, are the documentation for your system. Along with the program code, the design definition will become a package that is necessary for future changes.

When a system is to be changed or enhanced, the programmer will refer to the documentation package for a clearer understanding of the system. This will enable the programmer to find the easiest way to make the enhancement. A poorly assembled documentation package can make changes difficult, if not impossible, to implement.

Some companies keep outdated computer equipment, some dating back to the early 1960s. Why? Because the programs were written then, and the documentation has become scattered, scrambled, and lost during the interim. In some cases, the source language for the program itself has been lost, rendering all change impossible. The executives' attitude toward this is "The programs still work well, and we don't have the time to rewrite and redocument the system." Usually, the cost of keeping the old equipment is much greater than the cost of developing a new, rewritten and documented system.

The point of this is that the documentation package is important to you and to your business. Write it well, and keep two copies of everything!

Readability

Since the source code of the program is to become part of the documentation package, it is important to write it in a readable manner. Even the pseudocode or flowchart should be painstakingly written, so that when you come back to it later, you can understand how the process works. Many professional programmers find themselves working on systems they designed and wrote years in the past and scratching their heads in wonder at how they could have forgotten what they did. With readable, understandable documentation, reworking is a much easier task.

One way of making programs (and pseudocode) more readable is to indent subordinate code. Any code that is inside a loop should be indented to differentiate it from the main code. This one act alone makes the program much easier to read.

Another method of making a program easier to read is to start each function at the top of a new page. In some languages, it is necessary to put comments in the code, showing the break between the end of one subfunction, and the start of the next.

Finally, comment statements are available in virtually all computer languages. Use them to your advantage. By commenting effectively and changing those comments when necessary, you can put some documentation directly into the code. This is especially helpful when a complicated process is present; you can explain the process in plain language to programmers who might change the program in the future. Remember, it could be you!

MAKING SURE THE PROGRAM WILL WORK

There are two types of errors associated with program coding. They are *syntax errors* and *logic errors*. The logic errors should be obvious in the process design. Process designs (pseudocode) should be carefully examined not only by the creator, but by other, even disinterested, parties. This can be done in an informal or formal walk-through of the pseudocode. Each decision point can be evaluated, and errors can be worked out before coding begins.

Syntax errors are usually discovered when the program is run on the computer. They can also be avoided or minimized by careful examination of the coded program. It is also good to have the dBASE II manual handy (and open) while coding a program.

Testing During Coding

When the coding of a major function is complete, testing can begin, and from then on, testing can progress simultaneously with coding. Higher level functions can be tested with stubs at the lower levels. When the high-level function works, the stubs may be filled in. Every decision path in the function should be tested before the next module is included for testing. Testing in this fashion means that any errors that appear are usually the fault of the last subroutine that was added, making error detection and correction much easier.

Using Test Data

At this point, some form of test input data is necessary. This should be, whenever possible, actual live data, gleaned from already existing files. In the case of a new system, all of the test data may have to be generated by the tester. For each item of test input, there should be a written document stating the expected results when the program is presented with that item. Test data should include erroneous and invalid information.

The test data can also become part of the documentation package. The test data can be listed, along with the expected results. If, when testing a program, unexpected results occur, either the expected results are incorrect or there is a problem in the program (most likely). Unexpected results should not be blamed on the weather, cosmic rays striking the computer, or the computer itself. The problem lies with the program in most cases, and sometimes with the interpretation of the expected results.

Most of the time, the responsibility for creating test data falls to the programmer. This may not be a good idea. Usually, the programmer is the person most closely involved with the system, and therefore he could, either consciously or unconsciously, test the program with slanted data that will produce the desired results while not testing every possible program path. One company had a system that worked well for six years. One day, a transaction was entered and the system failed. Why? That particular type of transaction was never tested, not once, during the testing phase of the project; in fact, it was never entered until that fateful day when the system came crashing down at 2:00 A.M. early one Friday. Poor testing practices can let errors slip in when you least expect them as the poor on-call programmer found out that morning.

One solution to this is to have some other party create the test data. This may not be possible in small shops, where one person is responsible for everything. Once the test data is created, the programmer can evaluate the transactions and write expected results for them. This will help maintain integrity in the system, while possibly testing for conditions not envisioned by the programmer.

Test It Again

When coding is complete for the entire major function, test it again. Any final errors encountered should be small and easy to fix. The expected results should be compared to the actual results and then compared against the results required by the problem definition. When all this has been satisfied, the system is ready for use and can be implemented as a new office procedure.

DESIGNING DATA

Just as important as developing the process is designing the database. Since systems are restricted by the data they have access to, deciding what data is necessary is an important step in development. This is why the output specifications are written before the input is defined. When a new system is being developed, care must be taken to include all information necessary for the system, as well as for any forseen future uses.

dBASE II Data Types

In dBASE II there are three types of data. You have seen character and numeric data before. Character fields are those that hold data that is not used in calculations. Numeric fields are those numbers and quantities that are to be used in calculations.

There is also a type of data called *logical data*. This type of data has only two values, true and false. Logical data is made up of the answers to "YES/NO" or true/false questions such as "Is this person a veteran?" or "Does this person have security clearance?" Logical data fields can be used as the conditional expression in an IF-THEN-ELSE statement. They can also be used in complex conditions with other logical data fields or conditional expressions.

Identifying Records

The first data items in a record should be those data items that provide a unique identification for the record. In a personnel system, the name of the employee is not a good primary identification item, but could be used as a secondary identification item. A better primary identification item would be a social security number, because it is unique to each employee. In a payroll or personnel system, the social security number would probably be the first data item in the record and would be the major *key* that identifies the record. A social security number is a good example of a data item that is all numbers, but is defined as character data because it is not used or manipulated in any calculations.

Arrangement of Data

An important guideline in deciding on the arrangement of data items in a record is that you should keep related fields together. The name information would be immediately followed by the address information if these are commonly used together in the output.

A third guideline is that you should describe the data in terms of *entities*. An entity is composed of all fields necessary to producing the output. This concept is most useful when more than one file is involved. In a personnel system, the major entity would be described as *employee*, even if name and address information was in one file, the rate of pay in another, and hours worked in still another. This happens often in systems that use data that was intended for other purposes and would be costly to reenter. By using the entity approach, the system can be designed as if all data resided in the same place.

Let the Computer Do the Work

One final guideline: do not include fields in the record that can be calculated from other fields already available. The computer should do any calculations—that is its purpose. Data entry people should not have to do any calculations, and their decisions should be kept to a minimum. The computer can do these things faster and more accurately, and the data entry process can be shortened accordingly.

SUMMARY

In Chapters 5 and 6 you have seen the seven step method of program design:

1. Define the problem.
2. Define the output.
3. Define the input.
4. Define the process.
5. Code.
6. Test.
7. Evaluate.

Also discussed were the three fundamentals of a good program:

Generality
Modularity
Hierarchy

You also learned the basic types of statements found in a computer language:

Assignment Statements
Input/Output statements
Decision Statements
Loop Control Statements

You also saw the workings of decision statements, and you were introduced to the last phase in program development, the coding phase. Finally, Chapter 6 discussed documentating and testing the program, and designing and arranging data fields. In the last two sections of this book, using data with dBASE II will be discussed in more detail.

Chapter 7

Business Considerations

This book so far has tried to generally describe some suggestions that apply to all sizes of business—from megabuck corporations to mom-and-pop operations. However, the method by which individual steps are accomplished changes with the size of the business.

LARGE VERSUS SMALL

Large corporations have large staffs of programming specialists and data entry personnel. Projects that these staffs perform can take years to complete and can cost the company a lot of person-power. The cost of the project is carefully measured against the benefits and savings that the company will realize.

On the other end of the business spectrum, even a small retail outlet can benefit from the use of a computer. The projects that would be undertaken would be shorter in duration, however; and all data entry and programming probably would be per-formed by the same person. Possibly the owners would have to do everything by themselves. This could mean that programming will be done during off hours and weekends, and even be forgotten for long periods of time as the problems of running the business intervene.

In large businesses, a given department can go to the programming staff with a business problem, and the staff is expected to develop the answer. Small businesses do not have this advantage. Small business managers must decide the uses of auto-mation themselves. They should ask themselves some questions such as "What takes the most time away from customer services? What part of my job is boring, repetitious? What information must be saved for long periods of time, and would take a lot of space to store?" Once these questions have been answered, the small business manager should have some idea of what aspects of the business to auto-mate.

ADMINISTRATIVE AUTOMATION

By using the guidelines presented in this book, even the business manager who has to program on weekends can be involved in the development of an automated system. Commonly, the first type of system that a small business would create is a payroll/personnel system. This area is often the most significant function of a company that is not directly related to increasing sales or profits. By automating administrative functions, the small business releases resources to concentrate on the profit-making areas of the business, which usually include customer relations. Automation can help you with your business, not run your business for you; data processing is notoriously a service function.

As the small business programmer becomes familiar with the equipment and language of automation, more and more uses will occur to him. It is important to adhere to the system development method described in this book while working on the second and third automation projects. This will prevent something that professional programmers know as "second system syndrome;" that is, adding too many functions to a simple system. A system that has too many bells and whistles hanging off it will be unwieldy to use and manage effectively. Remembering the KISS maxim (Keep It Simple, Stupid) will make development more manageable.

INTERACTIVE PROGRAMMING

As mentioned earlier, the advent of terminals and microcomputers has made possible the use of a programming style known as interactive programming. In the past, programs were written to run without interruption from the operator. The process used files, and sometimes "parameter" cards, to communicate changing information such as report date (usually different from the real date), start/cutoff dates, and the like. This type of information is specific to the time and this date that the

program is to be run and would have to be entered at run time. This idea of batch processing meant that once the program had started, the user had to wait while the program ran all its coded instructions without interruption.

Interactive programming is just that—having a conversation with the program. The program prints certain questions on the screen, and the user must answer them to allow the program to continue running. In the cases mentioned above, the program might print ENTER REPORT DATE:, and the user would enter the date that should appear at the top of the report.

The problem with doing this in the past was that terminals were not widely used to perform program execution. They were used to enter and modify programs. The computer operations staff, the trained professionals that actually run the computer in large installations, were too busy doing their job to answer questions from the program. Now, terminal operators, who may or may not be programmers, are running their own jobs at the terminal. Since each one is the operator for his little piece of the system and would probably just sit and watch the program run anyway, he has time to respond to questions from the program. This not only gets needed data to the program, but also eliminates some boredom on the part of the operator. It is a way of letting him know that the program is working for him.

Microcomputing

Microcomputers have brought the idea of interactive programming to its peak usage. Game programs are the most obvious and notorious type of interactive program. They translate the input of the game controller (joystick) into motions of graphic characters on the display screen and dole out rewards and punishments (for the improper use of the controller). Interactive business programs do much the same thing—if the data is entered incorrectly, the program will send an error message to the user who will immediately reenter the data.

The microcomputer has another advantage: the system is not being used by anyone other than the operator. This means that all resources available to the system are available to you with no waiting. Since you are the operator, the questions and answers that you use to interact with your program can be individualized to you. This can make the programming process more fun, and the dry data entry jobs less boring and more accurate.

Menus

One way of interacting with programs is with full screen menus. Menus are lists of functions that you may want to perform using the system and that you have programmed previously. For instance, let's say that you have created some dBASE II programs that you can use to do all your home budgeting functions. You might have a checkbook balancing program, a loan calculation program, a bill register, and a check-writing program. To produce a menu system from this, you would add the top level of the hierarchy, a new module called BUDGET perhaps. This module would display the choices available and ask you to enter an option number that is listed beside the name of the option.

As an option is selected, BUDGET would then call the program that performs the chosen function. As the number of uses for the microcomputer grow, they may be added to the menu, or a new, higher-level menu could be implemented. Now when you choose BUDGET from that higher menu, the menu that was just discussed would appear on the screen. You could then choose a function from that menu.

Another hierarchy has developed: a hierarchy of menus that should mirror the hierarchy of functions discussed earlier. Note that in the example above, functions were added from lower to higher. This is a minor deviation from the top-down approach, and would not have happened at all if the future uses for the computer had been forseen. If you are using the machine to do budget work and suddenly decide to put a name and address list on the computer as well, you now have two functions that are unrelated. By adding a higher level to the hierarchy, you can bring the functions together in a bigger package, possibly called HOME MANAGEMENT. Nothing detrimental such as developing something "bottom-up", was done, but functions were merged into a new hierarchy whole. This change will make use of the system easier because the list of functions is clear to any operator. The programmer has not undermined his control of the system.

Chapter 8

Fred's Friendly Fish Market

Now that you have seen some of the activities involved in creating and using an automated system, let's develop a system that could be used for either business or personal purposes. For the purpose of this example, let's introduce a small businessperson named Fred. Fred's business is small, that is, not him!

Fred owns a wholesale fish market. Fred is growing larger each month. Not Fred, his business! He sells all types of fish and seafood to area restaurants, supermarkets, and other smaller fish markets. Fred has decided that, in order to grow larger, he must be able to operate his business more efficiently. He is spending too much time running the business and not enough time with the lobsters and crabs. Fred's fish are ready to enter the computer age!

Fred sends circulars to his regular customers every month. This means that Fred himself needs to address every circular by hand each month, and this is excruciatingly boring work to Fred. He'd much rather be spending time with his family or improving the business, not typing out a hundred envelopes or so every month. So, after careful research, Fred has decided to purchase a personal computer that can use dBASE II software. Fred did this because he knows that, although this is the first use he has thought of for automating his business, there will be more uses in the future.

Before Fred purchased that personal computer, he defined his business problem in general terms: "I want to print labels, store an address/ phone list, and produce a directory of these people."

Fred's purchase-decision was based on his immediate needs (a computer, a disk drive for storage, and a printer). Looking ahead to the future, Fred decided that buying a good all-purpose machine with a reliable service contract and useful, generalized software now and expanding his uses later was his best bet in automating his business.

PROBLEM DEFINITION

Now that he has decided on his resources, even if he hasn't made the purchase yet, he can start designing the program he will use. As shown in Fig. 8-1, the definitions of the problem is the basis upon which the whole system is built. Fred now adds more detail to his problem definition.

I need to enter and store information to be printed on mailing labels and on plain paper

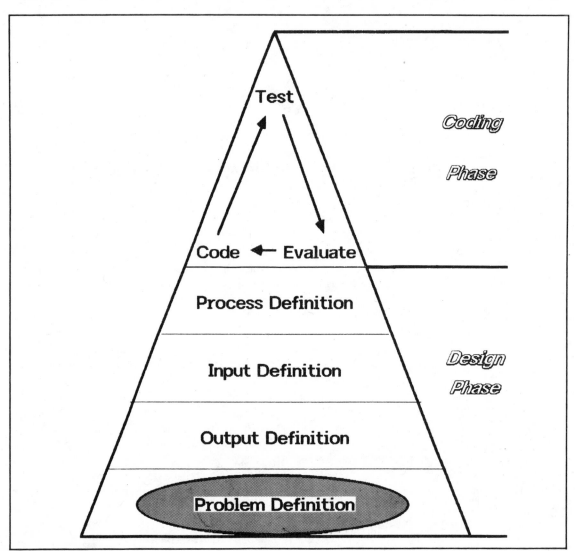

Fig. 8-1. The problem definition.

for a directory for use in mailing those darn circulars.

The dBASE II software that I have chosen can automatically handle data entry, storage, and editing when I supply disks to store the information on.

Also, I will need backup copies of these disks, as well as backup copies of the software.

On the mailing labels I need to have customer name, street address, city, state, and zip code.

On the directory I also need to have the telephone number.

Now that Fred has written the definition in this form, breaking functions onto separate lines, he can see that the program will not be too difficult to write, and there is no calculation to be performed on the data. dBASE II will supply an entry and update facility for the information, so the thing to do now is to design the data.

DEFINING THE OUTPUT DATA

Since Fred decided to computerize his customer list, he must define precisely what he will need on that list. Fred knows that the customer directory and mailing labels are of utmost importance. Fred starts by thinking about what fields are needed in order to prepare those darn mailing labels and produce a customer directory.

The first field is "name." Fred decides that, since he wants all output to be in alphabetical order by last name, he will put last name first in his database. He could put all names in one field called NAME, in last—first order. However, Fred is still thinking of the future; someday, he might want to send personalized letters to his customers, and he would need to print the name in first—last order. Fred defines his first piece of output data as two fields: FNAME, and LNAME. They are character data items, and each will be twenty characters long.

The next data item is "address." Fred creates ADDRESS as a character field, up to 25 characters long. This field will hold the street address.

The "city name" field, Fred decided, would be fifteen characters long, with the name CITY. Fred is being very careful not to use meaningless names in identifying his data items, so that future enhancements will be easier. Good old Fred, always thinking about the future.

The "state" field is easy, says Fred, "Just two characters identify every state in the USA, and I only have customers in three!" So the field becomes STATE, character data, two positions long.

Now comes a toughy, Fred thought. Zip code used to be five digits long, but isn't it supposed to be changed to nine digits in the near future? Fred decides to make zip code nine digits long to be sure; although, he could have easily changed this at a later time with dBASE II. A zip code is an excellent example of a number that is not used in calculations. It could be defined as a character field. However, Fred wants dBASE II to edit the input data for him, and if he defines it as character data, the system would allow any character in the field. By defining it as a numeric field, it will accept only numbers nine positions long.

The last step is taking care of the phone number, so Fred uses the same reasoning as for ZIPCODE and comes up with PHONE, which will be ten digits long and numeric.

Fred's output description looks like this:

Field	Data Type	Length
FNAME	character	20
LNAME	character	20
ADDRESS	character	25
CITY	character	15
STATE	character	2
ZIP	numeric	9
PHONE	numeric	10

The output definition is part of the evolving system design. Since it is still a design, the definition can be changed to reflect new requirements and developments. This definition is not "cast in stone!"

The Format of the Output

Part of the output definition is also defining exactly what the output reports will look like. In a name/address file this is usually easy because there are few fields to contend with, and because the format of mailing labels is defined by the post office and is rarely changed. (Look how long it will take American businesses to implement the nine digit zip code—7 years!)

Format of the Mailing Labels

Fred has decided to buy blank labels that are three across a page, or *3-up* as they are referred to. That means that three labels must be printed at one time, or the labels on the right side of the page will go to waste. The format that would be used if there are eight names on the mailing list is shown in Fig. 8-2.

The layout of the labels does not provide enough details to be useful as an output definition. The field names are really not enough. The length of each field should be part of the label definition to ensure the proper fit and alignment. Producing this type of format for the label will show the smallest possible size the label should be. The following shows a single label. Note that the space from one X to the next is the field length as defined previously.

```
X-------FNAME-------X X------LNAME------X
X---------ADDRESS---------X
X----CITY-----X, ST
X--ZIP--X
```

These field definitions reflect the largest possible variable that each field can hold.

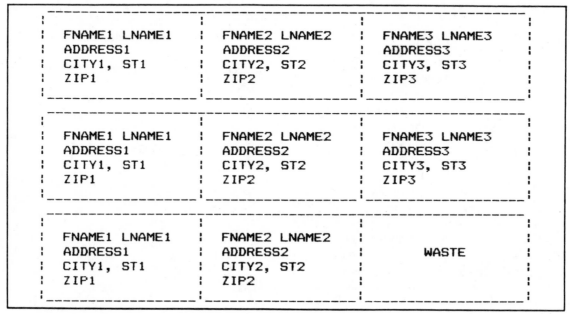

Fig. 8-2. Mailing labels.

40

Format of the Directory

The only real document Fred has to design is the directory he wants printed. This should lead to more questioning on Fred's part—does he want a hand-held, book size directory, or does he want it printed on 3 × 5 cards. Some printers can only handle forms with sprocket feed holes on the sides; some work with regular typing paper. Fred has to take these details into consideration as well.

So Fred, for the time being, has decided on 8½ × 11 inch paper because he has pin feed paper for his new printer. If at a later time he wishes to convert to ROLIDEX, he can do so without too many problems. And, if he ever runs out of the special forms, he can always convert to plain paper.

Fred decided to make his directory one column wide, with as many names as fit on each page. This is the most efficient form that he can think of, and it will probably not be used that often anyway. He just needs it to look up a name or phone number when he is not near the computer.

Fred now defines the format for an entry in the directory:

```
X------LNAME-------X, X------FNAME-------X
                      X------ADDRESS----------X
                      X----CITY-----X ST  X--ZIP--X
```

The format shows the maximum length of each field. This is because the maximum length of the fields must be allowed for on the output forms. Otherwise, the fields may get chopped off, or *truncated*, if other fields on the form compete for the same space. Also the fields could print past the edge of a narrow form, which wastes ink and time, and doesn't do your printer much good either.

Now Fred can figure out how many of these entries will fit on a page. He already decided that he would use regular paper with a length of 11 inches for this listing. Fred's printer prints 6 lines per inch, so this means that there will be 66 lines

available per page. Each individual entry takes 5 lines, and Fred wants 2 lines between entries; thus each entry will require 7 lines in all. Also, Fred decided that he didn't want the first and last entries on each page to print too near the top or bottom. He decides to leave 5 blank lines at the top and bottom of each page or a total of 10 blank lines. With a little math, Fred figures

66 total lines − 10 margin lines = 56 effective lines

56 lines / 7 lines per entry = 8 entries per page.

Fred decides that he will print eight entries per page. Each entry will be formatted as shown previously.

TWO THINGS AT ONCE

Fred has defined his output pretty well. His next discovery is that he has also defined the input. This is because it's Fred's first stab at automation: he has no existing files, and all data that is needed will have to be present in the input or calculated from the input. Since there is no calculation involved in the solution to Fred's business problem, he has done the remarkable feat of defining his input and output in one step. Up-front planning has already paid off in this admittedly simple system.

Fred's input description looks just like his output description because there are no calculations:

Field	Data Type	Length
FNAME	character	20
LNAME	character	20
ADDRESS	character	25
CITY	character	15
STATE	character	2
ZIP	numeric	9
PHONE	numeric	10

REEXAMINING THE DESIGN

Now the problem has been defined and the output specified, and Fred is ready to tear into his process definition. As he looks carefully at the documents he has created, he notices that there is not much processing to do at all. The information has only to be retrieved from wherever it is now and placed on the output form. Fred takes the sensible approach and decides to look over his requirements one more time.

On closer inspection, he notices two things. First, the nine digit zip code is broken into two parts: the five digit zip code and the new four digit part are separated by a hyphen. He decides not to create a ZIP1 and ZIP2 field for the two parts.

Second, the telephone number, when entered as a single number, is awkward to look at and needs to be divided into three parts: area code, exchange, and number. Instead of breaking up the phone number into its component parts, Fred decides that he will make the field a character field and enter all punctuation manually. Now the numeric edit will not work, so Fred will have to edit the contents of the phone number field by himself. He is prepared to do that to save processing time. So, both the zip code and the phone number fields will be character fields. The zip code will be ten characters long and have the form NNNNN-NNNN. The phone number

will have the form (AAA)NNN-NNNN and will be thirteen characters long.

FRED DIVIDES TO CONQUER

Now that Fred has defined his output and input, he is ready to chart the hierarchy of the functions in the system. He first draws a square on the empty sheet of paper and labels it CUSTOMER SYSTEM. This is the overall name of the major function. He then draws six more boxes in a line an inch or two under the first box. He labels these boxes, from left to right, ADD CUSTOMER, CHANGE CUSTOMER, REMOVE CUSTOMER, PRINT MAILING LABELS, PRINT MAILING LIST. These are the overall kinds of actions that Fred will need his system to perform. He then connects the boxes with lines, denoting the hierarchy of the functions. The result is shown in Fig. 8-3.

Fred now adds a third level of boxes about an inch under the second row. He puts two boxes underneath PRINT MAILING LABELS box. He connects them to the box using the hierarchy lines and labels them as in Fig. 8-4. Since the function PRINT MAILING LABELS will automatically print the labels each time a row of three labels are for-

Fig. 8-3. The main function hierarchy chart.

42

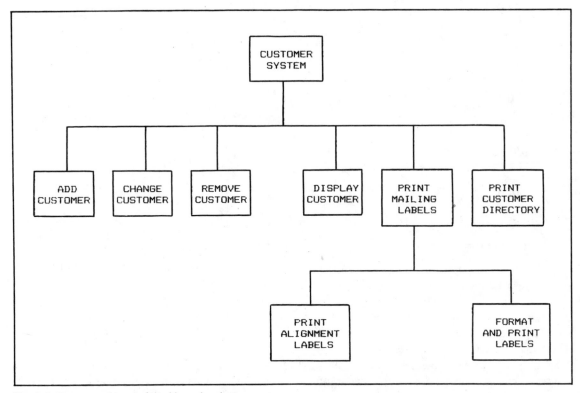

Fig. 8-4. The second level of the hierarchy chart.

matted, it is shown as a part of the second hierarchy rather than as a separate third level.

Fred feels that his hierarchy is now complete, and he is ready to start his screen design.

DESIGNING SCREENS

At this point in the design, Fred (or you) can take a look at how the data is to be entered. When a new customer is to be added to the file, all of the input fields must be entered; the record concerning the customer does not exist in computer-usable form. So, in order to "capture" this information, Fred designs the data input screen for customer additions to look like the screen shown in Fig. 8-5.

With this screen, Fred can enter all the information needed for each customer. Notice that he

allowed for the full length of each field; he also included a heading for the screen and a label for each field. You may notice a large space between the heading and the first field. Later you will learn how error messages and informational messages can also be programmed to appear in this space.

For the CHANGE CUSTOMER function, Fred needs approximately the same screen as was defined for the ADD CUSTOMER function, except that when it appears, it should have all the information already displayed. Then it can be changed and the record updated. With this type of process, however, Fred will have to tell his program which customer to change. He will need the screen shown in Fig. 8-6.

The name information will give the program a

```
------------------------------------------------
:                                              :
:       FRED'S FRIENDLY FISH MARKET            :
:            CUSTOMER ADDITIONS                :
:                                              :
:                                              :
:                                              :
:     LAST NAME:   LNAME---------------X       :
:     FIRST NAME: FNAME---------------X        :
:                                              :
:     ADDRESS: ADDRESS-------------------X     :
:     CITY:      CITY----------X               :
:                                              :
:     STATE: ST     ZIP: ZIP-----X             :
:                                              :
:     PHONE NUMBER: PHONE-------X              :
:                                              :
------------------------------------------------
```

Fig. 8-5. The screen design for adding customers.

clue that indicates which record is to be retrieved for changes. If the record is not found the computer can be programmed to display an error message as shown in Fig. 8-7. The user will be requested to reenter the name. When the record is retrieved, it will be displayed on the screen as shown in Fig. 8-8, with all the information filled in. Fred then has the ability to change any field on the screen. After changes have been made, he can tell the system to put the record with the changes back into its place in the file.

The screens for DISPLAY CUSTOMER, shown in Figs. 8-9 and 8-10, will look almost the same as those for CHANGE CUSTOMER shown, except that no data can be changed.

For the DELETE CUSTOMER function, Fred will need a screen to enter the name of the customer to be deleted, and some way of confirming the delete. If, by chance, the name was entered incorrectly, or the wrong name was entered, he wants the ability to abort the deletion. The program should ask if the retrieve record is the correct one

Fig. 8-6. The screen design for customer search.

```
------------------------------------------------
:                                              :
:       FRED'S FRIENDLY FISH MARKET            :
:            CUSTOMER CHANGES                  :
:                                              :
:  *** ENTER CUSTOMER TO BE CHANGED ***        :
:                                              :
:    LAST NAME:   LNAME---------------X        :
:    FIRST NAME: FNAME---------------X         :
:                                              :
:                                              :
:                                              :
:                                              :
:                                              :
:                                              :
:                                              :
------------------------------------------------
```

```
  ----------------------------------------
  :                                        :
  :        FRED'S FRIENDLY FISH MARKET     :
  :            CUSTOMER CHANGES            :
  :                                        :
  :    *** NAME NOT FOUND - TRY AGAIN ***  :
  :                                        :
  :     LAST NAME:   LNAME--------------X  :
  :     FIRST NAME:  FNAME--------------X  :
  :                                        :
  :                                        :
  :                                        :
  :                                        :
  :                                        :
  :                                        :
  ----------------------------------------
```

Fig. 8-7. An example of a screen error message.

to remove from the file. Notice how Fred is using informational messages in the message area of the confirmation screen shown in Fig. 8-11.

After creating the screens for the customer data entry and the maintenance functions (called *file maintenance* in programmer talk), Fred turns to the actual application screen. The add, change, delete, and display functions are also applications, but they are support functions; that is to say, they exist only to facilitate the operation of the functions PRINT MAILING LABELS, and PRINT DIRECTORY.

These last two are the output generators, the functions for which the system was written in the first place.

The input screen for the PRINT MAILING LABELS function is designed as shown in Fig. 8-12.

This screen asks if alignment labels are to be printed. When a Y is entered, the test labels will be printed. The alignment routine will print a series of Xs across the labels so the operator can properly adjust the printer. The <cr> symbol means *car-*

Fig. 8-8. The Customer change data screen.

```
  ------------------------------------------------
  :                                                :
  :          FRED'S FRIENDLY FISH MARKET           :
  :              CUSTOMER CHANGES                  :
  :                                                :
  :                                                :
  :                                                :
  :      LAST NAME:    LNAME--------------X        :
  :      FIRST NAME:   FNAME--------------X        :
  :                                                :
  :      ADDRESS:   ADDRESS------------------X     :
  :      CITY:      CITY----------X                :
  :                                                :
  :      STATE: ST     ZIP: ZIP-----X              :
  :                                                :
  :      PHONE NUMBER: PHONE------X                :
  :                                                :
  ------------------------------------------------
```

```
 ----------------------------------------
i                                        i
i     FRED'S FRIENDLY FISH MARKET        i
i          CUSTOMER DISPLAY              i
i                                        i
i  *** ENTER NAME TO BE DISPLAYED ***    i
i                                        i
i    LAST NAME:   LNAME---------------X  i
i    FIRST NAME: FNAME---------------X   i
i                                        i
i                                        i
i                                        i
i                                        i
i                                        i
i                                        i
i                                        i
i                                        i
 ----------------------------------------
```

Fig. 8-9. The screen for a customer search.

riage return and means that the operator should press the enter or return key. After the alignment labels are printed, this screen is displayed again. When Fred has aligned the printer to his satisfaction, he presses the enter key, and the customer labels are printed.

The PRINT DIRECTORY function really does not need a screen, since the plain paper forms can be aligned without using the method described for the PRINT MAILING LABELS function. Fred decides to display a screen anyway, to confirm that the

PRINT DIRECTORY function is the one that the operator wanted. So he designs the screen shown in Fig. 8-13.

When this screen is displayed, Fred will have to tell the program to start printing the directory. If he chose the option by mistake, he could abort it.

On closer examination of his screens, Fred decides that this screen could also be used in the PRINT MAILING LABELS function in the same way. Since this project is still in the design phase, writing another piece of paper is an easy task. This

Fig. 8-10. The customer display screen.

```
 ------------------------------------------------
i                                                i
i          FRED'S FRIENDLY FISH MARKET           i
i               CUSTOMER DISPLAY                 i
i                                                i
i                                                i
i    LAST NAME:   LNAME---------------X          i
i    FIRST NAME: FNAME---------------X           i
i                                                i
i    ADDRESS:  ADDRESS-------------------X       i
i    CITY:       CITY----------X                 i
i                                                i
i    STATE: ST     ZIP: ZIP-----X                i
i                                                i
i    PHONE NUMBER: PHONE-------X                 i
 ------------------------------------------------
```

46

```
 ----------------------------------------
:                                         :
:     FRED'S FRIENDLY FISH MARKET         :
:            CUSTOMER DELETION            :
:                                         :
:  ENTER "D" TO CONFIRM DELETE ===>  __   :
:                                         :
:     LAST NAME:    LNAME--------------X  :
:     FIRST NAME:   FNAME--------------X  :
:                                         :
:     ADDRESS:  ADDRESS-------------------X :
:     CITY:      CITY----------X          :
:                                         :
:     STATE: ST     ZIP: ZIP-----X        :
:                                         :
:     PHONE NUMBER: PHONE----X            :
:                                         :
:                                         :
:                                         :
 ----------------------------------------
```

Fig. 8-11. The deletion confirmation message.

sort of change should be noted in the design, rather than changed when the full system is implemented. Fred now changes the Mailing Label screen to look like the one shown in Fig. 8-14.

Fred has one more screen to design—the menu screen for the entire customer system. This screen (and program) is the top level on the hierar-chy chart, and will allow Fred to initiate any of his functions by entering a number or letter. Fred's menu screen is shown in Fig. 8-15.

The ENTER SELECTION line is where the selection is entered. This is called a *prompt* because you are prompted for the right answer. If you enter anything besides 1-6 or X, the system will prompt

Fig. 8-12. The mailing label print screen.

```
 ----------------------------------------------
:                                              :
:       FRED'S FRIENDLY FISH MARKET            :
:          MAILING LABEL PRINT                 :
:                                              :
:                                              :
:                                              :
:     ENTER "Y" FOR ALIGNMENT PRINT            :
:        OR <cr> TO BEGIN PRINT                :
:                                              :
:       ====>  ___                             :
:                                              :
:                                              :
:                                              :
:                                              :
:                                              :
:                                              :
 ----------------------------------------------
```

```
------------------------------------------
:                                          :
:                                          :
:      FRED'S FRIENDLY FISH MARKET         :
:      CUSTOMER DIRECTORY PRINT            :
:                                          :
:                                          :
:                                          :
:      ENTER <cr> TO BEGIN PRINT           :
:        OR "N" TO ABORT PRINT             :
:                                          :
:          ====> ___                       :
:                                          :
:                                          :
:                                          :
:                                          :
:                                          :
:                                          :
:                                          :
------------------------------------------
```

Fig. 8-13. Customer directory and screen.

you for a correct answer by printing INVALID SELECTION—TRY AGAIN on the message area of the screen.

Now, Fred is ready to tackle the design of the processes his system will perform.

A MENU SYSTEM

Fred envisions the top level of the hierarchy as a menu that will invoke the next lower level of functions. This means that when he runs the program, a list of choices will appear on the screen, with an option number beside each one. The operator (probably Fred) will enter the number of his choice, and that function will be performed. It's just like ordering food in a restaurant, thought Fred. No wonder they are called menus.

Fig. 8-14. The revised mailing label print screen.

```
---------------------------------------------------
:                                                   :
:          FRED'S FRIENDLY FISH MARKET              :
:            MAILING LABEL PRINT                    :
:                                                   :
:                                                   :
:                                                   :
:                                                   :
:       ENTER "Y" FOR ALIGNMENT PRINT,              :
:            "A" TO ABORT PRINT,                    :
:          OR <cr> TO BEGIN PRINT                   :
:                                                   :
:              ====> ___                            :
:                                                   :
:                                                   :
:                                                   :
:                                                   :
:                                                   :
:                                                   :
---------------------------------------------------
```

48

```
----------------------------------------
:                                        :
:    FRED'S FRIENDLY FISH MARKET         :
:       CUSTOMER SYSTEM MENU             :
:                                        :
:                                        :
:                                        :
:    ENTER SELECTION ===> __             :
:                                        :
:       1 - ADD CUSTOMER                 :
:       2 - CHANGE CUSTOMER              :
:       3 - REMOVE CUSTOMER              :
:       4 - DISPLAY CUSTOMER             :
:                                        :
:       5 - PRINT MAILING LABELS         :
:       6 - PRINT DIRECTORY              :
:                                        :
:       X - EXIT SYSTEM                  :
:                                        :
----------------------------------------
```

Fig. 8-15. The main customer system menu.

Fred then writes the pseudocode shown in Fig. 8-16 for his menu program:

Inside the DO WHILE loop, Fred placed a CASE construct to test for the options he listed on his menu screen. He includes an OTHERWISE unit in case the number entered was not one listed on the screen. Fred then ends the DO WHILE loop with an ENDDO and notes that this will be the end of the program, because it has fulfilled all the functions.

```
SET EXIT TO "N"
DISPLAY MENU SCREEN
READ OPTION
DO WHILE EXIT = "N"
   CASE
      WHEN OPTION = 1 PERFORM "ADD CUSTOMER"
      WHEN OPTION = 2 PERFORM "CHANGE CUSTOMER"
      WHEN OPTION = 3 PERFORM "REMOVE CUSTOMER"
      WHEN OPTION = 4 PERFORM "DISPLAY CUSTOMER"
      WHEN OPTION = 5 PERFORM "PRINT MAILING LABELS"
      WHEN OPTION = 6 PERFORM "PRINT MAILING LIST"
      WHEN OPTION = X SET EXIT TO "Y"
      OTHERWISE WRITE "INVALID OPTION"
      DISPLAY MENU SCREEN
      READ OPTION
   ENDCASE
ENDDO
```

Fig. 8-16. Pseudocode for a menu program.

```
SET EXIT TO "N"
DO WHILE EXIT = "N"
   CASE
      DISPLAY MENU SCREEN
      READ OPTION
      WHEN OPTION = 1 PERFORM "ADD CUSTOMER"
      WHEN OPTION = 2 PERFORM "CHANGE CUSTOMER"
      WHEN OPTION = 3 PERFORM "REMOVE CUSTOMER"
      WHEN OPTION = 4 PERFORM "DISPLAY CUSTOMER"
      WHEN OPTION = 5 PERFORM "PRINT MAILING LABELS"
      WHEN OPTION = 6 PERFORM "PRINT MAILING LIST"
      WHEN OPTION = X SET EXIT TO "Y"
      OTHERWISE WRITE "INVALID OPTION"
   ENDCASE
ENDDO
```

Fig. 8-17. Redesigning the pseudocode.

Fred uses a switch, which is called EXIT, to determine if the operator has chosen the exit option. The first statement sets the switch for exiting the system to no exit. As long as this code is N, the menu is to be displayed so that another option can be chosen. Fred wrote the statement DISPLAY MENU and then used a DO WHILE to see if the exit option (he called it option X) had been chosen.

Walking Through the Menu Program

Fred now "walks-thru" his pseudocode to determine if it is correct and performs the processes he wants when he wants. He writes EXIT on a separate sheet of paper and writes below it. After EXIT he adds OPTION and writes an X below it, showing that he has chosen the EXIT SYSTEM option on his (as yet) imaginary menu. Fred has decided to test this option first (a very good idea).

EXIT	OPTION
N	X

The next statement to be performed is the DO WHILE. The condition asks if EXIT is equal to N. Looking at his sheet of paper, Fred sees that EXIT is equal to N, because N was assigned to it in the first statement; EXIT has not been changed by another assignment. "This isn't right," thought Fred. The program should not get into the loop if the X option was chosen. On close examination of the code, Fred sees that the condition would be met on the next time through the loop, but only after the menu is displayed another time.

So, Fred makes a modification to the pseudocode as shown in Fig. 8-17.

Now when he chooses option X, the WHEN unit for the condition OPTION-X is performed, and the value of EXIT is changed to Y. Control jumps out of the CASE figure to the ENDDO, and the condition is tested. Since EXIT now equals Y, the condition is no longer true, so control then passes out of the DO WHILE to the statement following the ENDDO.

THE FUNCTIONS

Now Fred begins to code the functions on the second level of the hierarchy chart. As he looks at the functions, Fred realizes that the add, change, remove, and display functions are probably performed easily in a powerful database manager like dBASE II.

Since the major purpose of a database management program is to add, change, delete, and display records in a database file, he can probably use very few dBASE II commands to perform these functions. His pseudocode for these functions look like this:

```
ADD A CUSTOMER

   ACCESS CUSTOMER FILE
   ADD CUSTOMER DATA IN LAST NAME ORDER
   CLOSE FILE


CHANGE A CUSTOMER

   ACCESS CUSTOMER FILE
   ENTER CUSTOMER NAME
   VERIFY AND RETRIEVE RECORD
   CHANGE CUSTOMER DATA
   CLOSE FILE


REMOVE CUSTOMER

   ACCESS CUSTOMER FILE
   ENTER CUSTOMER NAME
   VERIFY AND DELETE RECORD
   CLOSE FILE


DISPLAY CUSTOMER

   ACCESS CUSTOMER FILE
   ENTER CUSTOMER NAME
   VERIFY AND DISPLAY CUSTOMER
   CLOSE FILE
```

Fred has now pseudocoded all but the last two functions the system is to perform. These functions are a little more involved:

```
PRINT MAILING LABELS

   PERFORM "ALIGNMENT PRINT"
   ACCESS CUSTOMER FILE
   READ A CUSTOMER RECORD
   DO WHILE MORE RECORDS
   PERFORM "FORMAT FOR LABELS"
     IF LABEL COUNTER = 3
       THEN
          PRINT A ROW OF LABELS
          RESET LABEL COUNTER
     ENDIF
     READ NEXT RECORD
   ENDDO
   CLOSE FILE
```

In this program, notice that Fred has put off defining the two subfunctions in the PERFORM statements. No matter how simple they may be, they are still on the next level of the hierarchy, and the second level is not finished yet:

```
PRINT MAILING LIST

   ACCESS CUSTOMER FILE
   READ CUSTOMER RECORD
   DO WHILE MORE RECORDS
     PRINT DIRECTORY ENTRY
     READ NEXT RECORD
   ENDDO
   CLOSE FILE
```

Again, Fred has postponed the definition of the third-level modules until later. Notice that these programs will still be valid, no matter what format the final labels or directory take. This means that if Fred starts out using sheets that contain 3 labels across the page, *3-up labels* and later switches to 2-up labels, the only modules that need to be changed are the PRINT ALIGNMENT and FORMAT FOR LABELS modules. This is an advantage of modular programming—changes to the lower level functions do not require the recording of any higher modules.

THE SUBFUNCTIONS

Now Fred turns to his third and final level:

```
PRINT ALIGNMENT LABELS

   ASK IF ALIGNMENT NEEDED
   DO WHILE ALIGNMENT NEEDED
     PRINT LABEL WITH X'S FILLING EVERY
     FIELD
     ADVANCE TO NEXT LABEL
     ASK IF ALIGNMENT IS NEEDED
   ENDDO


FORMAT FOR LABELS

   ADD 1 TO LABEL COUNTER
   MOVE CUSTOMER FIELDS TO LABEL 1, 2 OR 3,
       DEPENDING ON LABEL COUNTER
```

These two functions could probably be coded in the PRINT MAILING LABELS pseudocode. Do not be tempted to join short modules, however. Always break the process down into functional components, as Fred has done. Always traverse the module hierarchy from top to bottom; beware of short-cuts.

Fred now codes the final function:

```
PRINT DIRECTORY ENTRIES

    PRINT THE DIRECTORY ENTRIES
    BLANK OUT THE DIRECTORY FIELDS
    ADVANCE PAPER
    IF TOO CLOSE TO BOTTOM OF PAGE FOR MORE
      ENTRIES
        THEN ADVANCE TO TOP OF PAGE
ENDIF
```

Notice that Fred did not say just exactly how he is going to know when the printer is nearing the bottom of the page. This will have to be done in dBASE II code, and Fred hasn't learned it yet. Therefore, he leaves the pseudocode statements deliberately vague; he will not be tied down to a particular method.

An important advantage of top-down coding is that the basic system can be made available quickly, before all the modules are coded in dBASE II. In the customer system example, the ADD CUSTOMER function could be the first one done. Then, while Fred is coding the other modules, someone else can be entering the customer data (Fred's wife Elsa, for instance). Then, when the PRINT functions are ready to be placed *on-line*, the data will be available to test them, and the system will be ready to go.

Chapter 9

Fred Gets Ambitious

Fred has finished the design for his customer information system. He is feeling very proud of himself but, he still doesn't feel perfect; it seems too easy! Fred wants to automate as much as he can. He thinks of other sections that he can automate most easily.

"Gee whiz," I should automate orders next. There are so many each day that we work many hours after the docks close just to do the paperwork. Also, we could do the daily inventories so we know what to order each day. My brother Frank always orders too much mackeral and not enough lobster. He says, "Don't worry, what we sell, we sell." But I do worry; we need to track our inventories so we don't run out. Murphys Restaurant came to us for crab last week, and we were out; they haven't ordered from us since. So, I want to automate our customer orders and our inventories. That way I will know what my customers are ordering and what I need to have in our warehouse.

Finally, I want to automate the payroll here. We are always paying too much to the dockhands or the checks are late or something. I will do all these things.

Fred has gone off the deep end! Because of one success, he is ready to tackle the world (and all he has done is the design). The next logical step is to chart the whole system. This will become the new top level of the hierarchy chart, and everything else will move down one level. The customer system becomes part of a bigger system and will be represented as such. The resulting hierarchy chart is shown in Fig. 9-1, and the Main Menu screen is shown in Fig. 9-2.

After charting and designing his Main Menu screen, Fred thinks he is now ready to tackle the rest of the system. He remembers that a beginner should design a little at a time. One module can be finished before the others are started.

Fred is now ready to automate the next part of

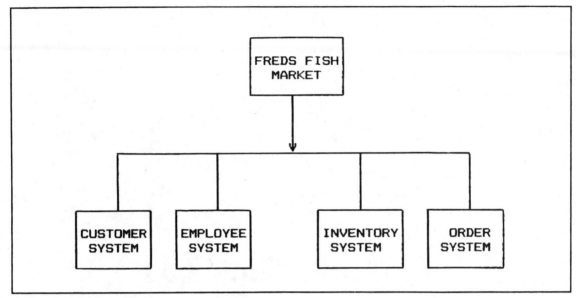

Fig. 9-1. Fred's Fish Market system hierarchy chart.

his system, the ordering system. When customers place orders with Fred, the smallest part of the process that he goes through is actually sending out the order. The rest of the process is filling out the order form, keeping track of the inventory, and keeping orders on the file for long periods of time.

Fred has just about outgrown his four-drawer file cabinet. In the fish business there are no backorders. If you don't have it, the customer will go somewhere else to get it. There are many standing orders. One of Fred's customers, The Fish Depot in Somersville, has a lobster special twice a week.

Fig. 9-2. Fred's Fish Market main screen design.

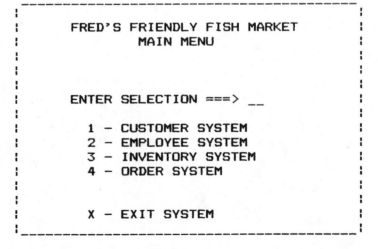

They expect sixty-two 1-pound lobsters every Tuesday and Saturday. They don't even call in the order; the lobsters are expected to be there (and its a long walk). They do call in other items each day, though. Fred and Frank (his brother) spend a lot of time remembering who gets what, and when.

So with one design already under his belt, Fred starts the design for the Customer Order System.

THE PROBLEM DEFINITION

Fred needs certain information to create this system. In processing orders now, he has

customer information
an order number to uniquely indentify orders
the date of the order
the quantity, description, and price of each item ordered

As Fred examined his current way of processing orders, he saw that there were two forms of output: the order form that goes to Fred's shipping department to indicate what is to be packed and shipped, and the shipping form (bill of lading), which is also the invoice (Fred's Fish is C.O.D. only—not codfish, cash on delivery—he doesn't give credit).

Fred defined his problem like this:

Fred immediately noticed that the shipping form has some information on it that can be retrieved from the customer system he has just finished designing! That means that he will not have to reenter the information; he will just have to retrieve it when he wants.

THE OUTPUT DEFINITION

Now Fred defines the fields he will need for his output:

Field	Type	Length
FNAME	Character	20
LNAME	Character	20
ADDRESS	Character	25
CITY	Character	15
ST	Character	2
ZIP	Character	10
ORDER NUMBER	Numeric	5
DATE ORDERED	Character	8
QUANTITY	Numeric	3
ITEM	Character	25
PRICE	Numeric	5.2

Six out of the eleven items of output that Fred defined are fields from his previous system! Since that information will be available in computer-usable form, Fred doesn't have to worry about entering it again. Fred wonders how to retrieve it

```
"I need to record and store
order information
to be used to produce
order forms and shipping labels.
The order forms should have:
    the order number and customer name
    each item and quantity number.
The shipping form should have:
    the order number and all customer information
    each item and quantity
    along with prices and a total."
```

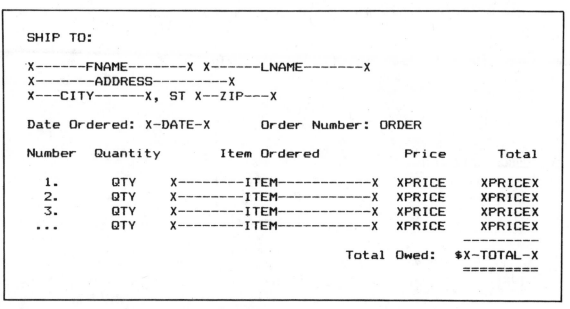

```
    SHIP TO:

    X-------FNAME-------X  X------LNAME-------X
    X--------ADDRESS---------X
    X---CITY------X, ST X--ZIP---X

    Date Ordered: X-DATE-X       Order Number: ORDER

    Number   Quantity        Item Ordered          Price        Total

      1.        QTY     X---------ITEM-----------X  XPRICE      XPRICEX
      2.        QTY     X---------ITEM-----------X  XPRICE      XPRICEX
      3.        QTY     X---------ITEM-----------X  XPRICE      XPRICEX
     ...        QTY     X---------ITEM-----------X  XPRICE      XPRICEX
                                                               ---------
                                            Total Owed:  $X-TOTAL-X
                                                               =========
```

Fig. 9-3. The shipping form field definition.

from the customer file, but he realizes that should be figured out as a part of the input design.

The length of the PRICE field is 5.2. This means it will contain a total of 5 characters, with two representing pennies. The largest price you could have would be 99.99 because the decimal occupies a space.

Fred defines the shipping form so that it will look just like the ones he wrote by hand. The shipping form is shown in Fig. 9-3.

The order form would be the same but would not have prices or the customer's address.

THE INPUT DEFINITION

The total price fields including the TOTAL OWED would not be input fields. They can be calculated by multiplying QTY times PRICE as the items are printed on the form.

Fred now can define his input. The fields from the customer system can be retrieved, so the only fields that need to be input for the order system are

ORDER NUMBER	Numeric	5
DATE ORDERED	Character	8
QUANTITY	Numeric	3
ITEM	Character	25
PRICE	Numeric	5.2

Now Fred can address a question that has been bothering him. "How can I use my customer file with my new order file? Each order must be related to a unique customer, and if, at some point, I have two customers named Bill Smith; how could the program tell them apart using the information I have given it?"

A good question: as things are designed now, there is no unique identification for a customer, apart from the customers last and first names. When Fred was envisioning his customer system, it wasn't important. If he somehow asked to delete the wrong customer, he could always abort the delete and find the next record that had the name he entered. Now, however, when he will be accessing that file from a program, Fred cannot rely on his own judgment because a computer cannot make judgments of this type. Another way must be found.

Fred decides that he must change his customer system to include a field called Customer Number. This will be a unique indentifier, will be first on the record, and will be assigned by Fred when the customer data is initially added to the file.

Fred has also decided to add something he always wanted and never even did in the manual system—the customer's business name. When Fred started, he sold mainly to other distributors. He always dealt with the owner and would ship the items with the owners name on the label. As Fred has gotten larger (the business, not Fred: he only weighs 130 lbs), he has not been able to meet all of his customers. The business name is more important than the owner's or seafood buyer's name in a large supermarket chain.

Fred's new input description for the customer system looks like this:

Field	Data Type	Length
CUSTNO	Numeric	5

Field	Data Type	Length
COMPANY	Character	20
FNAME	Character	20
LNAME	Character	20
ADDRESS	Character	25
CITY	Character	15
STATE	Character	2
ZIP	Character	10
PHONE	Character	13

Fred makes this change to his customer system design, and looks for more changes. He knows that his customer information screens will change; for example, the Add Customer screen now will have to include customer number and company, as shown in Fig. 9-4.

Also, the screens for Change Customer, Delete Customer, and Display Customer can be changed to retrieve the customer record by the customer number, rather than by the more unreliable customer name. For example, the Change Customer screens would look like the one shown in Fig. 9-5.

Fred had to make these changes to the customer name screens for Delete Customer, and Dis-

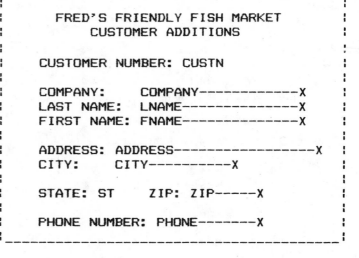

Fig. 9-4. A new customer additions screen.

```
-----------------------------------------------
:                                               :
:        FRED'S FRIENDLY FISH MARKET            :
:             CUSTOMER ADDITIONS                :
:                                               :
:    CUSTOMER NUMBER: CUSTN                      :
:                                               :
:    COMPANY:      COMPANY--------------X        :
:    LAST NAME:    LNAME--------------X          :
:    FIRST NAME:   FNAME--------------X          :
:                                               :
:    ADDRESS:  ADDRESS------------------X        :
:    CITY:     CITY----------X                   :
:                                               :
:    STATE: ST    ZIP: ZIP-----X                 :
:                                               :
:    PHONE NUMBER: PHONE-------X                  :
:                                               :
-----------------------------------------------
```

```
------------------------------------------------
:  :                                        :  :
:        FRED'S FRIENDLY FISH MARKET        :
:             CUSTOMER CHANGES              :
:                                           :
:                                           :
:                                           :
:     CUSTOMER NUMBER: CUSTN                :
:                                           :
:     LAST NAME:   LNAME---------------X    :
:     FIRST NAME: FNAME---------------X     :
:                                           :
:     ADDRESS: ADDRESS-----------------X    :
:     CITY:     CITY----------X             :
:                                           :
:     STATE: ST     ZIP: ZIP-----X          :
:                                           :
:     PHONE NUMBER: PHONE-------X           :
:  :                                        :  :
------------------------------------------------
```

Fig. 9-5. A Revised Customer Change Screen.

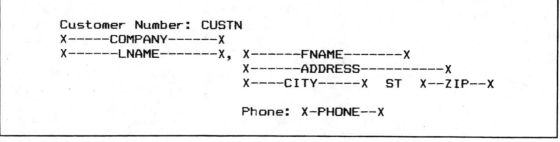

```
        Customer Number: CUSTN
        X-----COMPANY------X
        X------LNAME-------X,  X------FNAME-------X
                              X------ADDRESS----------X
                              X----CITY-----X  ST  X--ZIP--X

                  Phone:  X-PHONE--X
```

Fig. 9-6. A revised directory format.

play Customer as well. He also had to make the change to his directory format as shown in Fig. 9-6.

With these changes made, Fred feels that he can now produce an input definition for the order system:

Field	Type	Length
ORDER NUMBER	Numeric	5
CUST NUMBER	Numeric	5
DATE ORDERED	Character	8
QUANTITY	Numeric	3
ITEM	Character	25
PRICE	Numeric	5.2

A TWO FILE SYSTEM

Now that Fred has decided on the input fields, he looks at the design of the data. One order record, as just defined has one item associated with it. "This is no good," Fred thought. "Most of the orders I process are for more than one item." He could put ITEM1, ITEM2, etc., directly on the order record, but this would make the record very large and difficult to use. This would also limit the number of items that could be assigned to one order number. Fred is about to experience the realities of relational database design, (and he doesn't even know what that means—yet).

In the Database section of this book, you will learn in detail how to analyze and design databases. For now, only a brief mention of the *two-file* system is necessary.

The solution is for Fred to create two files: one for order number, customer number, and date; and another for the quantities, items, and prices. The "bridge" between the files is the order number which will appear in both. In the order file one record will appear for each order. In the order items file, one record will appear for each different item ordered. The order number will be placed in the order items file, and all item records with the same order number will be the corresponding order on the order file.

The order file itself will be a bridge between the customer file and the order items file, because of the inclusion of the customer number. The definitions that Fred has arrived at are:

ORDER FILE

Field	Type	Length
ORDER NUMBER	Numeric	5
CUST NUMBER	Numeric	5
DATE ORDERED	Character	8

ORDER ITEMS FILE

ORDER NUMBER	Numeric	5
QUANTITY	Numeric	3
ITEM	Character	25
PRICE	Numeric	5.2

By using the two-file approach, Fred has made his system easier to use. Also, he can have any number of items on a single order. This has made the system more flexible.

THE FUNCTION HIERARCHY

Fred's major function is called the Order System. What would an order system consist of? Well,

Fred has a good example of an order system right now—the one he uses currently. So, he examines what exactly it is that he does now with orders. Figure 9-7 presents a comparison between a manual order system and an automated order system.

One thing he does now is write new orders as they come in. Therefore, the system will need a function for ENTER ORDERS.

Now, when a customer calls to change an order, Fred makes the correction using a pencil, crossing off and adding items in the list. Also, if a customer calls and says "Forget it," he just throws that order form away (after a few choice words). So, his system will need to perform the functions CHANGE ORDERS, and DELETE ORDERS.

Another thing that Fred does is look up an order in that old four-drawer file cabinet when there is a question about it. A DISPLAY ORDER function is also necessary. Fred also needs to have standing orders on the system. These are orders that are basically the same each week. Fred decides to input those once and use the order number over and over again, changing the date.

Finally, the system will need a function to print the order forms that are to be sent to the shipping department and the shipping forms with the prices that Fred has already defined in his output definition. The shipping department will enter the prices and make any changes for any out-of stock items after the order has been packed. Remember, there are no backorders in the fresh fish business—only lost sales—and Fred doesn't want to see any get away! The function hierarchy chart, showing the main functions, is presented in Fig. 9-8. Now, Fred can design his main menu for the order system as shown in Fig. 9-9.

All system functions are available from this menu—or will be when Fred gets the system coded and tested!

Fred's pseudocode for the menu program looks like this:

```
SET EXIT TO "N"
DISPLAY MENU SCREEN
DOWHILE EXIT = "N"
   READ OPTION
   CASE
      WHEN OPTION = 1 PERFORM "ADD ORDERS"
      WHEN OPTION = 2 PERFORM "CHANGE ORDER"
      WHEN OPTION = 3 PERFORM "REMOVE ORDER"
      WHEN OPTION = 4 PERFORM "DISPLAY ORDER"
      WHEN OPTION = 5 PERFORM "PRINT ORDER FORMS"
      WHEN OPTION = 6 PERFORM "PRINT SHIPPING FORMS"
      WHEN OPTION = X SET EXIT TO "Y"
      OTHERWISE WRITE "INVALID OPTION"
   ENDCASE
ENDDO
```

Fig. 9-7. A comparison between a manual order system and an automated order system.

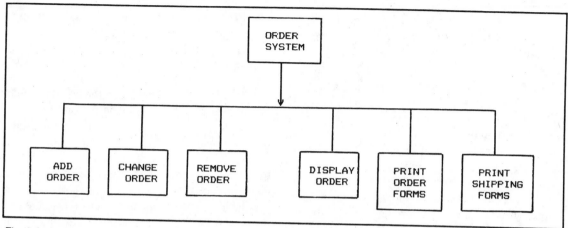

Fig. 9-8. An order system hierarchy chart.

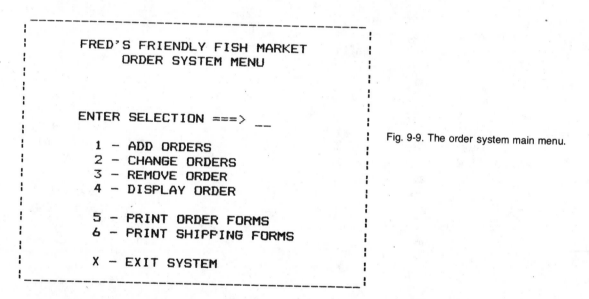

Fig. 9-9. The order system main menu.

With the menu out of the way, Fred moves to the next level of his hierarchy chart. The establishment of an add order function is the first and most important step in creating an order system, so Fred tackles this function first.

THE ADD ORDER FUNCTION

Something about this system has been bothering Fred. Each time an order is entered, one or more items are going to be entered. How can the items be entered at the same time as the order is created?

Fred can land this fish by accessing both files in his program. The first screen will ask for information that is specific to that order; in other words, the customer number and order date. When this information is entered, the program will display a second screen for adding items.

The second screen will have room for the operator to enter ten items. If there are more than ten items, the screen will be redisplayed with enough space for the next ten items. Each screen will allow ten items to be entered under that order number; by redisplaying the screens, the operator can add any number of items.

What if the order number that is entered already exists on the order file? This would be an invalid condition, since according to Fred's design, the order number is supposed to be unique. It would be irritating to enter the customer number and date, just to find out that the order number already exists, and the information must be reentered.

One way of eliminating this problem is to use an entry screen. An entry screen is a preliminary screen that would ask for the order number and customer number. Then, if an order with that number already exists, an error message could be displayed. Otherwise the order would be new (and valid), and the customer number could be used to pull the necessary customer fields from the customer file. The customer number would be checked to make sure that it did exist on the customer file, as the system can't retrieve information that is not there. By adding this entry screen, Fred makes his system more reliable, because duplicate orders would not be possible.

Fred's first input screen, the entry screen, is shown in Fig. 9-10.

He can then create the next screen in the sequence, the order additions screen shown in Fig. 9-11.

In this figure, you can see the customer information that was drawn from the customer file. This information is displayed on the add order screen so that the operator can judge whether or not the correct customer number was chosen. If the customer did not exist on the customer file, an error message would be displayed, but there is no way that Fred can guard against an incorrect customer number entry. The computer can't read minds! Therefore Fred displays the customer information immediately, so the operator will be able to double check to see that the customer's name matches what he believes is the customer number.

Finally, Fred creates the add items screen as shown in Fig. 9-12.

Notice that the company and name information is displayed on this screen, also. This is another double-check; if the operator gets confused about which order is being entered, the name information will help him figure it out.

The quantity and item number for ten items can be entered on this screen. If there are less than ten items, the operator enters the orders and enters blanks on the next line (actually just presses the enter key again), and the order is filed. If there are more than ten items, the operator fills up the ten

Fig. 9-10. The order additions preliminary screen.

```
------------------------------------------------
:                                              :
:      FRED'S FRIENDLY FISH MARKET             :
:            ORDER ADDITIONS                   :
:                                              :
:                                              :
:                                              :
:    ORDER NUMBER:        ORDRN                :
:                                              :
:    CUSTOMER NUMBER:     CUSTN                :
:                                              :
:_____:
```

```
---------------------------------------------
:                                             :
:        FRED'S FRIENDLY FISH MARKET          :
:             ORDER ADDITIONS                 :
:                                             :
:                                             :
:    ORDER NUMBER:       ORDRN                :
:                                             :
:    CUSTOMER NUMBER:  CUSTN                   :
:                                             :
:    COMPANY:      COMPANY------------X       :
:    LAST   NAME:  LNAME--------------X       :
:    FIRST NAME:   FNAME--------------X       :
:                                             :
:                                             :
:    DATE ORDERED: MM/DD/YY                    :
:                                             :
---------------------------------------------
```

Fig. 9-11. The order additions screen.

items on the first screen, presses enter, and receives a fresh screen with room to add ten more items. The # field changes to show records eleven to twenty. When a blank line is entered on the screen, the program will know that the operator is finished adding items.

Fred is almost ready to begin pseudocoding the add order function, but first, he notices that he needs to make a small change to the hierarchy chart. The add items function would go under the add order function in the hierarchy chart.

Fred has broken this function into its smallest

Fig. 9-12. The Order Items Additions Screen.

```
----------------------------------------------------
:                                                    :
:           FRED'S FRIENDLY FISH MARKET              :
:              ORDER ITEM ADDITIONS                  :
:                                                    :
:                                                    :
:    ORDER NUMBER:        ORDRN                      :
:                                                    :
:    COMPANY:        COMPANY------------X            :
:    LAST   NAME:    LNAME--------------X            :
:    FIRST NAME:     FNAME--------------X            :
:                                                    :
:        #    QUANTITY   ITEM NUMBER                 :
:                                                    :
:        1      QTY        ITEMN                     :
:        2      QTY        ITEMN                     :
:        3      QTY        ITEMN                     :
:       ...     QTY        ITEMN                     :
:       10      QTY        ITEMN                     :
----------------------------------------------------
```

parts. He can now design the process of adding items. The pseudocode Fred created for add order looks like this:

```
ADD AN ORDER

    ACCESS ORDER FILE
    SET ORDER NUMBER TO NOT BLANK
    DO WHILE ORDER NUMBER NOT BLANK
       DISPLAY SCREEN
       ENTER ORDER NUMBER AND CUSTOMER NUMBER
       IF ORDER NUMBER NOT BLANK
         VERIFY ORDER NUMBER
         IF NEW NUMBER
            THEN
                ACCESS CUSTOMER FILE
                VERIFY CUSTOMER NUMBER
                IF FOUND
                  THEN
                      DISPLAY CUSTOMER DATA
                      ENTER DATE FIELD
                      ADD TO ORDER FILE
                      PERFORM "ADD ITEMS"
                  ELSE
                      WRITE "CUSTOMER NUMBER NOT FOUND"
                ENDIF
            ELSE
                WRITE "ORDER NUMBER ALREADY ON FILE"
         ENDIF
       ENDIF
    ENDDO
```

In this program, Fred decides that the operator entering of a blank order number will signal the end of the process. As long as the operator continues to enter order numbers and customer numbers on the screen, the program will continue to add orders to the file. This is done with the DO WHILE loop in conjunction with the IF statement; each time the screen is displayed, the IF statement checks for an order number. If it is blank, control shuttles around the processing to the end of the loop. The DO

WHILE condition then becomes false, and control passes out of the loop to the end of the program.

Within the first IF statement, "verify order number" means to check the order file for an identical order number.

The IF NEW NUMBER statement following the VERIFY order number statement sees if a duplicate order number is found. If a duplicate is found, control passes to the ELSE unit, which causes an error message to be displayed. Within the THEN unit of the IF NEW NUMBER statement, the customer number is treated in much the same way.

Once the order number and the customer number are verified, the display screen for add order is presented. The operator can see the customer information that was retrieved from the customer file and can enter the order date. When this screen is entered correctly, control passes to the add items function for the addition of items to the order.

Satisfied with this pseudocode, Fred moves on to define the add items process.

ADD ITEMS

```
        ACCESS ORDER FILE
        ACCESS ORDER ITEM FILE
        SET ITEMCOUNT TO 1
        SET QUANTITY TO NOT BLANK
        DO WHILE QUANTITY NOT BLANK
          DISPLAY SCREEN AND EXISTING ITEM NUMBERS
          ENTER QUANTITY AND ITEM NUMBER
          IF QUANTITY NOT BLANK
            VERIFY ITEM NUMBER
            IF FOUND
              THEN
                RETRIEVE PRICE
                WRITE RECORD TO ORDER ITEM FILE
                INCREMENT ITEMCOUNT BY 1
              ELSE
                WRITE "ITEM NUMBER NOT ON FILE"
            ENDIF
          ENDIF
          IF ITEMCOUNT IS A MULTIPLE OF 10
            THEN REDISPLAY ITEM SCREEN
          ENDIF
        ENDDO
```

In this program, the add items screen has ten lines for item numbers and quantities. Each time a line is entered, the program verifies that the item number exists on the item file, and if it does, it retrieves the price. It then places the newly ordered item into the order items file. If the item number is not on the file, an appropriate error message is displayed.

As long as the item number entered is not blank, the system will continue to add records to the file. Each time the operator has entered ten records an IF statement will clear the display and update the item number counter.

THE CHANGE ORDER FUNCTION

Fred is now ready for the next leg on the hierarchy—the change order function. In this function, Fred envisions that the only changes that should be necessary will be changes to the items. The customer number should never be incorrect as it is double checked at entry time. Fred has learned that some controls are necessary, but too many controls or redundant controls only slow down processing and make the system overly complicated.

Other functions that come under the change order heading are: add items, change the quantity of

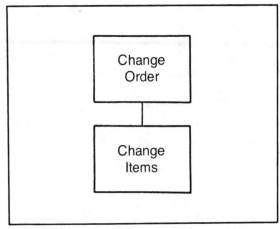

Fig. 9-13. The updated change order hierarchy.

an item, change an item number, and remove an item. On the advice of a friend, Fred has decided to combine them into one function. Fred's new hierarchy chart for the change order items function is shown in Fig. 9-13.

Now Fred can create the screens that the program will use. He again uses the entry screen method, but with a minor difference as shown in Fig. 9-14.

On this entry screen, Fred does not ask for the customer number. Why not? Because it already exists on the order file, thus there is no need to enter it again! The customer number had to be entered on the add order entry screen because the order did not exist yet and the customer number

Fig. 9-14. The order changes preliminary screen.

```
----------------------------------------------------------
:                                                        :
:           FRED'S FRIENDLY FISH MARKET                  :
:                  ORDER CHANGES                         :
:                                                        :
:                                                        :
:         ORDER NUMBER:        ORDRN                     :
:                                                        :
:                                                        :
:                                                        :
:----------------------------------------------------------
```

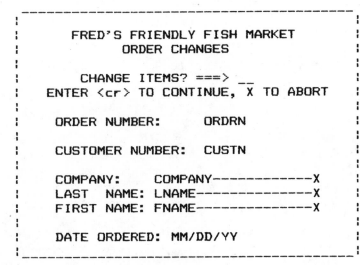

Fig. 9-15. The order changes screen.

```
----------------------------------------------------
:                                                  :
:       FRED'S FRIENDLY FISH MARKET                :
:              ORDER CHANGES                       :
:                                                  :
:       CHANGE ITEMS? ===>  __                     :
:    ENTER <cr> TO CONTINUE, X TO ABORT            :
:                                                  :
:    ORDER NUMBER:        ORDRN                    :
:                                                  :
:    CUSTOMER NUMBER:    CUSTN                      :
:                                                  :
:    COMPANY:       COMPANY-------------X          :
:    LAST  NAME: LNAME-------------X               :
:    FIRST NAME: FNAME-------------X               :
:                                                  :
:    DATE ORDERED: MM/DD/YY                        :
:                                                  :
----------------------------------------------------
```

was needed to retrieve the customer information. Now the order record already exists on the file and can provide the customer number.

The next screen to develop is the order changes screen. This screen is merely a *pass-through* to the change order items function. A pass-through screen is one that is displayed but allows no input to the system. The screen in Fig. 9-15 allows Fred to make sure that he has the right order before moving on to the change items function.

When this screen is displayed, the program asks the operator if there are changes to be made to the items in the order. If there are, and the operator answers affirmatively, Fred will have the program display the change items screen.

Since the change items function seems a little tricky to Fred, he decides to first pseudocode the change order pass-through screen.

Fred first verifies that the order exists, and if it does, he has the program display the order changes screen. The customer's number, company name, and contact's name are displayed to make sure that the right order has been retrieved. Then the operator can enter a carriage return to continue (<cr>), or an X to abort changing that particular order number. When the operator enters a blank order number, the system will return to the main order menu. After a carriage return is entered the order items change screen is displayed.

Originally, Fred was going to have functions that would add, change, and remove items. After thinking about it for several days, in between his arguments with Frank, the only design he could envision was a simple design that would show one item at a time and allow it to be changed. Fred knows he can improve on this. He doesn't want to watch each and every item appear before him just to

```
CHANGE AN ORDER

    ACCESS ORDER FILE
    SET ORDER NUMBER TO NOT BLANK
    DO WHILE ORDER NUMBER NOT BLANK
       DISPLAY SCREEN
       ENTER ORDER NUMBER
       IF ORDER NUMBER NOT BLANK
          VERIFY ORDER NUMBER
          IF FOUND
             THEN
                ACCESS CUSTOMER FILE
                RETRIEVE CUSTOMER INFORMATION
                DISPLAY "CHANGE ITEMS" MESSAGE
                READ CHOICE
                IF CHOICE NOT X
                   THEN PERFORM "CHANGE ITEMS MENU"
                ENDIF
             ELSE WRITE "ORDER NUMBER NOT FOUND"
          ENDIF
       ENDIF
    ENDDO
```

change the twenty-second item. He wants a system that allows him to enter the quantity and item number he wants to change or delete. He will worry about adding items later. He finished his design just as a friend of his named Myron strolled into the retail area of Fred's Friendly Fish. He showed his design to Myron who promptly talked him into trading three lobsters and a pound of scallops for a more difficult-to-implement but easier-to-use design. (Myron already computerized his business, a local personnel agency that does some computer work too.)

Fred had explained to Myron that it was important that the operator be able to see all the items at once and be able to add, change, or remove items from the same screen. Myron told Fred that because of the screen size limitations the addition of only 10 items could be displayed at a time. Through a *scroll* function, more items could be displayed after the first ten. The resulting screen is shown in Fig. 9-16.

Myron also explained that there is a difference between adding items to a new order and adding items to an existing order. The change items menu displays ten items at a time, like the add items menu. However, only the items that already exist for that order will be placed on the change items menu for review and selection. Fred wondered how an item could be added. The answer struck him like a ton of mackerel. "If there are less than ten items on the screen, there will be some blank lines on the menu. If the operator (probably Fred or Elsa) asks to change a blank line, the item number and quantity that are typed for that line will be added to the file.

The best way to handle the change, or removal of items was to think of each function as a variety of the change function. The easiest way to do that was to make changes or deletions one part of an IF statement and the additions another part. Myron impatiently explained to Fred: "If you retrieve an item that exists on the file, you can do two things to it; change the quantity, item number, or both, or

Fig. 9-16. The order items changes screen.

```
-------------------------------------------------
:                                               :
:      FRED'S FRIENDLY FISH MARKET              :
:           ORDER ITEM CHANGES                  :
:                                               :
:       ENTER SELECTION ===>  __                :
:       C/CHANGE, S/SCROLL, X/EXIT              :
:                                               :
:      ORDER NUMBER:      ORDRN                  :
:                                               :
:      COMPANY:       COMPANY------------X      :
:      LAST  NAME:  LNAME--------------X        :
:      FIRST NAME:  FNAME--------------X        :
:                                               :
:        #   QUANTITY   ITEM NUMBER             :
:                                               :
:        1      QTY        ITEMN                 :
:        2      QTY        ITEMN                 :
:        3      QTY        ITEMN                 :
:       ...     QTY        ITEMN                 :
:       10      QTY        ITEMN                 :
:                                               :
-------------------------------------------------
```

68

```
--------------------------------------------------
:                                                :
:        FRED'S FRIENDLY FISH MARKET             :
:           ORDER ITEM CHANGES                   :
:                                                :
:       RECORD NUMBER ==>  __                     :
:    ENTER RECORD NUMBER TO BE CHANGED           :
:                                                :
:    ORDER NUMBER:      ORDRN                     :
:                                                :
:    COMPANY:       COMPANY------------X          :
:    LAST  NAME: LNAME--------------X             :
:    FIRST NAME: FNAME--------------X             :
:                                                :
:      #   QUANTITY   ITEM NUMBER                 :
:                                                :
:      1     QTY          ITEMN                   :
:      2     QTY          ITEMN                   :
:      3     QTY          ITEMN                   :
:     ...    QTY          ITEMN                   :
:     10     QTY          ITEMN                   :
:                                                :
:------------------------------------------------:
```

Fig. 9-17. The order items change screen.

Fig. 9-18. The order items change screen.

```
   --------------------------------------------------
:                                                    :
:          FRED'S FRIENDLY FISH MARKET               :
:             ORDER ITEM CHANGES                     :
:                                                    :
:     QUANTITY: QTY   ITEM NUMBER:  ITEMN            :
:                ENTER CHANGES                       :
:                                                    :
:      ORDER NUMBER:       ORDRN                      :
:                                                    :
:      COMPANY:        COMPANY------------X           :
:      LAST  NAME: LNAME--------------X               :
:      FIRST NAME: FNAME--------------X               :
:                                                    :
:        #   QUANTITY   ITEM NUMBER                   :
:                                                    :
:        1     QTY          ITEMN                     :
:        2     QTY          ITEMN                     :
:        3     QTY          ITEMN                     :
:       ...    QTY          ITEMN                     :
:       10     QTY          ITEMN                     :
:                                                    :
:----------------------------------------------------:
```

```
 ---------------------------------------------
|                                             |
|      FRED'S FRIENDLY FISH MARKET            |
|           ORDER ITEM CHANGES                |
|                                             |
|      RECORD NUMBER ==>  __                   |
|   ENTER RECORD NUMBER TO BE CHANGED          |
|                                             |
|    ORDER NUMBER:        ORDRN                |
|                                             |
|    COMPANY:       COMPANY-------------X      |
|    LAST  NAME:  LNAME---------------X        |
|    FIRST NAME:  FNAME---------------X        |
|                                             |
|       #   QUANTITY   ITEM NUMBER             |
|                                             |
|      11     QTY        ITEMN                 |
|      12     QTY        ITEMN                 |
|      13     QTY        ITEMN                 |
|                                             |
|                                             |
|                                             |
 ---------------------------------------------
```

Fig. 9-19. The order items scroll screen.

you could remove the item by changing the quantity to zero.

Fred understands, Myron leaves. He can use the record numbers shown on the screen to retrieve the data. If there is no data for that record number, the record will be added. If there is data, the item is changed if the quantity is set to anything besides zero. The item is deleted if the quantity is set to zero. The first option listed on the menu is C for change, which means add, change, or delete items. The S will allow Fred to page forward through the displayed items ten at a time. The X function will allow Fred to exit this function and return to the main order change screen to change other orders.

The next logical step is to design the screen to be displayed when the C option, change an item, is requested. The screen is shown in Fig. 9-17.

This screen allows the operator to specify the record number of the items they wish to change. The record number is the first field on the item list.

The user must choose one of the record numbers displayed on an error message will be displayed. Once the record number is entered and the record found, the next screen, shown in Fig. 9-18, will display the item to be changed.

Fred can now enter any changes he wishes. He can also not enter changes, which will leave the item as is. Fred decides that there is no need for a delete confirmation. If the operator changes the quantity to 0, that is a very conscious decision. Fred is beginning to understand the use of controls.

These are all the screens needed for the change items function. Figure 9-19 shows a sample of the screen that would be displayed if the S command were entered. It shows a screen with items 11, 12, and 13. The operator would have to enter a number greater than 13 to add an item to the file.

Prior to pseudocoding the change items subfunction, Fred comes up with the final hierarchy chart for the order system as shown in Fig. 9-20.

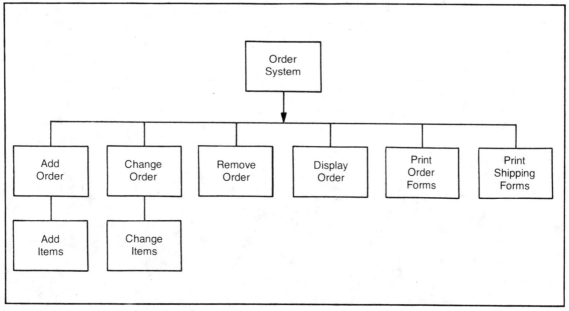

Fig. 9-20. The order system hierarchy chart.

Fred starts the pseudocoding with the main part of the menu for changing items. He builds the menu just like other menus he has built before, using the CASE statement.

```
CHANGE ITEMS

  SET EXIT TO 'N'
  DISPLAY MENU SCREEN
  DO WHILE EXIT = 'N'
    DISPLAY ITEMS
    DISPLAY SELECTION
    READ SELECTION
    CASE
      WHEN SELECTION = 'X'
        SET EXIT TO 'Y'
      WHEN SELECTION = 'C'
        CHANGE RECORDS
      WHEN SELECTION = 'S'
        ADD 10 TO SCROLL COUNTER
    ENDCASE
  ENDDO
```

Here, Fred has the program look for C, S, or X. Option C causes the section used to change the items to be accessed. Option S will add ten to the counter that keeps track of the record numbers displayed and causes the next ten to be displayed the next time the screen is shown. The X option is chosen when the operator wants to leave the menu and return to the change order function.

Pseudocoding the Change Items Menu

Now that Fred is finished with screen design for the change order items function, he feels he understands the process better. With a little help from his friend, he will turn his hand to pseudocoding; Myron gets more lobsters. The resulting code is shown in Fig. 9-21.

Fred performs all three functions (add, change, and delete) in this one piece of pseudocode. This may or may not be a good idea, from the standpoint of modularity, because the fewer func-

71

```
CHANGE ITEMS

 SET EXIT TO 'N'
 DISPLAY MENU SCREEN
 DO WHILE EXIT = 'N'
    DISPLAY ITEMS
    DISPLAY SELECTION
    READ SELECTION
    CASE
      WHEN SELECTION = 'X'
         SET EXIT TO 'Y'
      WHEN SELECTION = 'C'
         ACCESS ORDER ITEM FILE
         SET RECORD NUMBER TO NOT BLANK
         SET SCROLL COUNTER TO 10
         DO WHILE RECORD NUMBER NOT BLANK
            DISPLAY SCREEN
            ENTER RECORD NUMBER
            IF RECORD NUMBER NOT BLANK
              THEN
                 VERIFY RECORD NUMBER IN THE 10 DISPLAYED
                 IF IN THE 10
                   THEN
                      RETRIEVE RECORD
                      DISPLAY QTY AND ITEMN
                      IF BLANK
                        THEN
                           DISPLAY ADD MESSAGE
                      ENDIF
                      ENTER CHANGES
                      IF QTY AND ITEMN NOT BLANK
                        THEN                              /* ADD RECORD */
                           IF OLD QUANTITY BLANK
                             THEN
                                VERIFY ITEM NUMBER
                                IF FOUND
                                  THEN
                                     RETRIEVE PRICE
                                     WRITE RECORD TO ORDER ITEM FILE
                                  ELSE
                                     WRITE "ITEM NUMBER NOT ON FILE"
                                ENDIF
                           ENDIF
```

```
                        IF QTY OR ITEM NUMBER DIFFERENT THEN ORIGINAL
                    THEN                              /* DELETE RECORD */
                        IF QTY = 0
                        THEN
                            REMOVE RECORD FROM ORDER ITEM FILE
                        ELSE                          /* CHANGE RECORD */
                            VERIFY ITEM NUMBER
                            IF FOUND
                                THEN
                                    RETRIEVE PRICE
                                    WRITE RECORD TO ORDER ITEM FILE
                                ELSE
                                    WRITE "ITEM NUMBER NOT ON FILE"
                            ENDIF
                        ENDIF
                    ENDIF
                ENDIF
                ELSE
                    WRITE "RECORD NUMBER NOT ON DISPLAY"
            ENDIF
        ENDIF
        ENDDO
    WHEN SELECTION = 'S'
        ADD 10 TO SCROLL COUNTER
    ENDCASE
ENDDO
```

Fig. 9-21. The order item changes pseudocode.

tions a module is to perform, the easier it is to code later. However, Fred does (wisely) separate the functions within the pseudocode with some extra comments.

The first step in the pseudocode is to display the screen that requests the record number. All functions require the record number, and it is immediately checked to determine if that record number is currently displayed on the screen. If that record is not displayed, an error message is sent to the operator and another record number can be entered.

If the record is currently displayed on the

screen, the change item panel is displayed, allowing the operator to change the quantity and item number shown on the screen. The program determines whether or not the line for that record number was blank by checking to see if the old fields were blank. If they are, this item is to be added and after verifying the item number, the record is added to the item file.

If the quantity of the chosen item is changed to zero, Fred has the program recognize this as a delete function, and the record is removed from the order items file.

If the item number is changed, Fred's program

```
 -------------------------------------------------
:                                                 :
:       FRED'S  FRIENDLY  FISH  MARKET            :
:              ORDER  REMOVAL                     :
:                                                 :
:                                                 :      Fig. 9-22. The preliminary order removal
:       ORDER  NUMBER:        ORDRN               :      screen.
:                                                 :
:                                                 :
:                                                 :
 -------------------------------------------------
```

decides that this is a change to the item, checks to make sure that the new item number is on the item file, and retrieves the price. Finally the changed record is updated in the order item file.

Now, Fred adds pseudocode for the scroll function to the bottom of the pseudocode, and he is done. In this small program, Fred creates a *scroll counter* to keep track of the top item on the menu screen. The scroll counter is set to one in the change order program. The first item and the following nine items are then displayed on the menu. When the S option is chosen, this program adds ten to the scroll counter, and the eleventh through twentieth items are displayed. No matter how many items are in the file for this order, the scroll program will display ten at a time, scrolling forward only.

Fred has completed the toughest design he has

Fig. 9-23. The order removal screen.

```
 -------------------------------------------------------
:                                                        :
:          FRED'S  FRIENDLY  FISH  MARKET                :
:                 ORDER  REMOVAL                         :
:                                                        :
:      ENTER  D  TO  CONFIRM  DELETE  ==>  __            :
:                                                        :
:                                                        :
:      ORDER  NUMBER:        ORDRN                       :
:                                                        :
:      COMPANY:         COMPANY-------------X            :
:      LAST   NAME:  LNAME---------------X               :
:      FIRST  NAME:  FNAME---------------X               :
:                                                        :
:      DATE  ORDERED:  MM/DD/YY                          :
:                                                        :
:         #   QUANTITY   ITEM  NUMBER                    :
:                                                        :
:         1      QTY        ITEMN                        :
:         2      QTY        ITEMN                        :
:         3      QTY        ITEMN                        :
:        ...     QTY        ITEMN                        :
:        10      QTY        ITEMN                        :
:                                                        :
 -------------------------------------------------------
```

74

had to tackle so far in his short data processing career, and he is now free to move on to the next function in the system.

THE REMOVE ORDER FUNCTION

For the remove order function, Fred again decided to use an entry screen to confirm that the order exists before any processing is performed. In the case of a delete operation, this is particularly important. It is easier to go through an extra confirmation step than it is to reenter an entire order that was deleted by mistake.

The entry screen looks like the change order entry screen and is shown in Fig. 9-22.

Figure 9-23 shows the next screen that Fred designs, the confirmation screen for the delete.

This screen looks like the other item screens; however, only the first ten items are displayed. Fred has decided not to give the delete function a scrolling capability. "Anyone can tell if the order is the correct one from the first ten items," said Fred. "Why bother with unnecessary processing?"

So Fred pseudocodes the delete order function like this:

```
REMOVE ORDERS

        ACCESS ORDER FILE
        SET ORDER NUMBER TO NOT BLANK
        DO WHILE ORDER NUMBER NOT BLANK
          DISPLAY SCREEN
          ENTER ORDER NUMBER
          IF ORDER NUMBER NOT BLANK
            VERIFY ORDER NUMBER
            IF FOUND
              THEN
                 RETRIEVE ORDER
                 ACCESS CUSTOMER FILE
                 RETRIEVE CUSTOMER INFORMATION
                 DISPLAY ORDER
                 ACCESS ORDER ITEMS FILE
                 DISPLAY 1ST 10 ITEMS
                 ENTER DELETE CONFITMATION
                 IF CONFIRM = D
                   THEN
                      DELETE MAIN ORDER RECORD
                      DELETE ALL ITEM RECORDS
                 ENDIF
              ELSE
                 WRITE "ORDER NOT ON FILE"
            ENDIF
          ENDIF
        ENDDO
```

```
----------------------------------------
:---------------------------------:    :
:                                  :    :
:    FRED'S FRIENDLY FISH MARKET   :    :
:          ORDER DISPLAY           :    :
:                                  :    :
:                                  :    :
:    ORDER NUMBER:      ORDRN      :    :
:                                  :    :
:                                  :    :
:                                  :    :
:---------------------------------:    :
```

Fig. 9-24. The preliminary order display screen.

After the order number is entered from the entry screen, the order is looked up in the order file. If it does not exist, an error message is displayed. If it does exist, the order, customer, and ordered items information is retrieved from their respective files, and the delete order confirmation screen is displayed. If a D is entered from this screen, the order will be removed from the order file, and all items with that order number will be removed from the ordered items file.

Fred is satisfied with the documentation of his system so far. He is ready to dive into the next function.

THE DISPLAY ORDER FUNCTION

Fred can now design the display order func-

Fig. 9-25. The order display screen.

```
------------------------------------------
:                                         :
:      FRED'S FRIENDLY FISH MARKET        :
:             ORDER DISPLAY               :
:                                         :
:        ENTER <cr> TO CONTINUE           :
:                                         :
:                                         :
:    ORDER NUMBER:       ORDRN            :
:                                         :
:    CUSTOMER NUMBER:    CUSTN            :
:                                         :
:    COMPANY:        COMPANY-------------X :
:    LAST   NAME: LNAME----------------X  :
:    FIRST NAME: FNAME----------------X   :
:                                         :
:    DATE ORDERED: MM/DD/YY               :
:                                         :
:                                         :
:       #   QUANTITY   ITEM NUMBER        :
:                                         :
:       1      QTY        ITEMN           :
:       2      QTY        ITEMN           :
:       3      QTY        ITEMN           :
:      ...     QTY        ITEMN           :
:      10      QTY        ITEMN           :
:                                         :
------------------------------------------
```

tion, and he designs it almost like the remove order function. If you look closely at the screens and pseudocode, you can see many similarities. Instead of deleting orders, Fred has the program display the information on the screen. He also allows the scrolling forward through the items by pressing the enter key. The screens are shown in Figs. 9-24 and 9-25. The pseudocode looks like this:

```
DISPLAY ORDERS

    ACCESS ORDER FILE
    SET ORDER NUMBER TO NOT BLANK
    DO WHILE ORDER NUMBER NOT BLANK
      DISPLAY SCREEN
      ENTER ORDER NUMBER
     IF ORDER NUMBER NOT BLANK
        VERIFY ORDER NUMBER
        IF FOUND
          THEN
              RETRIEVE ORDER
              ACCESS CUSTOMER FILE
              RETRIEVE CUSTOMER INFORMATION
              DISPLAY ORDER
              ACCESS ITEM FILE
              DO WHILE MORE RECORDS
                 DISPLAY 10 ITEMS
                 ENTER CONTINUE CONFIRMATION
              ENDIF
          ELSE
              WRITE "ORDER NOT ON FILE"
        ENDIF
      ENDIF
    ENDDO
```

First, the order number is entered and checked against the order file. If the order exists, the order and customer information is displayed, along with the first ten item records for that order. By placing the item displays within a DO WHILE loop, Fred has taken care of the scrolling facility. When the enter key is pressed, more items are looked for in the order items file, and if found, they are displayed. When there are no more item records for that order, the process is complete, and the entry screen is displayed again.

Now Fred has all the administrative functions out of the way. The add, change, delete, and display functions all exist for only one purpose: to add and manipulate the information necessary to produce the output, the order form and the shipping form.

THE PRINT ORDER FORM FUNCTION

To print the order form, Fred uses the entry screen concept to find the order in the file. If the order is not present, an error message is displayed. The entry screen, shown in Fig. 9-26, looks almost like the other order number entry screens.

Another design consideration is the way the printed order form will appear on paper. Fred will

```
--------------------------------------------------
|                                                |
|       FRED'S FRIENDLY FISH MARKET              |
|          ORDER FORMS PRINT                     |
|                                                |
|                                                |
|      ORDER NUMBER:        ORDRN                 |
|                                                |
|                                                |
|                                                |
--------------------------------------------------
```

Fig. 9-26. The print order forms screen.

use the form he uses now, so he defines his output to assure that he remembers all the fields and can easily code the line and column numbers in his final program. The layout of the form is shown in Fig. 9-27.

Since this function does not require a "confirm" screen, like remove order, Fred can jump right into his process definition:

In this program, the entry screen is displayed, and the order number is entered by the operator. The program searches the order file for that order number and when it is found, the program retrieves the customer information. The order and customer information is printed, and then the order item file is searched for all items belonging to that order. As each item record is retrieved, the item file is

```
PRINT ORDER FORM

        STORE BLANK TO ORDER NUMBER
        DO WHILE ORDER NUMBER NOT BLANK
           DISPLAY SCREEN
           ENTER ORDER NUMBER
           IF ORDER NUMBER NOT BLANK
             ACCESS ORDER FILE
             VERIFY ORDER NUMBER
             IF FOUND
               THEN
                   PRINT HEADER OF ORDER
                   ACCESS CUSTOMER FILE
                   RETRIEVE CUSTOMER INFORMATION
                   DISPLAY ORDER INFORMATION
                   ACCESS ORDER ITEM FILE
                   DO WHILE MORE RECORDS
                      RETRIEVE QUANTITY AND ITEM NUMBER
                      ACCESS ITEM FILE
                      RETRIEVE DESCRIPTION
                      PRINT RECORD
                   ENDDO
               ELSE
                   WRITE "ORDER NUMBER NOT ON FILE"
             ENDIF
           ENDIF
        ENDDO
```

```
            Order Number: ORDRN

            X------COMPANY------X
            X-------FNAME-------X  X-------LNAME-------X

            Order Date: MM/DD/YY

 ITEM #       QUANTITY        ITEM NUMBER              DESCRIPTION

   1            QTN             ITEMN        X----------DESC---------X
   2            QTN             ITEMN        X----------DESC---------X
   3            QTN             ITEMN        X----------DESC---------X
   4            QTN             ITEMN        X----------DESC---------X
   5            QTN             ITEMN        X----------DESC---------X
   6            QTN             ITEMN        X----------DESC---------X
   7            QTN             ITEMN        X----------DESC---------X
   8            QTN             ITEMN        X----------DESC---------X
```

Fig. 9-27. The order form print layout.

```
    FRED'S FRIENDLY FISH MARKET
        SHIPPING FORMS PRINT


    ORDER NUMBER:       ORDRN
```

Fig. 9-28. The print shipping forms screen.

searched for that item number so that the item description may be printed on the order form. The program then loops back, using the inner DO WHILE loop, to search for more items.

THE PRINT SHIPPING LABEL FUNCTION

The last function of Fred's order system is to print the shipping label for an order from the stored order information. Again, the entry screen concept is used, as it was in the print order form function. The screen is shown in Fig. 9-28.

The final design consideration is the way the printed shipping form will appear on paper. Fred will use the form he uses now so he defines his output to assure that he remembers all the fields and can easily code the line and column numbers in his final program. The format of the output is shown in Fig. 9-29. The pseudocode looks like this:

```
PRINT SHIPPING FORM

    STORE BLANK TO ORDER NUMBER
    DO WHILE ORDER NUMBER NOT BLANK
       DISPLAY SCREEN
       ENTER ORDER NUMBER
       IF ORDER NUMBER NOT BLANK
          ACCESS ORDER FILE
          VERIFY ORDER NUMBER
          IF FOUND
            THEN
                PRINT HEADER OF ORDER
                ACCESS CUSTOMER FILE
                RETRIEVE CUSTOMER INFORMATION
                PRINT ORDER INFORMATION
                ACCESS ORDER ITEM FILE
                SET TOTAL TO 0
                DO WHILE MORE RECORDS
                   RETRIEVE QUANTITY AND ITEM NUMBER
                   ACCESS ITEM FILE
                   RETRIEVE DESCRIPTION AND PRICE
                   AMOUNT = QUANTITY X PRICE
                   ADD AMOUNT TO TOTAL
                   PRINT RECORD
                ENDDO
                WRITE TOTAL
                DISCOUNT AMOUNT = DISCOUNT/100 X TOTAL
                WRITE DISCOUNT
                SUBTRACT DISCOUNT FROM TOTAL
                WRITE AMOUNT DUE
            ELSE
                WRITE "ORDER NUMBER NOT ON FILE"
          ENDIF
       ENDIF
    ENDDO
```

In this process, the order number is searched for on the order file, and if it is not present, an error message is displayed. If an order is on file, however, the order and customer fields are retrieved and printed on the shipping form. Then, Fred has the program search for the items that belong to the order. As each item is found, the item description and its price are retrieved from the item file. The program calculates the price to the customer for each item by multiplying quantity times the item price. The total is accumulated, so that the bottom line, the total cost can be printed on the form. The program then loops to get any further items for the order.

If Fred has decided that a particular customer gets a discount, the discount percentage is retrieved from the customer file; the amount of the discount is then calculated and subtracted from the

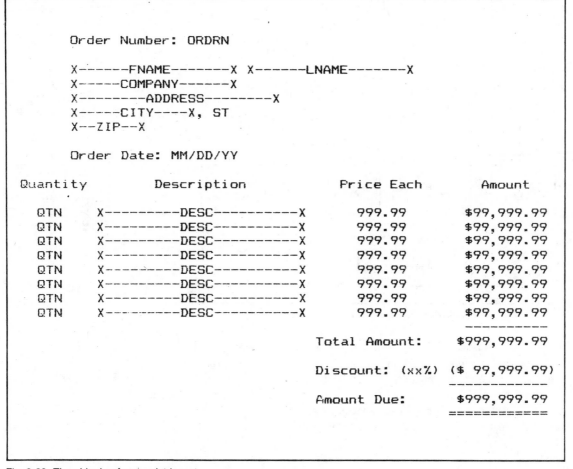

```
    Order Number: ORDRN

    X-------FNAME-------X X-------LNAME-------X
    X-----COMPANY------X
    X--------ADDRESS--------X
    X-----CITY----X, ST
    X--ZIP--X

    Order Date: MM/DD/YY

Quantity          Description              Price Each        Amount

   QTN     X---------DESC----------X         999.99      $99,999.99
   QTN     X---------DESC----------X         999.99      $99,999.99
   QTN     X---------DESC----------X         999.99      $99,999.99
   QTN     X---------DESC----------X         999.99      $99,999.99
   QTN     X---------DESC----------X         999.99      $99,999.99
   QTN     X---------DESC----------X         999.99      $99,999.99
   QTN     X---------DESC----------X         999.99      $99,999.99
   QTN     X---------DESC----------X         999.99      $99,999.99
                                                         -----------
                                      Total Amount:     $999,999.99

                                      Discount: (xx%)  ($ 99,999.99)
                                                         -----------
                                      Amount Due:       $999,999.99
                                                         ===========
```

Fig. 9-29. The shipping forms print layout.

total price of all items on the order. Last, but definitely not least (in Fred's eyes), the total cost is printed at the bottom of the form.

THE INVENTORY SYSTEM

Fred's friend Myron made some other suggestions for Fred to try. One of these is to incorporate an inventory system. This is a logical extension of the item file that Fred would like to build. Fred hasn't realized yet, but he has to find a way to add, change, or delete items in the item file. Fred has produced the design shown in Fig. 9-30 and will tackle it in the future. For now, Fred will simply establish the item file using the dBASE II user functions.

SUMMARY

In the last two chapters, you have followed Fred as he designed systems for his business. You saw the logical constructs at work in his pseu-

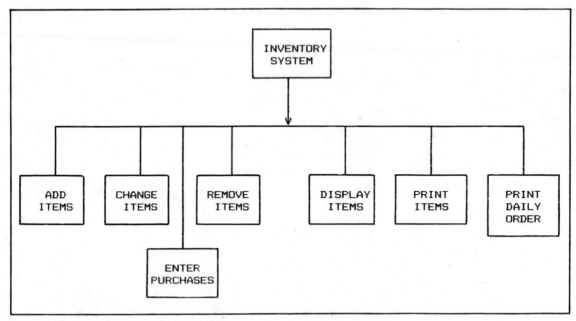

Fig. 9-30. The inventory system hierarchy chart.

docode, saw him develop his systems from scratch, and you saw his documentation package slowly grow as he aimed to automate his entire business.

Fred had to change his original design for the customer system as other systems started to need access to that data. His design was growing and evolving, bending to his needs as he defined his business problems.

You will be seeing more of Fred in the next two sections of this book, as he learns dBASE II, and sees how to turn his designs into working reality.

Section II
Database Fundamentals

Chapter 10

What is a Database?

Database is a term given to the physical area and logical means of storing your data in a computer system. A database is simply data that has been transformed into meaningful information by logically grouping and storing it.

There are endless numbers of databases in the world. One of the more common databases in any business is the file of customers. This file in its simplest form would contain the customer's name, address, and phone number. The database might contain many other files such as customer accounts, and lists of items the customers have purchased. In a retail business there would be other files such as inventory files, price files, stock number files, and description files. Together, all these files make up the database for the business. The terms *database* and *files* are used interchangeably in this book, although you could think of all related files as being a database.

Another example of a database is a dictionary system. The files that make up the database would include the dictionary file and the thesaurus file. The dictionary file would include a single entry for each word. The entry would contain three fields: the word, the type (noun, verb, etc.), and the definition. The thesaurus file would contain many entries for each word. Each entry would contain the word from the dictionary file along with other words that mean the same thing.

A database is an organized collection of records. Such things as newspapers or magazines are not databases. An index of magazine articles that tells the subject, magazine name, and date is a database. Information must be in some order and must be retrievable by some orderly means. This is the difference between information and chaos.

Why would you need a database? This is a commonly asked question. A database will allow you to ask questions and quickly receive answers about your data. "How many customers bought

$200 worth of product this month?" "Which of my customers live in Connecticut?" "How many customers in New England pay their bills on time?" These are all typical questions that you might ask if you had a database.

What can a database management system like dBASE II do for you? Besides being able to allow you to easily enter, change, and delete data, it allows you to change the description of your records at any time. For example, for ten years you have had two stores in Connecticut. Now you are adding stores in Massachusetts, Rhode Island, and New York. Your database has a place for store name and city but not state. If you have many records already on a computer, would you have to change them all? The answer is yes. With most languages this would be a difficult process. With a database manager like dBASE II it is simple and easy.

A database manager can also let you ask questions in many forms. "How many fish did we sell this month? the last 3 months? how about all year?." "How many customers live outside of CT?" Questions such as these are simple to ask using dBASE II. It's almost as simple as asking them in English! dBASE II also lets you produce reports with just one command. The true beauty of dBASE II, however, is that apart from being a database manager, it is also a programming language.

In the first section, you learned about how to program. That section discussed the proper design of a program and all the logical constructs. In this chapter, you will learn more about how to plan your database and use dBASE II programming commands to manipulate the database. First, let's learn a little bit more about databases.

dBASE II is a relational database management system. This means that each record is stored just as you entered it. Each record is the same size and has the same fields, each the same size. The records are collections of related fields. Each file is a collection of records; one or several files can constitute a database. With microcomputers you can think of a database as being all the files on your disk. If these terms still confuse you, read the explanations on the following pages carefully.

Usually, when you are using several files in a database system, you have to have some way to use them together. This is where the concept of a *common key* comes in. In the customer example a key might be the customer name. If you had one file with the customer name, addresses, and phone numbers, while another file had the customer names and account balances, you could use the name as a key to retrieve information from both files.

These keys allow you to tie many files together. For example, a parts file from a typical business might look like this:

```
          DESCRIPTION FILE
PART:NO   WEIGHT       DESCRIPTION
6HD       6oz.      Heavy Duty Nails
8LT       8oz.      Light Weight Nails
8LTS      8oz.      Light Weight Screws
6BT       6oz.      Light Weight Bolts
10WA      10oz.     Heavy Duty Washers
6RN       6oz.      Roofing Nails
ES-28     -         28 in. Electric Saw
```

This file can be accessed, and information concerning the part number and its corresponding description can be retrieved. But in this example, there are two other pieces of information needed: the price of a part and the number in stock. This company has several files in their databases; the other files are shown in Fig. 10-1.

To produce a report that will include the part number, description, price per item, and quantity in stock, you would have to check three different files. Here, you see that each file contains the same part numbers, but they have no other common information. This is one way to organize your information. The part number is called the key; all other information is related to it.

The part number need not be the only key field in the database. For example, in the inventory file, location may also be used as a key field. This file

```
                         PRICE FILE
        PART:NO      UNIT      PRICE:EA    PRICE:10    PRICE:100
          6HD        1000        22.34      182.30      1595.00
          8LT        1000        22.34      162.70      1256.00
          8LTS        100         3.56       33.50       295.00
          6BT         100         4.35       41.30       386.00
          10WA       1000        18.45      174.50      1663.00
          6RN        1000        22.34      162.70      1200.00
          ES-28         1        89.50      695.00      5950.00


                       INVENTORY FILE
        PART:NO    QTY:INSTK   ORDER:QTY   ORDER:LVL   LOCATION
          6HD        63000       50000       10000      WHSE1
          8LT        56000       50000       15000      WHSE2
          8LTS        3000        5000        4000      BIN37
          6BT         5000        5000        4000      WHSE4
          10WA        6000       20000       10000      WHSE2
          6RN        12000       10000        5000      WHSE3
          ES-28          78          50          25      STORE
```

Fig. 10-1. Sample price and inventory files.

might have the building location, the hours the building is open, and the state it is in. The concept of key fields is an important one in organizing your data and retrieving it again later.

Files

Each database is made up of files. Figure 10-2 is an example of a file. This one is aptly named CUSTOMER FILE. All the information in the file makes up the file, or as some people refer to it, the database. As described above, there really is no key associated with this file. A likely key would be the name, field; however, if you are interested in loca-

tion, state, or zip codes, any of these might be keys instead.

Records

A database file is made up of records. Each record would be a line in the table. In the customer file, each record consists of a name, several address fields, and the phone number. There are three records in this file: one each for Joe Smith, Bill Jones and Mark Ames.

Fields

Each field is a column in the table and has its

```
                          CUSTOMER FILE
        NAME           STREET            CITY      ST    ZIP     PHONE
    Joe Smith    23 Daring Lane      Enfield    CT   06268   5552345
    Bill Jones   156 East St         Windsor    CT   06234   5551645
    Mark Ames    10 South Rd         Branford   CT   05455   5553774
```

Fig. 10-2. An example of a file.

own title. The customer file has the following fields: NAME, STREET, CITY, ST, ZIP, and PHONE. These fields are defined when the database is created. Whenever you wish to use this data you must call each field by its name. Later, if you want to print the information, you could change the column header from NAME to PERSON'S NAME or anything else you want. The field names exist only to help you use the data in the program.

DATABASE STRUCTURES

The *database structure* is the dictionary to your data. You will sometimes hear the database structure referred to as the *data dictionary*. The database structure is made up of several elements including the database name, the name of each field, the maximum size each of field, and the field type.

Database Names

The database name should be something meaningful. Actually all names you use in a computer system should be meaningful. Remember, some day someone else may have to use this program. Even though you have two lovely children named Sue and Bobby, these names are inappropriate in your computer system. Choose names that will indicate what the database contains. In dBASE II there are three rules for creating the database name:

A maximum of eight characters may be used.
The name must start with a letter.
No blanks are allowed in the name.

Good database names include CUSTOMER for a customer file, INVENTORY for an inventory file, and SALE:OCT for an October sales file. Examples of illegal names are 1957SALE (the name must start with a letter), CUSTOMERS (the name is too long), and CAR PART (no blanks are allowed). By properly naming your files, you will be able to

easily recognize and use your databases—and so will everybody else!

Field Names

Records do not have names. They can be identified by their record number; each record is assigned a number by dBASE II. Usually this number reflects the sequence of creation. The first record entered is record 00001, the next record 00002, and so on. When the records are sorted, they will have different numbers—but more about that later.

Each field has a field name. It is this name that you use when you search, sort, report, change, or do anything to the database. Each field name in a file must be unique; that is, no two can be the same. You can use the same name in different files; when two files share a common key the same field name should be used.

As with database names, each field name should be meaningful. Use NAME to represent a person's name, and ZIP:CODE for the zip code. Remember, these names will be used extensively in your program so they should be easily recognizable and if possible, short. Short field names can be used in calculations or expressions without causing them to go on forever.

Field names have rules just like database names:

A maximum of 10 characters may be used.
The name must start with a letter.
No blanks are allowed in the name.

Examples of good names include CUSTOMER, QTY, CITY:ST. Unacceptable names include CUSTOMER:NAME (there are more than 10 characters), CITY ST (there are no blanks allowed), or "52:WKS" (the name must start with a letter).

Fields

Field names allow us to identify a column of

data such as NAME, or ZIP:CODE, but what is actually in those columns? Why the data, of course. Each data item is called a field, or variable. This is because the NAME in record 00003 may be changed at any time. It's value can vary but the program will never change the value unless you tell it to.

You will find there are many ways to change a field. You can directly input data into the field; you can edit a value already there; you can use an assignment statement to change it. No matter what, you always have control over the contents of a field.

Field Types. There are three types of fields: character, numeric, and logical. Character fields are fields that will not be used in mathematical expressions. Character fields may contain any value: letters, numbers, special characters, anything! Don't forget that some numbers, such as zip codes and social security numbers, should be placed in character fields because they will never be used in calculations.

Numeric fields are just that—they contain numbers. The numbers may contain decimal points and even a negative sign on the left side. These are values that can be used in calculations. Amounts of any kind (prices, quantities, weights) are numbers.

Logical fields are data items which have only two possible values, true or false. They are always one position in length to contain either T or F.

These are used as a checklist type of variable. A field name of VETERAN may be a logical field. If the person is a veteran the field is set to T, if not, it is set to F.

Field Rules. As with field names the fields themselves are governed by a few rules to follow:

Character fields can contain a maximum 254 characters.

Numeric fields can contain a maximum 10 digits (with a calculation maximum of -1.8×10^{63} or 1.0×10^{-63}).

Logical fields can contain a maximum of 1 character, which must be T or F.

In the next chapter, you will learn how dBASE II allows you to create your data dictionary. There are a few things to remember first:

1. Every database has a name of 8 or less characters.
2. Fields are the columns of your database. Each field has a name of 10 characters or less. Each field has a type and a length.
3. Together, the fields make up the rows, which are the records.
4. Make your names mean something!

Chapter 11

Creating and Using the Database Structure

The first thing you will do after your program design is completed is to begin the database design. Your database should have all the fields needed for your program. Output fields are of no concern at this point; you have already used the output fields to determine the input fields. These input fields are the only fields that belong on your database. Any fields that can be calculated should not be on the database; they can be calculated at any time.

DESIGNING THE DATABASE

When you are creating a database keep these limits in mind:

Databases can have a maximum of 32 fields.
The total length of a record cannot exceed 1000 characters.
Databases cannot have more than 65535 records.

Let's take our small businessman Fred. The first task that Fred has decided to computerize is his customer file. So far you know that Fred has decided to include the customer's name, address, and phone number. Should his database look like this?

Fieldname	Type	Length
NAME	CHAR	20
ADDRESS	CHAR	29
PHONE	CHAR	10

Total		59

No, of course not! If you had defined your database this way, it would be very difficult to ask questions of it and to group common types of customers. Rather, let's divide up the database into a format that is easier to *query;* that is, get answers from:

Fieldname	Type	Length
LAST:NAME	CHAR	10
FIRST:NAME	CHAR	10
STREET	CHAR	12
CITY	CHAR	10
STATE	CHAR	2
ZIP:CODE	CHAR	5
AREA:CODE	CHAR	3
NUMBER	CHAR	7

Total		59

You can see that the size of the total database has not changed, but it is now easier to use if you wish to see a list of all customers in Connecticut or Massachusetts. This method of breaking each field into the smallest part is important in database design. Note that there is a field called STREET. You could have divided it into STREET#, STREET-NAME, and STREETTYPE, but this would not have made any sense. You would never care how many people lived on lanes as opposed to streets and roads. You would never ask to see customers who lived at addresses whose number was 32. You might, however, ask to see a list of all customers who live on Main Street. This can be done regardless of the street number, and you will see how later in this chapter.

The next activity is to create your database. When you run dBASE II, you will see a period on the screen. This dot is where you will type in dBASE II commands. The dot or period is called a *prompt* character; it appears when dBASE II is waiting for you to enter a command. The first command you will learn to use is the CREATE command.

CREATING THE DATABASE

Once you have entered dBASE II from your operating system, you type the CREATE command. This will allow you to create your database.

. CREATE
ENTER FILENAME:

dBASE II now asks you for the filename or database name. You must provide a name under which dBASE II will store the database. The filename on your disk will be the name that you enter followed by the suffix .DBF. If you name your database CUSTOMER, you will see the filename CUSTOMER.DBF when you list a directory of your disk. If you want your database on the disk in your default drive you would enter it as follows:

ENTER FILENAME: CUSTOMER

If you want the file on the disk in the B drive, you would enter the name with the drive specification:

ENTER FILENAME: B:CUSTOMER

Either way, this will set up the file CUSTOMER.DBF on the disk in the drive that was specified or in the default drive if no drive was specified.

So far the screen will look like this:

```
. CREATE
ENTER FILENAME: CUSTOMER
ENTER RECORD STRUCTURE AS
  FOLLOWS:
  FIELD          NAME,TYPE,WIDTH,
  DECIMAL PLACES
  001            _
```

dBASE II is now ready for you to describe the fields in each record in the file. Notice there are four items to enter for each field. The first three have been mentioned: NAME, TYPE, and WIDTH. The fourth is the number of decimal places in a field that is declared as numeric. Unless you need pennies in a dollar amount or a specific number of decimal places, you can ignore this item. If you need two decimal places in a field that can have amounts up to 99,999, you would want to describe the field as having a WIDTH of 7 and DECIMAL PLACES of 2. The WIDTH is the total width of the field including the decimals.

You are now ready to enter your fields. Enter each field's name, type, width, and optionally decimal places. Enter the field descriptions with commas between each item needed. Press the enter key after completing the field description. You may then enter the description for the next field. Below is a valid entry for the customer record:

```
. CREATE
ENTER FILENAME: CUSTOMER
ENTER RECORD STRUCTURE AS FOLLOWS:
    FIELD          NAME,TYPE,WIDTH,DECIMAL PLACES
    001            LAST:NAME,C,10
    002            FIRST:NAME,C,10
    003            STREET,C,12
    004            CITY,C,10
    005            STATE,C,2
    006            ZIP:CODE,C,5
    007            AREA:CODE,C,3
    008            NUMBER,C,7
    009

    INPUT DATA NOW? _
```

After entering the eight fields and pressing the enter key after each one, the information above should be on your screen. When dBASE II displays the line for the ninth entry, you just press the enter key to tell dBASE II you are done. dBASE II gives you the opportunity to enter data right away if you want. You can type N at this time and enter your data later.

USING THE DATABASE STRUCTURE

Once you have created the database, you can begin to use it. The first command you need is the command to OPEN the database. Opening the database means choosing the database you wish to

come more important than when you only have one.

To use the database, you must enter the appropriate dBASE II command. This command is USE. Below you see an example of this command:

. USE CUSTOMER

dBASE II knows to go to the default disk drive and open the file called CUSTOMER.DBF. In opening the database, dBASE II checks to make sure the file exists and then positions a pointer at the first record. You can always return to the top of a database with the USE command.

use. When you have many databases this will be-If the database is not on the default drive, that is, if your system is displaying the A> prompt but the database is on the B drive, you would open the database like this:

. USE B:CUSTOMER

The extension of DBF is used only by CP/M or DOS dBASE II knows that a file that is to be USEd must be a database file. Later, you will learn of other file extensions that dBASE II uses.

When you are done with the database you should close it. This will free memory and allow you to access other databases. In dBASE II, you don't have to CLOSE your database, but it is a good idea. dBASE II performs some of its updating only at the time the file is closed. If an error occurs while a file is open there can be problems.

To close a database, simply type USE by itself. dBASE II remembers the database in the original USE and closes it for you, for example

. USE

VIEWING THE DATABASE STRUCTURE

Now that you have learned how to USE a database, let's look at the one you've created. You can see it on your screen with a very simple command, DISPLAY STRUCTURE. Figure 11-1 shows the display.

As you can see, the database structure is displayed for you. In addition to the structure, the number of records that are in the file and the last update are displayed. To set the date in dBASE II type the command SET DATE TO mm/dd/yy, for example,

. SET DATE TO 02/15/84

CHANGING THE DATABASE

Up to this point, you have seen how to create a database and open it for use. You have not yet learned how to put data into it nor how to use this data. First, a very important subject is the problem of changing the database once it is defined. For now, assume there is no data in the database. Later you will learn how to change a full database without losing any of the records already in it.

So far, you have only created the database structure, the data dictionary if you will. Now you will see how to make a small change to it.

Fred decides that the street address is not enough. Some of his customers have internal mail addresses; some have post office boxes; others have apartment numbers or other secondary addresses. Fred realizes he needs a second address field. He will use the MODIFY STRUCTURE

```
.  USE CUSTOMER
.  DISPLAY STRUCTURE
STRUCTURE FOR FILE: CUSTOMER
NUMBER OF RECORDS:   00000
DATA OF LAST UPDATE 2/15/83
PRIMARY USE DATABASE
FLD      NAME          TYPE    WIDTH       DEC

001      LAST:NAME      C       010
002      FIRST:NAME     C       010
003      STREET         C       012
004      CITY           C       010
005      STATE          C       002
006      ZIP:CODE       C       005
007      AREA:CODE      C       003
008      NUMBER         C       007
** TOTAL **                    00059
```

Fig. 11-1. The database structure.

```
      . USE CUSTOMER
      . MODIFY STRUCTURE
      MODIFY ERASES ALL DATA RECORDS .. PROCEED(Y/N) Y


                        NAME          TYPE      LEN       DEC
           FIELD 01: LAST:NAME         C        010       000      :
           FIELD 02: FIRST:NAME        C        010       000      :
           FIELD 03: STREET            C        012       000      :
           FIELD 04: CITY              C        010       000      :
           FIELD 05: STATE             C        002       000      :
           FIELD 06: ZIP:CODE          C        005       000      :
           FIELD 07: AREA:CODE         C        003       000      :
           FIELD 08: NUMBER            C        007       000      :
           FIELD 09:                                               :
           FIELD 10:                                               :
           FIELD 11:                                               :
           FIELD 12:                                               :
```

Fig. 11-2. Changing the database structure.

command to add the field. The screen will look like this:

. USE CUSTOMER
. MODIFY STRUCTURE

MODIFY ERASES ALL DATA RECORDS . . . PROCEED (Y/N) -

Here dBASE II is warning Fred that changing his database structure will cause the erasure of all

```
                        NAME          TYPE      LEN       DEC
           FIELD 01: LAST:NAME         C        010       000      :
           FIELD 02: FIRST:NAME        C        010       000      :
           FIELD 03: STREET            C        012       000      :
           FIELD 04:                                                :
           FIELD 05: CITY              C        010       000      :
           FIELD 06: STATE             C        002       000      :
           FIELD 07: ZIP:CODE          C        005       000      :
           FIELD 08: AREA:CODE         C        003       000      :
           FIELD 09: NUMBER            C        007       000      :
           FIELD 10:                                                :
           FIELD 11:                                                :
           FIELD 12:                                                :
           FIELD 13:                                                :
           FIELD 14:                                                :
           FIELD 15:                                                :
           FIELD 16:                                                :
```

Fig. 11-3. Inserting a new field.

```
            . USE CUSTOMER
            . DISPLAY STRUCTURE
         STRUCTURE FOR FILE: CUSTOMER
         NUMBER OF RECORDS:   00000
         DATA OF LAST UPDATE 2/15/83
         PRIMARY USE DATABASE
         FLD       NAME          TYPE     WIDTH      DEC

         001       LAST:NAME      C        010
         002       FIRST:NAME     C        010
         003       STREET         C        012
         004       POBOX:APT      C        007
         005       CITY           C        010
         006       STATE          C        002
         007       ZIP:CODE       C        005
         008       AREA:CODE      C        003
         009       NUMBER         C        007
         ** TOTAL **                       00066
```

Fig. 11-4. The updated database.

records in the database. Later you will learn how to save them, but for now, since there are no records anyway, it doesn't matter if dBASE II deletes them.

Figure 11-2 shows the screen you would get after answering the proceed question affirmatively. The first twelve fields are listed including the field name, type, length, and number of decimal places. You now have the opportunity to change any existing field, add or insert a field, or delete a field. Adding or deleting fields require a special series of keys. These are known as *control keys*. On some computers there is a control key marked CTRL or CONTROL; on other computers the control symbol is above the 6 and looks like this: ^. The most common control sequences are:

```
CTRL-N  Insert Field above cursor
CTRL-T  Delete Field at cursor
```

```
CTRL-W  Save changes and exit
CTRL-Q  Quit without saving
```

The cursor can be moved normally around the display. Fred moves the cursor to FIELD 05 and types CTRL-N. Instantly the screen changes to prepare for the insertion of a new field as shown in Fig. 11-3.

Fred puts in the description of his new field and types CTRL-W. This will save his additions. He now uses the DISPLAY STRUCTURE command to review the change. The result is shown in Fig. 11-4.

Notice that the total reflects the change to the database structure. Fred now has enough room to put both the street address and a post office box or apartment number. There is no limit to the number of changes that can be made to a database structure, as long as the total number of fields is 32 or less and the total record length is 1000 characters or less.

Chapter 12

Database Records

Once the database structure has been created, you can begin to input records. When you first create the database structure, dBASE II asks you if you wanted to begin to input records immediately. If you had replied Y to that question, the screen shown in Fig. 12-1 would have appeared.

ADDING RECORDS

dBASE II automatically generates a form for you. You can fill in the form just like you would fill in any other form. You can now begin to input your data. As you press the enter key, the cursor will skip to the next field. After you enter the last field (NUMBER) and press the enter key, the record counter will be incremented by 1 and a new blank form will be displayed if you are in the add (AP-PEND) mode. To quit entering records, you would simply enter a blank record. This would return you to the "." prompt. You can enter as many records as you wish.

Entering character data is the easiest. Whatever you place in a field will be its value. Numeric fields work a little differently. As you enter the value, the number appears in the exact spaces that you type it into. When you press enter key, however, dBASE II will *right justify* the number. The number simply shifts to the right side of the bucket; whatever you typed is still there, just shifted over a little so that the rightmost figure is in the rightmost position.

This procedure takes care of entering data when you create the database, but how do you add data at other times? To add data at other times you use the APPEND command. The APPEND command allows you to enter data to the end of an existing database whenever you want. The append screen is shown in Fig. 12-2.

The procedure for entering data is the same whether you enter it after creating the database or use the APPEND command. If there are already

```
RECORD # 00001

LAST:NAME    :_          :
FIRST:NAME   :           :
STREET       :             :
POBOX:APT    :        :
CITY         :           :
STATE        :   :
ZIP:CODE     :      :
AREA:CODE    :     :
NUMBER       :       :
```

Fig. 12-1. The blank additions screen.

```
RECORD # 00001

LAST:NAME    :SMITH      :
FIRST:NAME   :JOHN       :
STREET       :PILGRIM WAY :
POBOX:APT    :        :
CITY         :PLYMOUTH   :
STATE        :MA:
ZIP:CODE     :05634:
AREA:CODE    :617:
NUMBER       :3442654:
```

Fig. 12-3. Entering the first record.

records in the database, dBASE II will position the record pointer to the last record on the file, and the new records will be placed after the existing ones. dBASE II takes care of adding the records regardless of the number of records in the database.

Figure 12-3 shows a sample record that has been added to the file.

After the first record has been entered, the screen will change to look like the one shown in Fig. 12-4. The first record has been added, and the second record is ready to be entered.

Assume that 15 records are now in the database. These records will be used to demonstrate some of the capabilities of the dBASE II database manager.

DISPLAYING RECORDS

There are many ways to display records. The easiest is to ask dBASE II to list all records. There are two ways to do this. The LIST command tells dBASE II to list all the records in the database. If you have a lot of records, you'd better be quick

```
. USE CUSTOMER
. APPEND

RECORD # 00001

LAST:NAME    :_          :
FIRST:NAME   :           :
STREET       :             :
POBOX:APT    :        :
CITY         :           :
STATE        :   :
ZIP:CODE     :      :
AREA:CODE    :     :
NUMBER       :       :
```

Fig. 12-2. The additions screen with APPEND.

```
RECORD # 00002

LAST:NAME    :_          :
FIRST:NAME   :           :
STREET       :             :
POBOX:APT    :        :
CITY         :           :
STATE        :   :
ZIP:CODE     :      :
AREA:CODE    :     :
NUMBER       :       :
```

Fig. 12-4. The screen display for Record #2.

```
.  USE CUSTOMER
.  DISPLAY ALL OFF
SMITH       JOHN        PILGRIM WAY                   PLYMOUTH    MA 05634 617 3442654
JONES       BILL        15 SAMOAN DR APT # 7          WESTVILLE   CT 04663 203 4662837
WILLIAMS    DANNY       17 ALOHA DR.                  HONOLULU    HA 67355 808 1257688
SMITH       ROBERT      15 APPIAN DR BOX 7            TRENTON     NJ 16645 207 5663343
ROBERTS     PHIL        GEORGIA LANE                  HARTFORD    CT 06105 203 4662777
CHARLES     LARRY       45 DOG LANE                   HARTFORD    CT 06105 203 2663885
CLARK       SEYMOUR     26 WHITE LN.                  E.HARTFORD  CT 06034 203 7546663
SMITH       KIRK        27 INN AVE.                   SPRINGS     MA 16646 413 2774883
YOUNG       SUE         27 VISTA DR. APT #7           WESTVIEW    MA 16646 413 3664828
JOHNSON     GEORGE      3445 OHIO LA                  DETROIT     MI 35535 574 2553773
MITCHELL    HENRY       23 DENNIS DR                  W.HARTFORD  CT 06117 203 7333232
YORK        JOHN        34 CAPE DR.                   HARTFORD    CT 06334 203 3664773
BATES       MARK        CHARLES RD.                   BOSTON      MA 46638 617 3552626
JAMES       GEORGE      24 PIE LANE                   S. WINDOW   CT 47744 203 3665737
SHERRI      JOE         14 CUP ROAD                   BUCKSVILLE  CT 46627 203 2663737
```

Fig. 12-5. Displaying Records.

because dBASE II will roll them right off the screen. A better way to display the records is with the DISPLAY command. This command by itself will display only the record that the record pointer is currently pointing to. Let's use the DISPLAY ALL OFF option to list the records in the database. The OFF option will suppress the display of the record numbers. The ALL option will cause all the

LAST NAME	FIRST NAME	STREET	POBOX APT	CITY	STATE	ZIP CODE	AREA CODE	NUMBER
----	-----	------	-----	----	-----	----	----	------
SMITH	JOHN	PILGRIM WAY		PLYMOUTH	MA	05634	617	3442654
JONES	BILL	15 SAMOAN DR	APT # 7	WESTVILLE	CT	04663	203	4662837
WILLIAMS	DANNY	17 ALOHA DR.		HONOLULU	HA	67355	808	1257688
SMITH	ROBERT	15 APPIAN DR	BOX 7	TRENTON	NJ	16645	207	5663343
ROBERTS	PHIL	GEORGIA LANE		HARTFORD	CT	06105	203	4662777
CHARLES	LARRY	45 DOG LANE		HARTFORD	CT	06105	203	2663885
CLARK	SEYMOUR	26 WHITE LN.		E.HARTFORD	CT	06034	203	7546663
SMITH	KIRK	27 INN AVE.		SPRINGS	MA	16646	413	2774883
YOUNG	SUE	27 VISTA DR.	APT #7	WESTVIEW	MA	16646	413	3664828
JOHNSON	GEORGE	3445 OHIO LA		DETROIT	MI	35535	574	2553773
MITCHELL	HENRY	23 DENNIS DR		W.HARTFORD	CT	06117	203	7333232
YORK	JOHN	34 CAPE DR.		HARTFORD	CT	06334	203	3664773
BATES	MARK	CHARLES RD.		BOSTON	MA	46638	617	3552626
JAMES	GEORGE	24 PIE LANE		S. WINDOW	CT	47744	203	3665737
SHERRI	JOE	14 CUP ROAD		BUCKSVILLE	CT	46627	203	2663737

Fig. 12-6. The main database.

```
. DISPLAY ALL OFF FOR STATE = 'CT'

JONES        BILL      15 SAMOAN DR APT # 7 WESTVILLE  CT 04663 203 4662837
ROBERTS      PHIL      GEORGIA LANE         HARTFORD   CT 06105 203 4662777
CHARLES      LARRY     45 DOG LANE          HARTFORD   CT 06105 203 2663885
CLARK        SEYMOUR   26 WHITE LN.         E.HARTFORD CT 06034 203 7546663
MITCHELL     HENRY     23 DENNIS DR         W.HARTFORD CT 06117 203 7333232
YORK         JOHN      34 CAPE DR.          HARTFORD   CT 06334 203 3664773
JAMES        GEORGE    24 PIE LANE          S. WINDOW  CT 47744 203 3665737
SHERRI       JOE       14 CUP ROAD          BUCKSVILLE CT 46627 203 2663737
```

Fig. 12-7. The Connecticut records only.

records to be displayed. Figure 12-5 shows the resulting display.

As you can see, all of the records have been displayed as they were entered, records 00001 to 00015. Later you will see how to sort these records by any of the fields. Now you will see some of the power of the display command. You can use the DISPLAY command to selectively display certain records, and at the same time, display only certain columns.

The complete database is shown in Fig. 12-6. Using other options of the DISPLAY command you can change the looks of the display. First, Fig. 12-7 shows only those customers with addresses in the state of CT.

The phrase FOR STATE = "CT" means to choose records that contain "CT" in the state field. Why is "CT" enclosed in quotation marks. This is to identify it as a literal value. "CT" is the value of STATE in the records to be displayed. If you wished to compare the variable STATE to a variable named CT the quotation marks would not be used with CT. When referring to a character value (also known as a *character literal*), you should enclose the value in quotation marks. Numbers do not have to be enclosed in quotation marks because variable names cannot begin with a number. With character fields, the quotation marks are the only way to tell the difference between a variable or field name and a character literal.

Figure 12-8 shows the display of only the names and phone numbers from all the records.

Notice that you are able to show only four of the fields by listing the names of the fields you want. Simply type the field names separated by commas to suppress the listing of all the fields. Also, you will notice that the fields are listed in the order you have specified.

Figure 12-9 shows how you can combine the two DISPLAY commands to list only those records that are from the state of CT.

Notice that you are able to display the Connecticut records without showing the state in the display.

Let's learn one more way of selecting records using the DISPLAY command along with the string command. The $ is a special symbol to dBASE II. It is used to search for partial matches. Let's assume that Fred wants to see his customers who live in any city that contains the word HARTFORD. Fred would type the command like this:

.DISPLAY ALL OFF FOR "HARTFORD" $CITY

The resulting display is shown in Fig. 12-10.
This form of the DISPLAY command allowed Fred to display all the records in the database whose city field included the word HARTFORD.

The DISPLAY command is extremely important for ad-hoc reports. In later chapters you will

```
.  DISPLAY ALL OFF FIRST:NAME,LAST:NAME,AREA:CODE,NUMBER

         JOHN       SMITH      617  3442654
         BILL       JONES      203  4662837
         DANNY      WILLIAMS   808  1257688
         ROBERT     SMITH      207  5663343
         PHIL       ROBERTS    203  4662777
         LARRY      CHARLES    203  2663885
         SEYMOUR    CLARK      203  7546663
         KIRK       SMITH      413  2774883
         SUE        YOUNG      413  3664828
         GEORGE     JOHNSON    574  2553773
         HENRY      MITCHELL   203  7333232
         JOHN       YORK       203  3664773
         MARK       BATES      617  3552626
         GEORGE     JAMES      203  3665737
         JOE        SHERRI     203  2663737
```

Fig. 12-8. Limiting the scope of the display.

learn how to save these reports with the REPORT command and how to add titles, column headers, totals, and subtotals (for your numeric fields). You will also learn some other commands for quick reporting, and learn how to use all these commands in *compound phrases*. A compound phrase provides ways of asking compound questions; for example, you could use a compound phrase if you want to see the names of people from Connecticut only if they live in Hartford. Compound phrases can produce very specific extractions from the database.

CHANGING RECORDS

After adding records, you might discover a mistake has been made. This is when the correction of records is necessary. To change a record you use the EDIT command. This command identifies the record by its record number. If you notice a record that has to be changed, you must find out its record number; then you may change the record as shown in Fig. 12-11.

After changing the record, move the cursor to the last field and press the ENTER key. The display

```
.  DISPLAY ALL OFF FOR STATE = 'CT' FIRST:NAME,
      LAST:NAME,AREA:CODE,NUMBER

         BILL       JONES      203  4662837
         PHIL       ROBERTS    203  4662777
         LARRY      CHARLES    203  2663885
         SEYMOUR    CLARK      203  7546663
         HENRY      MITCHELL   203  7333232
         JOHN       YORK       203  3664773
         GEORGE     JAMES      203  3665737
         JOE        SHERRI     203  2663737
```

Fig. 12-9. Limiting the search and the scope.

```
. DISPLAY ALL OFF FOR 'HARTFORD'$CITY

ROBERTS      PHIL       GEORGIA LANE      HARTFORD   CT  06105  203  466277
CHARLES      LARRY      45 DOG LANE       HARTFORD   CT  06105  203  266388
CLARK        SEYMOUR    26 WHITE LN.      E.HARTFORD CT  06034  203  754666
MITCHELL     HENRY      23 DENNIS DR      W.HARTFORD CT  06117  203  733323
YORK         JOHN       34 CAPE DR.       HARTFORD   CT  06334  203  366477
```

Fig. 12-10. Searching for a field.

will change to show RECORD # 00007. If you want to edit more records, you can continue until the end of the file, or you can end the process by typing CTRL-W.

DELETING RECORDS

In most computer systems, deleting records is a slow and arduous process, because as records are deleted, the file must somehow regain the use of the recovered space. In dBASE II, deleting records is a two-step process. First, you will use the DE-LETE command. This is very similar to the DIS-PLAY command; if you type the DELETE command, it will delete the record the pointer is currently pointing to. Giving the command DELETE FOR STATE = "MA" will delete only the first occurrence of a record with the state of MA. The most effective form is DELETE ALL FOR . . . . . This command will delete all the records for the given condition. For example, you may type

. DELETE FOR AREA:CODE = "808"
00001 DELETION(S)

and

.DELETE ALL FOR STATE = "CT"
00008 DELETION(S)

Figure 12-12 shows how the sample database will look after you have entered these two commands.

You will notice that all the records are there, but how can that be? You just deleted 9 of them! Notice the * in front of some records. The * indicates the records that are marked for deletion. Remember, this is a two-step process. The records won't physically disappear until the PACK command is issued. This command copies the file over without the deleted records. It takes a fair amount of time and should be done only after all deletions are completed. Do all your deletions first; then use PACK once! If you decide against deleting all the records marked with asterisks, you can issue the RECALL command. Let's bring back the records from Connecticut before packing the file:

```
. EDIT 6

RECORD # 00006
LAST:NAME    :CHARLES     :
FIRST:NAME   :LARRY       :
STREET       :45 DOG LANE :
POBOX:APT    :     :
CITY         :HARTFORD    :
STATE        :CT:
ZIP:CODE     :06105:
AREA:CODE    :203:
NUMBER       :2663885:
```

Fig. 12-11. Editing a record.

```
        A display of the sample database now shows this:

          . DISPLAY ALL OFF
  SMITH      JOHN        PILGRIM WAY            PLYMOUTH    MA 05634 617 3442654
 *JONES      BILL        15 SAMOAN DR APT # 7   WESTVILLE   CT 04663 203 4662837
 *WILLIAMS   DANNY       17 ALOHA DR.           HONOLULU    HA 67355 808 1257688
  SMITH      ROBERT      15 APPIAN DR BOX 7     TRENTON     NJ 16645 207 5663343
 *ROBERTS    PHIL        GEORGIA LANE           HARTFORD    CT 06105 203 4662777
 *CHARLES    LARRY       45 DOG LANE            HARTFORD    CT 06105 203 2663885
 *CLARK      SEYMOUR     26 WHITE LN.           E.HARTFORD  CT 06034 203 7546663
  SMITH      KIRK        27 INN AVE.            SPRINGS     MA 16646 413 2774883
  YOUNG      SUE         27 VISTA DR. AFT #7    WESTVIEW    MA 16646 413 3664828
  JOHNSON    GEORGE      3445 OHIO LA           DETROIT     MI 35535 574 2553773
 *MITCHELL   HENRY       23 DENNIS DR           W.HARTFORD  CT 06117 203 7333232
 *YORK       JOHN        34 CAPE DR.            HARTFORD    CT 06334 203 3664773
  BATES      MARK        CHARLES RD.            BOSTON      MA 46638 617 3552626
 *JAMES      GEORGE      24 PIE LANE            S. WINDOW   CT 47744 203 3665737
 *SHERRI     JOE         14 CUP ROAD            BUCKSVILLE  CT 46627 203 2663737
```

Fig. 12-12. Showing deleted records.

. RECALL ALL FOR STATE = "CT"
. 00008 RECALL(S)
. PACK
. PACK COMPLETE, 00014 RECORDS COPIED

Now, all of the unmarked records are copied. Notice that only 14 records were kept. The customer from Hawaii is gone. This is how dBASE II takes care of freeing up the space that was used by the now deleted records in the file. The use of the PACK command actually causes the unmarked records to be copied to a new file. The old file is then deleted, and the new file renamed.

Chapter 13

Sorting the Database

Most of the time you will want the records in your database in a certain order. You may want to see your customers in alphabetical order by last name; maybe you may want them listed according to the state they live in. There are even times you might want a list of your customers starting with the customer who owes the most money and ending with the one who owes the least money. No matter what order you wish to see the records in the database in, some type of arrangement will be necessary.

A NEW ORDER

The most common way to rearrange data in a file is to sort the data. This, however, means physically moving the records each time you want to change the way you see the data. This takes a great deal of computer time. To sort one thousand records using dBASE II will take five and one half minutes or more. This is unacceptable to most people. Unless you have very small databases that do not have too many fields, sorting the database takes too long.

There is also a problem caused by the need for multiple sorts. If you need to see your data in many different orders you will constantly be sorting your files.

There is a solution to the sorting dilemma. *Indexing* is a method that utilizes a separate list of pointers. This list contains the order of the records in the database based upon the sort criteria you have specified. A database can be indexed far more quickly than it can be sorted. This is because indexing a database means assigning values to a list of pointers, while sorting means physically rearranging the data. Updating indexes is also very quick as no physical rearrangement of the data is necessary.

To illustrate the concept of pointers, let's assume that you have the following data:

NAME	TEST SCORE	NAME	TEST SCORE
----	----------	----	----------
WILLIAM	85	ADAM	91
SAMUEL	57	CORY	34
FRED	63	FRED	63
GEORGE	98	GEORGE	98
ADAM	91	JOHN	89
JOHN	89	SAMUEL	57
ZACHARY	76	WILLIAM	85
CORY	34	ZACHARY	76

You can see that there is no special order to this sample file. A database can be sorted in ascending or descending order. If a database is sorted by an ascending key, the record with the lowest value in the field is the first record, and the record with the highest value in the key field is the last record. In a descending sort, the highest values come first. Character values are sorted from Z to A, and numbers from the largest positive value to the largest negative value; the opposite is true for an ascending sort.

Let's look at the data as if it had been sorted by name in ascending order. The data would be physically rearranged and would now look like this:

Sorting it by descending score yields:

NAME	TEST SCORE
----	----------
GEORGE	98
ADAM	91
JOHN	89
WILLIAM	85
ZACHARY	76
FRED	63
SAMUEL	57
CORY	34

Notice that in these two examples, the data itself was physically rearranged. Figure 13-1 shows a

NAME	TEST SCORE	ASCENDING NAME INDEX	DESCENDING TEST SCORE INDEX
----	----------	----------	----------
WILLIAM	85	7	4
SAMUEL	57	6	7
FRED	63	3	6
GEORGE	98	4	1
ADAM	91	1	2
JOHN	89	5	3
ZACHARY	76	8	5
CORY	34	2	8

Fig. 13-1. The Database with index pointers.

conceptual model of the same two sorts done with indexes.

As you can see there is a separate field (actually a separate field with the extension .NDX) that contains the order of each record for the sort desired. In this case, there are two separate index files.

For a final analogy describing the index pointers, imagine what you would do when you want to see a product that you know is in a software catalog, but you cannot remember the product name. The product you are searching for is indexed in several ways in the back of the catalog. Usually these indexes are in order by the product type, manufacturer, and by the product name itself. There are three separate indexes all pointing to the same page in the catalog.

SORTING THE DATABASE

The database above consisted of two fields, NAME and SCORE. If you wish to sort the database by name, you would issue the SORT command. Assume that the database name is TESTS.

```
. USE TESTS
. SORT ON NAME TO TESTSORT
. USE TESTSORT
```

Now there is a sorted copy of the database known as TESTSORT. The original database known as TESTS still exists in its original form. It is advisable to not sort your database into itself as you will lose your data if an error occurs while the copying and rearranging is being done. Since sorting is a special form of copying, the original data can remain safely in its own file.

To sort the database by descending test score you would enter the following:

```
. USE TESTS
. SORT ON TEST TO TESTSOR2;
    DESCENDING
. USE TESTSOR2
```

The problem of multiple keys has not yet been addressed. Using the customer file as an example, how would you sort the file if you wanted to report by STATE, and within the report for each state, you wished to see the names in alphabetical order. This would require *cascading* sorts and would take twice as long as a single sort. In order to do this, you would use the following commands.

```
. USE CUSTOMER
. SORT ON LAST:NAME TO CUSTSORT
. SORT ON STATE TO CUSTSOR2
```

The data is first sorted by LAST:NAME; the results of that sort are retained when the customers are divided into the STATE groups. The final sorted database is called CUSTSOR2, and must be referenced that way.

. USE CUSTSOR2

INDEXING THE DATABASE

Indexing the database is a much simpler task. Let's first look at the code to INDEX the TESTS database:

```
. USE TESTS
. INDEX ON NAME TO TESTSRT1
. USE TESTS INDEX TESTSRT1
```

In order to index the database, you simply use the INDEX command. When you want to use the database with the index, you will USE it with the index file. Unlike the sort, which must be redone every time a record is added, the index is automatically updated as you add records.

Let's look at the sort that was done according to descending test scores, this time using an index:

```
. USE TESTS
. INDEX ON -TEST TO TESTSRT2
. USE TESTS INDEX TESTSRT2
```

Here you see that, to index using a descending key, you place a - before the name of the filename being indexed. This indicated to dBASE II that it should create the descending index. Both of the previous examples produce the same result as the sort did—only much faster.

Finally, you must learn how to do a multiple index. You will use the CUSTOMER database and index by STATE. Within each state, the names will be sorted by LAST:NAME:

```
.  USE CUSTOMER
.  INDEX ON STATE + LAST:NAME;
      TO CUSTSORT
.  USE CUSTOMER INDEX CUSTSORT
```

Using Indexes

You can see how much simpler it is to index a database rather than to sort it. You can have one database of records and many different indexes that you can use. The example above shows indexing with multiple keys but using only one index file. You will always USE the database file; only the index will change!

When you search for records in a nonindexed file, dBASE II will check every record sequentially until it finds a match or reaches the end of the file. If there are thousands of records to search, this may take a long while. dBASE II will read the whole file just to find a single record. Using a database that has been sorted will not improve the situation. Sorting the database only rearranges the data; it does nothing to help dBASE II locate records faster.

Indexing, on the other hand, helps dBASE II locate records quickly. The typical find time on an indexed file is only two seconds when you are using a floppy disk system. Not only are indexes a better way to sort your data, they are also necessary for speed in your system.

Chapter 14

Searching the
Database—A Second Look

In this chapter you will see some advanced ways to search a database and begin to see the differences between using dBASE II as a database manager and using the dBASE II programming statements.

COMPOUND EXPRESSIONS

Compound expressions involve the use of connectors, such as AND, OR, and NOT. These allow you to ask far more specific questions than just querying the state someone lives in. With compound expressions, you can ask questions such as "Which of my customers live in apartments that are not in Connecticut or Massachusetts?" "How many customers do I have that have not made an order in two years but whose last order was over $20.00?" "Which of my largest ten customers owes the most money for more than 60 days?"

Obviously these pieces of data would have to be on the database in order for you to get a response to these types of questions, but without the compound expression, they could not be asked.

Let's discuss the first two connectors AND, and OR. AND is a connector that allows you to evaluate several comparisons and make a positive decision only if all the comparisons are true. (If you are asked to compare the variable AMT:SPENT to "less than 500" and the value of AMT:SPENT is less than 500, the expression is true. If AMT:SPENT is equal to or greater than 500, the expression is false.) Using AND you may ask a question such as the following:

IF AMT:SPENT < 500 .AND. STATE = "CT"
    PRINT THE CUSTOMER

This pseudocode representation illustrates the use of AND. Only if the customer has both spent less than 500 and been a resident of Connecticut will his name be printed. Merely living in Connecticut is not enough, the customer must also have spent less than 500.

The connector OR allows you to evaluate several expressions and take a certain course of action if any of the comparisons are true.

IF AMT:SPENT < 500 .OR. STATE = "CY"
    PRINT THE CUSTOMER

This pseudocode representation shows the use of OR. If the customer has spent less than 500 the expression is true regardless of the state he or she lives in. Likewise if he or she lives in Connecticut the expression is true regardless of the amount spent. Only if both parts of the expression are false is the expression false. For the expression in this example to be false, the person must not live in Connecticut and must have spent at least 500.

The final connector, NOT is always used only in conjunction with the expression itself. It does not allow two expressions to be combined. NOT causes the opposite of the expression to be true. For example

IF AMT:SPENT .NOT. < 500
PRINT THE CUSTOMER

is the same as:

IF AMT:SPENT > 500
PRINT THE CUSTOMER

You might notice that there are periods surrounding the AND, OR, and NOT connectors. This is the real syntax that dBASE II uses. This allows dBASE II to recognize these three words as connectors rather than as variable names.

DISPLAYING SELECTED RECORDS

Assume the database shown in Fig. 14-1. Let's take a look at several examples of DISPLAY command using compound expressions.

. DISPLAY ALL OFF FOR STATE = "CT" .AND.;
    BUY:THISYR = "Y"

You have asked for dBASE II to display all records for customers in Connecticut who have bought from you this year. Figure 14-2 uses italic type to indicate the records that were selected and displayed.

. DISPLAY ALL OFF FOR STATE = "CT" .OR.;
    BUY:THISYR = "Y"

Now you have changed what you are asking

LAST:NAME	FIRST:NAME	STATE	CUST:SINCE	BUY:THISYR	AMOUNT
SMITH	JOHN	MA	1981	Y	2356
JONES	BILL	CT	1979	Y	21533
ROBERTS	PHIL	NJ	1975	N	0
CLARK	SEYMOUR	CT	1973	Y	35689
SMITH	KIRK	MA	1975	N	0
YOUNG	SUE	MA	1971	Y	45680
JOHNSON	GEORGE	MI	1982	N	0
MITCHELL	HENRY	CT	1967	Y	8390
YORK	JOHN	CT	1969	Y	33612
JAMES	GEORGE	CT	1982	N	0

Fig. 14-1. A sample database.

SMITH	JOHN	MA	1981	Y	2356
JONES	BILL	CT	1979	Y	21533
ROBERTS	PHIL	NJ	1975	N	0
CLARK	SEYMOUR	CT	1973	Y	35689
SMITH	KIRK	MA	1975	N	0
YOUNG	SUE	MA	1971	Y	45680
JOHNSON	GEORGE	MI	1982	N	0
MITCHELL	HENRY	CT	1967	Y	8390
YORK	JOHN	CT	1969	Y	33612
JAMES	GEORGE	CT	1982	N	0

Fig. 14-2. Using the AND connector.

for. You want to see a customer's name if he or she lives in Connecticut or if he or she has bought from you this year. It doesn't matter which of those conditions were met; even if a given customer meets both requirements, you want to see his or her name. The results are shown in Fig. 14-30.

. DISPLAY ALL OFF FOR STATE .NOT. = "CT";
.OR. AMOUNT < 10000

Using the NOT expression, you will be able to see a customer's name if he or she has spent less than $10,000 or if he or she is not from Connecticut. Note that you want to see the names of those not residing in Connecticut no matter how much they have spent. The resulting display is shown in Fig. 14-4.

. DISPLAY ALL OFF FOR STATE = "MA".AND.;
(CUST:SINCE < = 1980 .OR. AMOUNT <;
1000)

In this example you see a *double compound* expression. Though there are three conditions, STATE ="MA," CUST:SINCE <=1980, and AMOUNT > 1000, the expression is reduced to two conditions, because of the placement of the parentheses. The first condition is simply that the customer must live in Massachusetts (STATE="MA"); the second is a complex expression itself and must be evaluated

SMITH	JOHN	MA	1981	Y	2356
JONES	BILL	CT	1979	Y	21533
ROBERTS	PHIL	NJ	1975	N	0
CLARK	SEYMOUR	CT	1973	Y	35689
SMITH	KIRK	MA	1975	N	0
YOUNG	SUE	MA	1971	Y	45680
JOHNSON	GEORGE	MI	1982	N	0
MITCHELL	HENRY	CT	1967	Y	8390
YORK	JOHN	CT	1969	Y	33612
JAMES	GEORGE	CT	1982	N	0

Fig. 14-3. Using the OR Connector.

SMITH	JOHN	MA	1981	Y	2356
JONES	BILL	CT	1979	Y	21533
ROBERTS	PHIL	NJ	1975	N	0
CLARK	SEYMOUR	CT	1973	Y	35689
SMITH	KIRK	MA	1975	N	0
YOUNG	SUE	MA	1971	Y	45680
JOHNSON	GEORGE	MI	1982	N	0
MITCHELL	HENRY	CT	1967	Y	8390
YORK	JOHN	CT	1969	Y	33612
JAMES	GEORGE	CT	1982	N	0

Fig. 14-4. Using the NOT connector.

before being evaluated in conjunction with the first condition.

The second expression is true if the customer has been a customer since 1980 or before. The second expression is also true if the customer has spent 1000. Finally, it is true if the customer has both been a customer since 1980 or before and has spent $1000. Only if the customer meets neither condition is the second expression false.

After evaluating the simple first expression and the compound second expression, you can evaluate the expression as a whole. Since there is an AND clause between them, both sides must be true to be true.

After careful examination, you realize that only people in Massachusetts who have been cus-

tomers since 1980 or have spent $10,000 should be listed. Figure 14-5 shows the resulting display.

. DISPLAY ALL OFF FOR BUY:THISYR = "Y";
  .OR. AMOUNT = 0

In the final example two opposite possibilities have been used. Logically, if someone has bought this year, their amount cannot be 0. Conversely, if their amount is 0 they could not have bought this year. By using the OR clause all records are selected, as shown in Fig. 14-6.

What would happen if you change this expression to AND? That's right—none of the records would have been selected.

SMITH	JOHN	MA	1981	Y	2356
JONES	BILL	CT	1979	Y	21533
ROBERTS	PHIL	NJ	1975	N	0
CLARK	SEYMOUR	CT	1973	Y	35689
SMITH	KIRK	MA	1975	N	0
YOUNG	SUE	MA	1971	Y	45680
JOHNSON	GEORGE	MI	1982	N	0
MITCHELL	HENRY	CT	1967	Y	8390
YORK	JOHN	CT	1969	Y	33612
JAMES	GEORGE	CT	1982	N	0

Fig. 14-5. A Double Compound Expression.

SMITH	JOHN	MA	1981	Y	2356
JONES	BILL	CT	1979	Y	21533
ROBERTS	PHIL	NJ	1975	N	0
CLARK	SEYMOUR	CT	1973	Y	35689
SMITH	KIRK	MA	1975	N	0
YOUNG	SUE	MA	1971	Y	45680
JOHNSON	GEORGE	MI	1982	N	0
MITCHELL	HENRY	CT	1967	Y	8390
YORK	JOHN	CT	1969	Y	33612
JAMES	GEORGE	CT	1982	N	0

Fig. 14-6. An example of conflicting search criteria.

LOCATE

When you are using dBASE II as a database manager and are querying your data with commands such as LIST and DISPLAY, you are asking dBASE II to search for records that meet a certain criteria and then show them to you on the screen. When you are using dBASE II as a programming language you will not use those commands as they do not give you very much flexibility when displaying the records on the screen.

When programming, you will want to know where it exists on the file. If it does exist, you will want to know where it exists. Once you determine the location of a record, you can use standard programming techniques to retrieve the record and display it any way you want.

The LOCATE command is used to help you to see if a record exists. The LOCATE command should only be used with nonindexed databases. It is used just like the DISPLAY command except all you can specify is the *search criteria* that is the characters the desired entry should contain. LOCATE will search the file beginning with the first record and continuing until it either finds the record or reaches the bottom of the file. If your file is very large, it may take a long time to go through it as every record must be read. If the desired record is on the bottom or not there at all, you will be in for a long wait.

LOCATE does not show you the record. If it finds the record, it responds by telling you the record number. If it doesn't find the record, it will tell you END OF FILE: for example,

```
. LOCATE FOR NAME = 'SMITH'
  RECORD 00025
```

and

```
. LOCATE FOR NAME = 'JONES' AND STATE= 'MO'
  END OF FILE
```

LOCATE also allows you to continue the search without returning to the *top* of the database. As you find a record, the record pointer moves to the record and the record number is displayed. If you issued another LOCATE command, dBase II would start again at the top of the file and only find the first occurrence of the record. The CONTINUE command allows you to keep searching:

```
  . LOCATE FOR NAME = 'SMITH'
    RECORD 00025

  . CONTINUE
    RECORD 00104
```

```
. CONTINUE
  RECORD 00684

. CONTINUE
  END OF FILE
```

In this example, records with the name of SMITH can be found in record numbers 25, 104, and 684. You can then use the location number to display those records, or in programs, you would display each record before using the CONTINUE phrase. In programming, you would have to check to see if the record information was equal to the information you were searching for after using the LOCATE or CONTINUE phrases. When END OF FILE is displayed, the record pointer is pointing to the bottom of the file.

FIND

The FIND command is used in the same manner as the locate command but is used with indexed databases to determine whether or not the indexed key exists. The FIND command knows what the indexed key is. You do not have to specify the field name or names that were used in the creation of the key. The FIND command will not tell you whether or not the record was found. You must query the record pointer variable. This is an internal variable known to dBASE II as # for instance, consider

```
. USE CUSTDATA INDEX CUST
. FIND 'SMITH'
. ? #
  25
```

and

```
. USE CUSTDATA INDEX CUST
. FIND 'JONES'
. ? #
  0
```

In the first example, the first occurrence of SMITH is in record number 25. The ? # command allowed you to see whether or not there was a SMITH in the database and to display the record number. The ? # command could have been fol-lowed by a DISPLAY command, which would have showed you record number 25, at which the record pointer is currently pointing.

In the second example, the record was not in the database. The pointer is set to 0, and no record could be displayed.

When you used the LOCATE command you were able to see subsequent occurrences of matching records by using the CONTINUE phrase. When using the FIND command, you must program this function. Since each keyed record is sequentially connected you can use SKIP commands and check the data.

```
. USE CUSTDATA INDEX CUST
. FIND 'SMITH'
. DISPLAY NAME,STATE
    SMITH   CT
. SKIP
. DISPLAY NAME,STATE
    SMITH   VT
. DISPLAY NAME,STATE
    SMITH   MA
. SKIP
. DISPLAY NAME,STATE
    STEBBINS AZ
```

As you can see, dBASE II does not know if it has found other occurrences of SMITH. The SKIP command simply runs through the database sequentially according to the indexed key, one record per SKIP. The FIND command lets you position the pointer and then search until there is no longer a match. However, you must use programming to determine when there is no longer a match, as shown below.

```
USE INDEXED DATABASE
FIND RECORD
IF # NOT 0
  THEN
    DO WHILE SEARCHFIELD = INDEXKEY
      DISPLAY RECORD
      SKIP
    ENDDO
  ELSE
    RECORD NOT FOUND
ENDIF
```

```
.  USE CUSTHIST INDEX CUSTST
.  DISPLAY ALL OFF

JONES        BILL        CT      1979            Y       21533
CLARK        SEYMOUR     CT      1973            Y       35689
MITCHELL     HENRY       CT      1967            Y        8390
YORK         JOHN        CT      1969            Y       33612
JAMES        GEORGE      CT      1982            N           O
SMITH        KIRK        MA      1975            N           O
YOUNG        SUE         MA      1971            Y       45680
SMITH        JOHN        MA      1981            Y        2356
JOHNSON      GEORGE      MI      1982            N           O
ROBERTS      PHIL        NJ      1975            N           O
```

Fig. 14-7. A look at the database.

```
.  USE B:CUSTHIST INDEX CUSTST
.  REPORT

   ENTER REPORT FORM NAME: CUST1
   ENTER OPTIONS, M=LEFT MARGIN, L=LINES/PAGE, W=PAGE WIDTH
   PAGE HEADING? (Y/N) Y
   ENTER PAGE HEADING: CUSTOMER HISTORY BY STATE
   DOUBLE SPACE REPORT? (Y/N) N
   ARE TOTALS REQUIRED? (Y/N) Y
   SUBTOTALS IN REPORT? (Y/N) Y
   ENTER SUBTOTALS FIELD: STATE
   SUMMARY REPORT ONLY? (Y/N) N
   EJECT PAGE AFTER SUBTOTALS? (Y/N) N
   ENTER SUBTOTAL HEADING: STATE OF
   COL      WIDTH,CONTENTS
   001      10,FIRST:NAME
   ENTER HEADING: FIRST;NAME
   002      10,LAST:NAME
   ENTER HEADING: LAST;NAME
   003      10,CUST:SINCE
   ENTER HEADING: CUSTOMER; SINCE
   ARE TOTALS REQUIRED? (Y/N) N
   004      10,AMOUNT
   ENTER HEADING: TOTAL;SPENT
   ARE TOTALS REQUIRED? (Y/N) Y
   005
```

Fig. 14-8. The report command.

REPORT

You have already seen how to use the DIS-PLAY command to display your records. The DIS-PLAY command allows you to display some or all of your records and also allows you to display only certain fields. The REPORT command will enable you to do all that using a more formal display. The REPORT command also allows you to save the format so you can see the formatted report whenever you want without having to redefine the format.

The REPORT command uses the FOR phrase,

```
PAGE NO. 00001
12/04/83

          CUSTOMER HISTORY BY STATE


     FIRST        LAST      CUSTOMER      TOTAL
     NAME         NAME       SINCE        SPENT

  * STATE OF CT
  BILL         JONES         1979        21533
  SEYMOUR      CLARK         1973        35689
  HENRY        MITCHELL      1967         8390
  JOHN         YORK          1969        33612
  GEORGE       JAMES         1982            0
  ** SUBTOTAL **
                                         99224


  * STATE OF MA
  KIRK         SMITH         1975        45680
  JOHN         SMITH         1981         2356
  ** SUBTOTAL **
                                         48036


  * STATE OF MI
  GEORGE       JOHNSON       1982            0
  ** SUBTOTAL **
                                             0


  * STATE OF NJ
  PHIL         ROBERTS       1975            0
  ** SUBTOTAL **
                                             0

  ** TOTAL **
                                        147260
```

Fig. 14-9. The report command output.

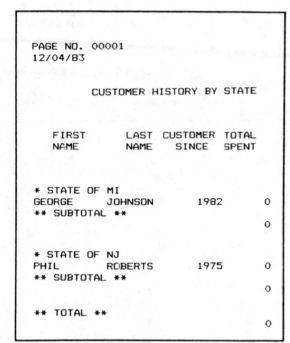

```
PAGE NO.  00001
12/04/83


          CUSTOMER HISTORY BY STATE


    FIRST       LAST   CUSTOMER  TOTAL
    NAME        NAME    SINCE    SPENT


  * STATE OF MI
  GEORGE     JOHNSON      1982      0
  ** SUBTOTAL **
                                    0


  * STATE OF NJ
  PHIL       ROBERTS      1975      0
  ** SUBTOTAL **
                                    0


  ** TOTAL **
                                    0
```

Fig. 14-10. The final report.

as does the DISPLAY command, to choose the records that will be selected for display.

Before using the REPORT command you must specify a database. Let's first USE and DISPLAY the complete database, as shown in Fig. 14-7.

Now you can use the REPORT command to see your data in a better format. Figure 14-8 shows how the formatting is done.

You can see there are many questions to answer after typing the REPORT command. These questions allow you to determine how your report will look. In this case you have chosen that your report should have subtotals by state, page heading that reads CUSTOMER HISTORY BY STATE, and have totals, which you later defined to be the total amount spent. You have chosen not to enter any values to change the margin or page width, or the number of lines per page. You did not want double spacing or new pages after each subtotal. You also told dBASE II that you did not want a summary report. The report shown in Fig. 14-9 was produced by answering the questions in the manner shown in Fig. 14-8.

The REPORT command will work with any database. It permits a simple way to customize column headers, subtotals, and totals. It does not allow the freedom to move fields and records anywhere on a page. Completely customized reporting will be demonstrated later in the programming section.

If you wanted to print this report on paper, you could have used the following command:

. REPORT TO PRINT

If you had already defined the report format, you could have typed

. REPORT FORM CUST1 TO PRINT

Finally, if you had only wanted the names of those customers who haven't bought anything this year, you could have typed

. REPORT FROM CUST1 TO PRINT FOR;
  BUY:THISYR = "N"

This command would have produced the report shown in Fig. 14-10.

Chapter 15

Data Relations

So far you have learned about using one database at a time. You have examined a customer database used to store such things as name, address, and phone number. You also examined a database that contained customers' names, and some history about their buying levels and longevity. These could easily fit in a single database. But, what about a file of customer purchases? One record could consist of all the items shown in Fig. 15-1.

What is shown is a symbolic record that has the customer name and address information along with shipping information and complete information concerning the 12 items on the order.

DATA REDUNDANCY

Can a record like this be created using a relational database manager such as dBASE II? Of course, but it would not be an efficient approach. Having a record like this would

1. require that every record have twelve different quantity, item number, list price, discount, net price, and amount fields whether there were twelve items on the order or one.

2. limit the record to twelve items. If the order had twenty items, you would have to split it up.

3. would make querying difficult. Each quantity, item number, and so on would have a different field name.

4. have 83 fields, many more than the 32 allowed in a record by dBASE II.

The way you can implement this type of data structure is by establishing a record for each quantity, item number, and so on. The record might contain the following fields:

```
ORDER:NO
CUST:NAME
BILL:STREET
BILL:CITY
BILL:STATE
BILL:ZIP
SHIP:STREET
SHIP:CITY
SHIP:STATE
SHIP:ZIP
PHONE
DATE
QTY
ITEM:NO
LIST:PRICE
DISC
NET:PRICE
AMOUNT
```

There will be a separate record for each item ordered. Notice the new field called ORDER:NO. This is the key. Each record that belongs to the order will have the same order number (along with all the same customer information). With the database structured in this fashion, you can easily query the database to see the items for each order number.

This database design solves the previous problems. You can query the database; there are less than 32 fields; and most importantly, if you have one item on the order, there will be only one record. You also have the ability to have an endless (or almost endless) number of items. If there are 75 items there would be 75 records. This, however, poses another problem; *data redundancy*.

Data redundancy occurs when *normalization* has not taken place. Normalization is a fancy term applied to database design. Simply put, normalization means having one data field in one place unless it is the key. You do have a key in your database— ORDER:NO. Each record for a specific order will have the same order number. But, look at the beginning of each record; the name, billing and shipping addresses, phone number, and date will be the

same for each record with the same order number. Only the fields that contain the quantity, item number, discount, and prices will be different. This is data redundancy at its worst.

There is a solution. Through the use of multiple databases, you will see how to transform this record structure into several smaller ones, save a lot of storage space, and eliminate data redundancy.

MULTIPLE DATABASES

Let's first define the present structure:

Field	Type		
ORDER:NO,	CHAR	005	000
CUST:NAME	CHAR	015	000
BILL:STREET	CHAR	015	000
BILL:CITY	CHAR	015	000
BILL:STATE	CHAR	002	000
BILL:ZIP	CHAR	005	000
SHIP:STREET	CHAR	015	000
SHIP:CITY	CHAR	015	000
SHIP:STATE	CHAR	002	000
SHIP:ZIP	CHAR	005	000
PHONE	CHAR	013	000
DATE	CHAR	008	000
QTY	NUM	003	000
ITEM:NO	CHAR	006	000
LIST:PRICE	NUM	005	002
DISC	NUM	003	000
NET:PRICE	NUM	005	002
AMOUNT	NUM	008	002
TOTAL		145	

Each record is 145 characters long. If an order has 15 items this will produce 15 records, each 145 characters long. Each record will have the same customer information with only the actual quantity and item information different. Looking at this, you will see that 15 records will cause 2175 characters to be added to the database. When you realize that the customer information, which includes name, addresses, phone number, and order date, need only be entered once, you will realize that of the 2175 characters added to the database, 1575 are redundant.

```
CUST:NAME
BILL:STREET
BILL:CITY
BILL:STATE
BILL:ZIP
SHIP:STREET
SHIP:CITY
SHIP:STATE
SHIP:ZIP
PHONE
DATE

QTY           QTY           QTY           QTY
ITEM:NO       ITEM:NO       ITEM:NO       ITEM:NO
LIST:PRICE    LIST:PRICE    LIST:PRICE    LIST:PRICE
DISC          DISC          DISC          DISC
NET:PRICE     NET:PRICE     NET:PRICE     NET:PRICE
AMOUNT        AMOUNT        AMOUNT        AMOUNT

QTY           QTY           QTY           QTY
ITEM:NO       ITEM:NO       ITEM:NO       ITEM:NO
LIST:PRICE    LIST:PRICE    LIST:PRICE    LIST:PRICE
DISC          DISC          DISC          DISC
NET:PRICE     NET:PRICE     NET:PRICE     NET:PRICE
AMOUNT        AMOUNT        AMOUNT        AMOUNT

QTY           QTY           QTY           QTY
ITEM:NO       ITEM:NO       ITEM:NO       ITEM:NO
LIST:PRICE    LIST:PRICE    LIST:PRICE    LIST:PRICE
DISC          DISC          DISC          DISC
NET:PRICE     NET:PRICE     NET:PRICE     NET:PRICE
AMOUNT        AMOUNT        AMOUNT        AMOUNT
```

Fig. 15-1. A sample database.

The solution is to break up this record structure and place portions of it in two databases. The first database will contain the order number and customer information. The second will contain the order number and order information:

```
CUSTOMER DATABASE
  ORDER:NO      CHAR    005    000
  CUST:NAME     CHAR    015    000
  BILL:STREET   CHAR    015    000
  BILL:CITY     CHAR    015    000
  BILL:STATE    CHAR    002    000
  BILL:ZIP      CHAR    005    000
  SHIP:STREET   CHAR    015    000
  SHIP:CITY     CHAR    015    000
  SHIP:STATE    CHAR    002    000
  SHIP:ZIP      CHAR    005    000
  PHONE         CHAR    013    000
  DATE          CHAR    008    000

  **TOTAL**             115
```

```
ORDER DATABASE
    ORDER:NO        CHAR     005   000
    QTY             NUM      003   000
    ITEM:NO         CHAR     006   000
    LIST:PRICE      NUM      005   002
    DISC            NUM      003   000
    NET:PRICE       NUM      005   002
    AMOUNT          NUM      008   002

    **TOTAL**                35
```

```
ORDERITM DATABASE
    ORDER:NO        CHAR     005   000
    QTY             NUM      003   000
    ITEM:NO         CHAR     006   000
    LIST:PRICE      NUM      005   002
    DISC            NUM      003   000
    NET:PRICE       NUM      005   002
    AMOUNT          NUM      008   002

    **TOTAL**                35
```

Now there are two databases. The CUSTOMER database will have only one record for each order, while the ORDER database will have one record for each item in the order. This procedure illustrates how large applications are designed using relational databases. This technique allows you to program large applications very efficiently.

The next step is to further eliminate redundancy. If there are many repeat customers who will have many different orders on the database, it would make a lot of sense to have a separate customer file. You could create a third database called CUSTOMER, while renaming the existing databases ORDER and ORDERITM. This would produce the following databases:

```
CUSTOMER DATABASE
    CUST:NO         CHAR     005   000
    CUST:NAME       CHAR     015   000
    BILL:STREET     CHAR     015   000
    BILL:CITY       CHAR     015   000
    BILL:STATE      CHAR     002   000
    BILL:ZIP        CHAR     005   000
    SHIP:STREET     CHAR     015   000
    SHIP:CITY       CHAR     015   000
    SHIP:STATE      CHAR     002   000
    SHIP:ZIP        CHAR     005   000
    PHONE           CHAR     013   000

    **TOTAL**                107
```

```
ORDER DATABASE
    ORDER:NO        CHAR     005   000
    DATE            CHAR     008   000
    CUST:NO         CHAR     005   000

    **TOTAL**                18
```

Let's do a quick analysis. Assuming 15 orders per customer with each order having 15 items, it would take the following amount of space to store the records:

ONE DATABASE
32,625 bytes

TWO DATABASES
9,600 bytes

THREE DATABASE
8,252 bytes

Let's not stop here. If you analyze the ORDERITM database, you can see some redundancies. The LIST:PRICE can be found on a separate file. The key for this file could be ITEM:NO. Creation of this file will save additional resources. Another possible reduction in storage space is to delete the NET:PRICE and AMOUNT fields. These fields are calculated and have no business being on the database. NET:PRICE is really LIST:PRICE × DISC; AMOUNT is really QTY × NET:PRICE. Let's make these changes and see the final database solution. The databases would look like this:

```
CUSTOMER DATABASE
    CUST:NO         CHAR     005   000
    CUST:NAME       CHAR     015   000
```

BILL:STREET	CHAR	015	000
BILL:CITY	CHAR	015	000
BILL:STATE	CHAR	002	000
BILL:ZIP	CHAR	005	000
SHIP:STREET	CHAR	015	000
SHIP:CITY	CHAR	015	000
SHIP:STATE	CHAR	002	000
SHIP:ZIP	CHAR	005	000
PHONE	CHAR	013	000
TOTAL		107	

PRICE DATABASE

ITEM:NO	CHAR	006	000
LIST:PRICE	NUM	005	002
TOTAL		11	

ORDER DATABASE

ORDER:NO	CHAR	005	000
DATE	CHAR	008	000
CUST:NO	CHAR	005	000
TOTAL		18	

ORDERITM DATABASE

ORDER:NO	CHAR	005	000
QTY	NUM	003	000
ITEM:NO	CHAR	006	000
DISC	NUM	003	000
TOTAL		17	

Let's do some more analysis. Assuming 15 orders per customer with each order having 15 items that are the same items each time, it would take the following amounts of space to store the records:

ONE DATABASE
32,625 bytes

TWO DATABASES
9,600 bytes

THREE DATABASES
8,252 bytes

FOUR DATABASES
4,213 bytes

This division would totally eliminate any redundancies. Notice that the amount of space necessary to store the 15 orders has been reduced from 32,625 characters to 4,213 characters. To put this in a better perspective, with a 320K disk you could have the following number of orders on a disk:

ONE DATABASE	147 orders
TWO DATABASES	500 orders
THREE DATABASES	582 orders
FOUR DATABASES	1,139 orders

You can see that the savings from the original design to the final design represents an almost eight-fold increase in space savings. The savings in disks alone would be worth the few minutes it might take to do a good database analysis.

JOINING MULTIPLE DATABASES

With dBASE II, commands such as DISPLAY, LIST, or REPORT only work with one database at a time. In relational database management, there is a command that allows the merging or JOINing of databases.

There are several ways you can join databases together in order to use your data effectively. In the third section of this book, you will learn the proper programming techniques to accomplish this without creating one large database from the small ones.

Even without programming you can merge separate databases in order to use the dBASE II query commands. The JOIN command allows you to combine databases. Let's assume the databases and data shown in Fig. 15-2.

Let's define a report you might wish to see. What about a report of all the orders in the file? You might want to see the customer's number, the date, and the quantity of each item, and the item number. You could use the following dBASE II commands shown in Fig. 15-3.

You will first notice the command SELECT SECONDARY. This command allows you to acti-

```
ITEM DATABASE
ITEMNO      DESC      PRICE

0001        HAMMERS    5.63
0002        PLIERS     7.94
0003        SCREWS      .04
0004        STAPLERS  17.46
0005        KNIVES     2.98

CUSTOMER DATABASE
CUSTNO      NAME        STREET          CITY         STATE    ZIP

0001        Fred Smith  24 Hall Blvd    Yalesville   CT      06354
0002        Bill Jones  19 Dry Gulch    Berlin       NH      07242
0003        John Wille  7 Seaton Rd.    Salem        NC      96738
0004        Susan James 41 Knott Dr.    Branford     MI      64483
0005        George Ho   63 Oahu Dr.     Maui         HA      82267

ORDER DATABASE
ORDNO       CUSTNO    DATE

0001        0003      6/15/83
0002        0005      6/15/83
0003        0001      6/16/83
0004        0002      6/16/83
0005        0003      6/17/83

ORDERITM DATABASE
ORDNO       QTY      ITEMNO

0001        15       0001
0001         9       0005
0001        100      0003
0002         3       0002
0002        16       0004
0003        23       0001
0003         7       0004
0003        20       0005
0003        800      0003
0003        35       0002
0004        40       0001
0005        12       0005
0005        15       0003
```

Fig. 15-2. Sample Databases.

```
.  USE ORDER
.  SELECT SECONDARY
.  USE ORDERITM
.  SELECT PRIMARY
.  JOIN TO ORDREP FOR P.ORDNO=S.ORDNO FIELD ORDNO, CUSTNO,
      DATE,QTY,ITEMNO
.  USE ORDREP
.  DISPLAY ALL OFF

      0001    0003    06/15/83        15        0001
      0001    0003    06/15/83         9        0005
      0001    0003    06/15/83       100        0003
      0002    0005    06/15/83         3        0002
      0002    0005    06/15/83        16        0004
      0003    0001    06/16/83        23        0001
      0003    0001    06/16/83         7        0004
      0003    0001    06/16/83        20        0005
      0003    0001    06/16/83       800        0003
      0003    0001    06/16/83        35        0002
      0004    0002    06/16/83        40        0001
      0005    0003    06/17/83        12        0005
      0005    0003    06/17/83        15        0003
```

Fig. 15-3. The JOIN Command.

vate or USE a second database. To join two databases it is necessary to SELECT a primary database and a secondary database.

The JOIN command allows you to take all the records from one database and merge the fields into the fields of another database. In the previous case the condition that the order numbers must be the same was imposed. Therefore, there are records in common in each of the database as shown in Fig. 15-4.

This report was sufficient, but there were too many codes. Let's get rid of those codes through a series of JOINs. Suppose you want to see the order number along with customer name, date, quantity, description, and cost of each item.

This result is accomplished using the following dBASE II commands:

```
.  USE ORDER
.  SELECT SECONDARY
.  USE ORDERITM
.  SELECT PRIMARY
.  JOIN TO ORD1 FOR P.ORDNO=S.ORDNO

.  USE ORD1
.  DISPLAY ALL OFF
      0001  0003  06/15/83  0001    15  0001
      0001  0003  06/15/83  0001     9  0005
      0001  0003  06/15/83  0001   100  0003
      0002  0005  06/15/83  0002     3  0002
      0002  0005  06/15/83  0002    16  0004
      0003  0001  06/16/83  0003    23  0001
      0003  0001  06/16/83  0003     7  0004
      0003  0001  06/16/83  0003    20  0005
      0003  0001  06/16/83  0003   800  0003
      0003  0001  06/16/83  0003    35  0002
      0004  0002  06/16/83  0004    40  0001
      0005  0003  06/17/83  0005    12  0005
      0005  0003  06/17/83  0005    15  0003
```

```
ITEM DATABASE

  ITEMNO       DESC       PRICE

   0001       HAMMERS      5.63
   0002       PLIERS       7.94
   0003       SCREWS        .04
   0004       STAPLERS    17.46
   0005       KNIVES       2.98

CUSTOMER DATABASE

  CUSTNO      NAME        STREET          CITY        STATE    ZIP

   0001     Fred Smith  24 Hall Blvd    Yalesville     CT     06354
   0002     Bill Jones  19 Dry Gulch    Berlin         NH     07242
   0003     John Wille  7 Seaton Rd.    Salem          NC     96738
   0004     Susan James 41 Knott Dr.    Branford       MI     64483
   0005     George Ho   63 Oahu Dr.     Maui           HA     82267

ORDER DATABASE

  ORDNO      CUSTNO       DATE

   0001       0003       6/15/83
   0002       0005       6/15/83
   0003       0001       6/16/83
   0004       0002       6/16/83
   0005       0003       6/17/83

ORDERITM DATABASE

  ORDNO       QTY        ITEMNO

   0001        15         0001
   0001         9         0005
   0001       100         0003
   0002         3         0002
   0002        16         0004
   0003        23         0001
   0003         7         0004
   0003        20         0005
   0003       800         0003
   0003        35         0002
   0004        40         0001
   0005        12         0005
   0005        15         0003
```

Fig. 15-4. Data in the Database.

```
. USE ORD1
. SELECT SECONDARY
. USE ITEM
. SELECT PRIMARY
. JOIN TO ORD2 FOR P.ITEMNO=S.ITEMNO
. USE ORD2
. DISPLAY ALL OFF
     0001 0003 06/15/83 0001    15 0001 0001 HAMMERS     5.63
     0001 0003 06/15/83 0001     9 0005 0005 KNIVES      2.98
     0001 0003 06/15/83 0001   100 0003 0003 SCREWS      0.04
     0002 0005 06/15/83 0002     3 0002 0002 PLIERS      7.94
     0002 0005 06/15/83 0002    16 0004 0004 STAPLERS   17.46
     0003 0001 06/16/83 0003    23 0001 0001 HAMMERS     5.63
     0003 0001 06/16/83 0003     7 0004 0004 STAPLERS   17.46
     0003 0001 06/16/83 0003    20 0005 0005 KNIVES      2.98
     0003 0001 06/16/83 0003   800 0003 0003 SCREWS      0.04
     0003 0001 06/16/83 0003    35 0002 0002 PLIERS      7.94
     0004 0002 06/16/83 0004    40 0001 0001 HAMMERS     5.63
     0005 0003 06/17/83 0005    12 0005 0005 KNIVES      2.98
     0005 0003 06/17/83 0005    15 0003 0003 SCREWS      0.04
```

Fig. 15-5. A Sample Database.

```
. USE ORD2

. SELECT SECONDARY
. USE CUSTOMER
. SELECT PRIMARY
. JOIN TO ORDREP FOR P.CUSTNO=S.CUSTNO FIELD ORDNO,NAME,DATE,
  QTY,DESC,PRICE
. USE ORDREP
. DISPLAY ALL OFF
     0001   John Wille      06/15/83    15 HAMMERS     5.63
     0001   John Wille      06/15/83     9 KNIVES      2.98
     0001   John Wille      06/15/83   100 SCREWS      0.04
     0002   George Ho       06/15/83     3 PLIERS      7.94
     0002   George Ho       06/15/83    16 STAPLERS   17.46
     0003   Fred Smith      06/16/83    23 HAMMERS     5.63
     0003   Fred Smith      06/16/83     7 STAPLERS   17.46
     0003   Fred Smith      06/16/83    20 KNIVES      2.98
     0003   Fred Smith      06/16/83   800 SCREWS      0.04
     0003   Fred Smith      06/16/83    35 PLIERS      7.94
     0004   Bill Jones      06/16/83    40 HAMMERS     5.63
     0005   John Wille      06/17/83    12 KNIVES      2.98
     0005   John Wille      06/17/83    15 SCREWS      0.04
```

Fig. 15-6. The Final JOIN.

ORDER REPORT

DATE	CUSTOMER NAME	QTY	DESCRIPTION	PRICE	AMOUNT
* ORDER NUMBER 0001					
06/15/83	John Wille	15	HAMMERS	5.63	84.45
06/15/83	John Wille	9	KNIVES	2.98	26.82
06/15/83	John Wille	100	SCREWS	0.04	4.00
** SUBTOTAL **					
					115.27
* ORDER NUMBER 0002					
06/15/83	George Ho	3	PLIERS	7.94	23.82
06/15/83	George Ho	16	STAPLERS	17.46	279.36
** SUBTOTAL **					
					303.18
* ORDER NUMBER 0003					
06/16/83	Fred Smith	23	HAMMERS	5.63	129.49
06/16/83	Fred Smith	7	STAPLERS	17.46	122.22
06/16/83	Fred Smith	20	KNIVES	2.98	59.60
06/16/83	Fred Smith	800	SCREWS	0.04	32.00
06/16/83	Fred Smith	35	PLIERS	7.94	277.90
** SUBTOTAL **					
					621.21
* ORDER NUMBER 0004					
06/16/83	Bill Jones	40	HAMMERS	5.63	225.20
** SUBTOTAL **					
					225.20
* ORDER NUMBER 0005					
06/17/83	John Wille	12	KNIVES	2.98	35.76
06/17/83	John Wille	15	SCREWS	0.04	0.60
** SUBTOTAL **					
					36.36
** TOTAL **					
					1301.22

Fig. 15-7. A Report with Subtotals.

This task began with joining the ORDER and OR-DERITM databases. As can be seen above, this allows you to combine the order number, customer number, and date with the order number, quantity, and item number. You will notice the order number appears twice as the required fields were not specified.

Next, the new database is joined to the ITEM database as shown in Fig. 15-5. This allows the ITEM records to be attached to the ORDER records. Notice that the resulting database has order number, customer number, date, order number, quantity, and item number. It also has the item number, description, and price taken from the ITEM file.

Finally, Fig. 15-6 shows the creation of the final database. The required fields were specified, the previous database was joined to the CUSTOMER database, and unneeded fields were eliminated.

Though the JOIN command is very powerful and allows you to connect many databases together,

```
. USE ORDREP
. REPORT
ENTER REPORT FORM NAME: ORDERRPT
ENTER OPTIONS, M=LEFT MARGIN, L=LINES/PAGE, W=PAGE WIDTH
PAGE HEADING? (Y/N) Y
ENTER PAGE HEADING: ORDER REPORT
DOUBLE SPACE REPORT? (Y/N) N
ARE TOTALS REQUIRED? (Y/N) Y
SUBTOTALS IN REPORT? (Y/N) Y
ENTER SUBTOTALS FIELD: ORDNO
SUMMARY REPORT ONLY? (Y/N) N
EJECT PAGE AFTER SUBTOTALS? (Y/N) N
ENTER SUBTOTAL HEADING: ORDER NUMBER
COL     WIDTH,CONTENTS
001     10,DATE
ENTER HEADING: DATE
002     15,NAME
ENTER HEADING: CUSTOMER NAME
003     5,QTY
ENTER HEADING: QTY
ARE TOTALS REQUIRED? (Y/N) N
004     15,DESC
ENTER HEADING: DESCRIPTION
005     8,PRICE
ENTER HEADING: PRICE
ARE TOTALS REQUIRED? (Y/N) N
006     10,QTY*PRICE
ENTER HEADING: AMOUNT
ARE TOTALS REQUIRED? (Y/N) Y
007
```

Fig. 15-8. Commands used to print the report.

```
.  REPORT FORM ORDERRPT FOR QTY >= 100

PAGE NO.  00001
12/04/83

                               ORDER REPORT


    DATE      CUSTOMER NAME    QTY    DESCRIPTION      PRICE      AMOUNT

* ORDER NUMBER 0001
06/15/83    John Wille        100 SCREWS               0.04        4.00
** SUBTOTAL **
                                                                   4.00


* ORDER NUMBER 0003
06/16/83    Fred Smith        800 SCREWS               0.04       32.00
** SUBTOTAL **
                                                                  32.00

** TOTAL **
                                                                  36.00
```

Fig. 15-9. Further selecting the records.

there are better techniques that can be used to prepare reports in dBASE II. You will see many of these in the third section of this book.

THE REPORT COMMAND REVISITED

Using the database just created, you can get a useful report. Let's prepare a report that shows the totals for each order. If you look back at the database in Fig. 15-6, you will see that there are some fields missing that will be needed on the report, which is shown in Fig. 15-7.

Most notable is the lack of data for the AMOUNT column. Remember that this information can be calculated as QTY × PRICE. This can be done in the REPORT command. The statements in

the REPORT command used to create the report are shown in Fig. 15-8.

You can see that AMOUNT was calculated by multiplying QTY × PRICE in the REPORT command. The REPORT command has been used to print totals. The date and customer name appear for each record; unless programming is used, it is very difficult to get rid of such multiple occurrences.

As a last example, let's reuse the REPORT form already created. Its name is ORDERRPT. You can get a report in the same form from any database by reusing the REPORT name. You can also impose other restrictions, such as asking to see only those items that have a quantity of at least 100. The resulting report is shown in Fig. 15-9.

Chapter 16

The Efficient Design and Use of Databases

There is a trade-off between speed and storage size in database design. If you are going to have many databases tied together by keys, you will find that your system will be fairly slow. It takes dBASE II nearly two seconds to access a file. If you have an order file whose data consists of order information and which is keyed by item number to a sales file and an order file, it will take at least six seconds to retrieve data from the different files. Access to three files at two seconds per file yields a six-second *response time*. On the other hand, it would make no sense to combine files that have no common bind just to speed up processing. Somewhere you have to make the decision whether a system will take up less room on a storage medium or will it run faster. A good database design can do both!

SPEED VERSUS STORAGE

As shown in the Data Redundancy section, you can control your storage size through normalization. Having your data in only one place is easiest when you update your databases, and will help insure data integrity. You must make decisions that will involve trade-offs between speed and storage. Let's use the following database:

	ORDER:NO	CUST:NAME	ADDRESS	CITY
fieldsize	4	15	15	15

	ST	ZIP	QTY	ITEM:DESC	PRICE
fieldsize	2	5	3	15	7

If each order needs to have the customer information, quantity, item description, and price, this record structure would be sufficient. If the record was indexed by ORDER:NO+CUST:NAME+QTY+ITEM:DESC, you could find a record in just two seconds. This technique assumes that the contents of the fields above would make the record unique. This however is a large index, and would take up a lot of room by itself.

What if every order had just five items, and you had 500 orders each month? It would take over 202K to store these orders each month. If you needed two second response time and didn't mind using 203K each month, there would be no problems.

What would happen if storage was more important? You could have two databases:

ORDER DATABASE

	ORDER:NO	CUST:NO	QTY	ITEM:DESC	PRICE
fieldsize	4	4	3	15	7

CUSTOMER DATABASE

	CUST:NO	CUST:NAME	ADDRESS	CITY	ST	ZIP
fieldsize	4	15	15	15	2	5

Each time you enter an order you would only enter the customer number. Later when you printed the order you could retrieve the customer information. It would take an additional two seconds to retrieve the customer information for each order, but the use of two files would save you 140K of storage each month. This would allow you to have many more orders on your storage device. It would also save you from entering the customer name and address from each order. The information would always be on a file of its own. Though the customer file will take up some space, usually it's not nearly as much space as it would take if the information were at the beginning of every record.

You can continue this process in order to save more storage by creating another database of item numbers, descriptions, and price as described in Chapter 15. This would increase the time it takes to retrieve an order by an additional two seconds for each item in the file, because an additional file access will be necessary for each item record. The main database would have the following fields:

MAIN DATABASE

ORDER:NO   CUST:NO   ITEM:NO

The system would use the CUST:NO field to access the customer file and the ITEM:NO field to access the item file. Though this would increase response time from two seconds, if there was only one file, to about six seconds in this multiple file system, the three file system will probably be desired. The obvious reason is that of saved storage. Many hundreds of thousands of bytes will be saved by separating the files and using common keys to retrieve the data when necessary. The index files will take some storage space, but the amount depends on the size of the index field. An index field such as a five byte order number will take slightly more than five bytes in the index file for each record in the order file.

There are much better reasons for splitting up the files. If the customer name and address information has to be entered for each record, there is a much greater chance for errors. What happens if the customer's address changes? All the records in any file that has the customer's address must be changed. The same is true for an item information. Each time the operator enters an item for an order, the price must be entered along with the item description. Much time is wasted entering item descriptions. The price is even more critical. Each time an item is entered, the price must be looked up. When the prices change, care must be exercised to make sure that the operator looks up the new prices even for common items. There are chances for errors in the price entry along with increased opportunities for fraud. If a $25.00 item is entered as $12.00 for the operator's friend, chances are nobody will ever catch the deception.

When these files are divided, the operator needs to enter only the three keys. The system will retrieve the up-to-date file information when the system runs. There is better error checking possible when the keys being entered can be verified against a master file. Data integrity is much easier to maintain when the data, such as customer addresses and item prices, are only in one place. This also saves entering them each time as they only need to be entered once in the master files; only the main key need be entered in the file that contains the data for each order.

Determining Speed

Speed is determined by how many times a database is accessed and searched. In an indexed database it does not matter where the record is in the database—it will take two seconds to find a record. In the previous example, you can assume that the customer file will only be accessed once for each order as the customer name is the same for each item on the order. So, by putting the customer information in a second file, you will only add two seconds to the overall access time for the order. But what about the item information? If you create a separate file for the item information you would save a considerable amount of storage, but you would increase the access time by two seconds per item.

If you have 500 orders per month with 5 items per order, you would save 45K of storage per month while increasing the overall waiting time per month by 83 minutes. Though it seems like a lot of waiting time, it averages only 12 seconds of extra time for each order. Maybe this extra 12 seconds is too much to accept, and you would not separate the files. When you normalize, remember the time implications. Is it one extra file access per unit or several accesses for each unit? By using special techniques described in the last section of this book, you will learn efficiency techniques that can reduce the number of file accesses or at least make subsequent accesses even faster.

DESIGNING WITH MULTIPLE DATABASES

The general rule is to normalize all the time, but the file design should minimize the number of total files. A good design should balance the file design with time considerations.

Database files should be indexed whenever possible. Later, in the third section of this book,

you will learn several techniques to use when databases must be indexed by several fields or indexed several different ways.

dBASE II is very slow when searching for records in a nonindexed database because it must check every record until it finds the one it is searching for. When you have a search on a non-keyed database it will take forever (or at least it seems that way). Every record must be searched until the requested record is found. Speed is determined by the number of bytes your computer can process per second. If you have 3000 records and each one is 50 bytes long, there are 150,000 bytes to be read. If your computer can read 500 bytes/second, it will take five minutes just to tell you that the record is not on the file. If the record you are searching for is on the file, its position will determine how much of the five minutes will be necessary to find it. As you can see, all files should be keyed or indexed in dBASE II to save a lot of time in searches. There may be times when you will want to index your file by some meaningless data field just to make searches faster. There is nothing wrong with this, as long as the order of the file is not important.

As discussed in the first section, the easiest way to design your program is to start by determining all the information necessary to produce the desired reports. In your program design, you already should have charted the hierarchy for the overall system. Most important to the database design were the input screens and the output reports that you learned to design in the first section. A study of the input screens and output reports will show you what you need in forms of input fields, output fields, and other fields necessary to get the output from the input. You can then begin to eliminate unneeded data fields by identifying any output fields that can be calculated from any of the input fields. If you have a person's birthday and today's date, you can easily calculate how old the person is. There is no need to store the person's age.

Likewise, if you have a quantity and a price, there is no need to keep the total amount (QTY × PRICE) as a field on the database.

Once you have determined all the fields necessary for the program, you should determine whether there will be one file or several files in your system. Group your files by common elements. Your main data files should not have to be updated too often. Daily is too often, unless there are many people accessing your databases. Sometimes it is easier, such as when you are dealing in the stock market, to enter the prices each time an order is given. In an industrial business, the prices may only change once a year. In the next chapter you will see some groupings of data fields into files that will not make sense at first, until you learn that some of the files are actually performing several duties.

MAINTENANCE OF DATABASES

There may be times when you have finished all your designing and have actually finished most of your programming, but in your testing, you discover that you left out a vital field from the database. Besides having to change your program, you will have to change your database structure and the test data in it. You may also need to change the database structure after your system has been running for a length of time. There is no way to foresee needed enhancements, and therefore no way to plan for them. By coding in a modular fashion you can minimize the *ripple effect*. The ripple effect is a term to describe how one module of a system interacts with another. If changing one module affects no other modules, the ripple effect has been eliminated.

Even if your code is tight and is effectively divided into modules, the most significant change you can make to a system is to change the input data. When you change the input data, you will probably have to add the item to your input screen and validation routines. This can be a simple process if your program is well designed and well written. But, how do you change your database? What if you already have 10,000 records? What happens if you have to add a new field to the cus-

```
.  USE CUSTOMER
.  DISPLAY STRUCTURE
STRUCTURE FOR FILE: CUSTOMER
NUMBER OF RECORDS:   00000
DATA OF LAST UPDATE 2/15/83
PRIMARY USE DATABASE
FLD     NAME          TYPE    WIDTH     DEC

001     LAST:NAME     C       020
002     FIRST:NAME    C       020
003     ADDRESS       C       025
004     CITY          C       015
005     STATE         C       002
006     ZIP:CODE      C       010
007     PHONE         C       013
**  TOTAL  **                 00105
```

Fig. 16-1. The customer file definition.

```
.  USE CUSTOMER
.  MODIFY STRUCTURE
MODIFY ERASES ALL DATA RECORDS .. PROCEED(Y/N) Y


                    NAME          TYPE      LEN       DEC
FIELD 01: LAST:NAME              C         020       000        :
FIELD 02: FIRST:NAME             C         020       000        :
FIELD 03: ADDRESS                C         025       000        :
FIELD 04: CITY                   C         015       000        :
FIELD 05: STATE                  C         002       000        :
FIELD 06: ZIP:CODE               C         010       000        :
FIELD 07: PHONE                  C         013       000        :
FIELD 08:                                                       :
FIELD 09:                                                       :
FIELD 10:                                                       :
FIELD 11:                                                       :
FIELD 12:                                                       :
```

Fig. 16-2. Changing the Database.

tomer file called CREDIT RATING, which is a numeric field with a length of one? What if you also have to change the address field from twenty-five characters to thirty characters? All of these problems are very difficult if you are using a language such as BASIC or Pascal. But dBASE II makes this type of task simple and easy.

Let's look again at the customer file you have seen in the programming section. It is shown in Fig. 16-1.

First, let's review how to change a database structure if you don't care about the records. You would use the MODIFY STRUCTURE command:

. USE CUSTOMER
. MODIFY STRUCTURE
    MODIFY ERASES ALL DATA RECORDS
    . . . PROCEED (Y/N) _

Remember that dBASE II is warning you that changing your database structure will cause erasure

of all records in the database. Figure 16-2 shows what you will see after giving a positive answer to the proceed question. The first twelve fields are listed with their field names, types, lengths, and numbers of decimals. You now have the opportunity to change any existing field, add or insert a field, or delete a field. Adding or deleting fields require a special series of keys. These are known as *control keys*. On some computers there is a control key marked CTRL or CONTROL; on other computers the control symbol is above the 6 and looks like this ∧. The most common control sequences are:

CTRL-N   Insert Field above cursor
CTRL-T   Delete Field at cursor
CTRL-W   Save changes and exit
CTRL-Q   Quit without saving

Let's change the address field to 30 characters and add a field called CREDIT. Using the control characters we make the changes, which are shown in Fig. 16-3, are made using the control characters.

After making the changes you will type CTRL-W to save the changes. But all your records are gone now! To prevent the loss of the data, it is fairly easy to save your existing file before modifying the structure, and then, after saving your changes, you can put your old data into the new file. Let's do that:

. USE CUSTOMER
. COPY TO TEMP
  nnnnn RECORDS COPIED

This command will copy your data to another file called TEMP. You can actually use any name you wish, but TEMP is easier to remember as it represents the temporary file. Every record is copied to TEMP, but the CUSTOMER database remains as it was. Next you will modify the structure as before.

. USE CUSTOMER
. MODIFY STRUCTURE
  MODIFY ERASES ALL DATA RECORDS
   . . . PROCEED (Y/N) Y

After changing the structure, you must still copy the records from the temporary database back to the new customer file:

. USE CUSTOMER
. APPEND FROM TEMP
nnnnn RECORDS APPENDED
. DELETE FILE TEMP
FILE HAS BEEN DELETED

This procedure will cause all the records from the temporary database to be copied back to the customer database, which has had its structure changed. The field CREDIT will be blank for all the records since the field did not previously exist. The ADDRESS field is the same as it was before, except that each record has five move blanks in the field, and addresses on new records can be thirty characters long instead of twenty-five. If you had deleted a field from the customer structure and then performed the append from the temporary file that had that field, dBASE II would have simply not copied that field. The APPEND command only copies fields that exist on the file that you are copying to.

The use of these techniques makes changing a database very easy. Though the old records will not contain any values for added fields, you can go back and add data to the new fields.

```
FIELD 01: LAST:NAME      C     020     000     :
FIELD 02: FIRST:NAME     C     020     000     :
FIELD 03: ADDRESS        C     030     000     :
FIELD 04: CITY           C     015     000     :
FIELD 05: STATE          C     002     000     :
FIELD 06: ZIP:CODE       C     010     000     :
FIELD 07: PHONE          C     013     000     :
FIELD 08: CREDIT         C     001     000     :
FIELD 09:                                       :
FIELD 10:                                       :
FIELD 11:                                       :
FIELD 12:                                       :
```

Fig. 16-3. Database After Changes.

PROGRAMMING AND DATABASES

Programming is programming whether you are using a database language or not. The database manager will perform a lot of functions that you normally have to take care of yourself. For example, changing the record structure is simple. However, there is one major difference between dBASE II and other programming languages when you need to access many files. You can only have two files open at a time using dBASE II. As you have learned, you open a file with the USE filename command. If you wish to close a file, you can use the USE command with no filename.

How do you handle the problem of needing several files open at one time? When you USE a file, the previously opened file is closed before the new file is opened. The solution to the problem lies in the use of the SELECT PRIMARY and SELECT SECONDARY commands. These commands allow you to have two files open at the same time and to access data from either one. Though there are many times you will want to have more than two files open at a time, you can always do anything you want by using two files at a time.

Let's look at an example of a situation in which you might want two files open at the same time. Assume you have two files called OLDPRICE, and NEWPRICE. Both files have the same item records, but most items have new prices. The object is to find out the percentage that each item went up or down in price. Each record structure is the same in both files.

```
FIELDNAME

ITEM:NO
PRICE
```

The following code will print a list of item numbers and percentage changes in the price:

```
. SELECT PRIMARY
. USE OLDPRICE
. SELECT SECONDARY
. USE NEWPRICE
. STORE S.PRICE/P.PRICE TO
    CHANGE looping instructions
```

The SELECT PRIMARY command in this example tells dBASE II to use the file that is named in the USE statement in the following line as the primary file. If a file has already been used as the primary file, dBASE II would move its file pointer to the last record accessed by the record pointer in that file. If a new file is then USEd, dBASE II will close the old primary file and position the record pointer to the top of the new file. The SELECT SECONDARY command assumes there is a primary file and opens a new file that can be pointed to by selecting the secondary file. Both files can be accessed at the same time. If a field name exists only on one file, the field can be accessed by the field name. If it exists on both files, you must use the P. and S. prefixes as shown above.

The SELECT command is also used for many purposes in the programming domain. In the programming section, you will see its many uses.

Chapter 17

Fred's Friendly Fish Market Revisited

In the Programming Fundamentals section, you learned about program design. Throughout Chapters 8 and 9 our small businessman, Fred, defined his problems. As you may remember, Fred wants to computerize his customer lists so he can have a directory at his fingertips. He wants to maintain a mailing list so he can print labels each month to send his monthly "fish specials" circular to his customers. He also wants a customer order system to keep track of his customer's orders, to help his shipping department ship the orders, and to help his billing department price and bill the orders.

FRED AND THE DATABASE DESIGN

Fred spent a lot of time defining the input data that he would need to produce his reports and forms. Without knowing it, Fred did most of his database design! However, Fred still needs to look at the big picture. Can he design even more flexibility into his programs with the database design? If

there are some special ways Fred may want to use his data in ad-hoc reports, he may want to add some fields to his database even if the defined reports don't need them.

For example, Fred could put a field called CREDIT in his customer file. This field would be maintained as a credit rating. Though Fred uses a cash-on-delivery system now, with a computer he could begin to extend credit to some customers. If a customer always pays his or her bills, he could put a 1 in the field. If he or she is always 30 days behind, perhaps a 2 could be placed there. He could set up the rating system any way he wants. Later, he could look up people that have bad ratings to see how much they buy. A customer who pays only twice a year but buys hundreds of dollars worth of fish may be worth having as a customer. The restaurant that buys only two lobsters every other month and then pays 6 months later may not be.

When designing a database, you should look at

all aspects of the database. You should begin by listing all the input files you have so far defined and deciding if there are any more fields that are necessary and if there are any fields that can be eliminated because of redundancy or because they can be calculated. Check to see if any databases can be split by a common key to create a new file and if any new files must be created (apart from keyed files). You should determine your indices or sorts for the file. Finally, you should calculate the amount of storage needed for your system before purchasing the hardware. dBASE II will run on almost any system, but you may want to buy a specific system for your own reasons.

FRED DEFINES HIS CUSTOMER DATABASE

There is little left to do in this area. Fred has done a wonderful job of defining his customer database. In Chapter 8, he used his head and was able to define his customer database almost perfectly. The record structure looks like this:

Fieldname	Data type	Length
FNAME	C	20
LNAME	C	20
ADDRESS	C	25
CITY	C	15
STATE	C	2
ZIP	C	10
PHONE	C	13

Fred could create his customer database right now, but remember that he must look at the big picture first.

In Chapter 9 Fred looked at the order system. When deciding on his input formats for his order system, he realized the need for a two-file system. He also realized the need for a key to the customer file. This meant rewriting the customer file to include the customer number. Fred discovered that without a customer number he could not tell the difference between John Smith of John's Seafood

and John Smith of Smiths Dairy Bar. Fred decided that it would also be nice to have the customer's business name in the file. As long as he only had to enter it once and could retrieve it at any time using the customer number, he decided that he would add the business name. Fred redefined his customer database like this:

CUSTOMER DATABASE

Fieldname	Data type	Length
CUSTNO	N	5
COMPANY	C	20
FNAME	C	20
LNAME	C	20
ADDRESS	C	25
CITY	C	15
STATE	C	2
ZIP	C	10
PHONE	C	13

He could enter this database into the system now, but Fred knows that he still hasn't finished looking at the big picture. As Fred continues there may be more to change.

FRED DEFINES HIS ORDER DATABASE

In Chapter 9, Fred defined his order databases. He began with the following conceptual design:

Fieldname	Data type	Length
FNAME	C	20
LNAME	C	20
ADDRESS	C	25
CITY	C	15
STATE	C	2
ZIP	N	9
ORDER NUMBER	C	5
DATE ORDERED	C	8
QUANTITY	N	3
ITEM	C	25
PRICE	N	5.2

Fred quickly realized that there were too many fields to enter each time. So he divided the fields into two databases. One of these is the customer database he had already defined. "Wow," thought Fred, "I am automating already! I can use the customer file for the orders. It takes me almost two hours each night just to write the names and addresses on the shipping forms and order forms. I can't wait until this is done. Elsa and Fred Jr. will be happy too."

Fred redefined his databases as follows:

CUSTOMER DATABASE

Fieldname	Data type	Length
CUSTNO	N	5
COMPANY	C	20
FNAME	C	20
LNAME	C	20
ADDRESS	C	25
CITY	C	15
STATE	C	2
ZIP	N	9
PHONE	C	10

ORDER DATABASE

ORDER NUMBER	N	5
CUSTOMER NUMBER	N	5
DATE ORDERED	C	8
QUANTITY	N	3
ITEM	C	25
PRICE	N	5.2

He now has his order file keyed to his customer file by the customer number. All Fred has to do is enter the customer's number, and the customer information will be retrieved when it is time to print the orders.

During the last analysis that Fred performed (described in Chapter 9) he realized that he would have many order-items records (one for each item ordered) for each order number. Though each order-items record has quantity, item description, and price fields, as well as the order number field, there is no need for each record to also have the customer number and date ordered. In more complex applications, there would probably be other information that is only in one file, such as shipping

address, customer purchase order number, and shipping method.

Fred realizes that he can save some space with the two-file system. He therefore has divided his order file into two files—an Order file and an order items file.

ORDER DATABASE

Fieldname	Data type	Length
ORDER NUMBER	N	5
CUSTOMER NUMBER	N	5
DATE ORDERED	C	8

ORDER ITEMS DATABASE

ORDER NUMBER	N	5
QUANTITY	N	3
ITEM	C	25
PRICE	N	5.2

The order file contains only the data needed for each order, while the order-items database contains only the data needed for each item of the order. Instead of each record having the extra burden of the customer number and date ordered, there is one record in the order file for each order, and as many records in the order-items file as there are items ordered.

FRED REDESIGNS THE ORDER FILES

So far, Fred has done a good job. He has almost normalized his data fully. He is able to analyze what he has done, and he says, "When I create an order I will add the main part of the order record to the order file and each item to the order-items file. When I add the order records the only other file that will be accessed will be the customer file (to obtain the customer information) and that is only accessed once for each record. I can add items to the order-items file about as fast as I can type. All I have to add is the quantity, item number, and price for each item. I can get the order number for each record from the main order file."

But wait! Fred is still thinking: "This still doesn't seem right. Why can't I make another file called item. This file can contain all the item descriptions and prices. I wouldn't have to look up the prices each day, since some change every week as the different boats bring different types of seafood to market. Why not set up a new file with the prices in it? That way we could enter any changes in prices in the morning, and as the orders came in, the new prices would be put on the orders. This would prevent us from undercharging or overcharging our customers."

Fred designs the new databases:

ORDER DATABASE

Fieldname	Data type	Length
ORDER NUMBER	N	5
CUSTOMER NUMBER	N	5
DATE ORDERED	C	8

ORDER ITEMS DATABASE

ORDER NUMBER	N	5
QUANTITY	N	3
ITEM	C	25

ITEM DATABASE

ITEM	C	25
PRICE	N	5.2

It is time for Fred to get some help. Do you see what is wrong? Sure, though Fred has made a new database, he didn't use his head. His key is a twenty-five character field, which is actually the item description. Fields like that do not make good keys. They are too long and are often entered incorrectly; they must be reentered when the data entry screen tells the operator "ITEM NOT FOUND." What about changing the order files to look like this:

ORDER DATABASE

Fieldname	Data type	Length
ORDER NUMBER	N	5
CUSTOMER NUMBER	N	5
DATE ORDERED	C	8

ORDER ITEMS DATABASE

ORDER NUMBER	N	5
ITEM NUMBER	N	5
QUANTITY	N	3

ITEM DATABASE

ITEM NUMBER	C	5
ITEM DESC	C	25
PRICE	N	5.2

Now Fred thinks he has the final order file design. The item file can now be used by the order system and can be updated separately. Look at the order-items database. All that will be stored is the order number, item number, and quantity. What happens if Fred wishes to do some analysis in later weeks? The price that would be retrieved from the item file would be the present price, instead of the price on the day the order was shipped. Fred realizes this, and after taking a nice break for a bowl of Elsa's clam chowder, he has an idea: "I will retrieve the price from the item file when the order is shipped, and then store the price in the order-items database. That way I will have the price that is correct for that day, and I still won't have to enter it each time I ship an order.

Fred is learning. Sometimes in the ever-changing world of data management, you must store something even though it exists somewhere else. There is a difference between storing data because a master file like the item file changes all the time, and storing data such as the customer information redundantly. If a customer changes the name of the company, you would still keep the same customer information. If a customer goes out of business, you might still keep the customer data for a while, or you could mark that customer by putting "out of business" in the company name field.

FRED GETS THE BIG PICTURE

Fred looks at his present database structures. He is again trying to get the big picture. He has made one subtle change. He has increased the size of the PHONE field to 13 characters. He has decided to display and store the phone number as (AAA) NNN-NNNN for easier readability.

CUSTOMER DATABASE

Fieldname	Data type	Length
CUSTNO	N	5
COMPANY	C	20
FNAME	C	20
LNAME	C	20
ADDRESS	C	25
CITY	C	15
STATE	C	2
ZIP	N	10
PHONE	C	13

ORDER DATABASE

ORDER NUMBER	N	5
CUSTOMER NUMBER	N	5
DATE ORDERED	C	8

ORDER ITEMS DATABASE

ORDER NUMBER	N	5
ITEM NUMBER	N	5
QUANTITY	N	3
PRICE	N	5.2

ITEM DATABASE

ITEM NUMBER	C	5
ITEM DESC	C	25
PRICE	N	5.2

Fred is satisfied. He thinks he is ready to think about the rest of the system. As he thinks, he realizes that he can make one more enhancement to the database and he decides to incorporate some new ideas.

Fred thinks aloud. "Ok, I have my customer file that will be used by both the customer system and the order system, and I have the item file that will be used by the order system. Am I missing anything? Oh, customer discounts! Each customer gets a discount on his order. Different customers get different discounts; That means that I can add DISCOUNT to the main customer file. When I retrieve the information for an order, I can retrieve the discount too. I will have to change my screen design again to input the discount, but at this time that's easy!"

Fred is performing good design analysis. You won't think of everything at once. Even though this is the final design phase, you may still think of new things. As long as your original design is good, additions are no problem.

FRED REMEMBERS THE INVENTORY SYSTEM

Fred also thought about two other systems, an inventory system and an employee system. Fred decides that the employee system is totally separate from the rest of his system and can wait until later. The inventory system, however, can use the item file. Fred decides to design the database now and design the rest of the system later.

The inventory system should have the quantity-on-hand of each item, and the quantity to be ordered when the on-hand amount drops below a certain number. Fred thinks quickly and decides that his inventory file will just be a reworking of his item file. He won't need to design a whole system to keep track of the items, descriptions, and prices. Just as the customer file is a file used by the order system but maintained by the customer system, which also uses it, the item file can be used by the order system but maintained by the inventory system. By doing the inventory system now, Fred will "catch two fish with one hook" (Is that how it goes?). He can add, change, and delete the items in the inventory system as well as alter the other inventory information. He redesigns the item database as follows:

ITEM DATABASE

Fieldname	Data type	Length
ITEM NUMBER	C	5
ITEM DESC	C	25
PRICE	N	5.2
ON HAND	N	5
STOCK LEVEL	N	5
ORDER AMOUNT	N	5
ORDER FLAG	L	1

The item number is the key that the order file uses to retrieve descriptions and prices. The ON HAND amount indicates what the present inventory is. Fred will use this file to determine when an item is out of stock, rather than checking the warehouse. The system can automatically subtract the amount of an order from the amount-on-hand and add to the on-hand amount when new seafood is delivered. The STOCK LEVEL is the amount of inventory that Fred wishes to maintain. If the STOCK LEVEL is 500, Fred wants to have at least 500 of that item at all times. STOCK LEVEL is sometimes called *EOQ* or *economic order quantity* when it is computed using a scientific method. In Fred's case, the quantity is selected based on years of experience. The ORDER AMOUNT is the amount Fred wants to buy when the ON HAND amount drops below the STOCK LEVEL. The ORDER FLAG is a logical field that indicates whether or not an order has been placed for the item. Fred has designed the inventory system in his head! Each day he will run a program that will run through all the items on the file and place orders for those whose ON HAND amount has fallen below the STOCK LEVEL. The ORDER FLAG is then turned on or changed to Y to indicate that an order has been placed with the fishermen. This is done

just in case the delivery takes a few days. Fred does not want to order the same thing twice!

FRED CALCULATES HIS STORAGE SIZE

Fred's final database design for the system (after all those changes) is the following:

CUSTOMER DATABASE

Fieldname	Data type	Length
CUSTNO	N	5
COMPANY	C	20
FNAME	C	20
LNAME	C	20
ADDRESS	C	25
CITY	C	15
STATE	C	2
ZIP	C	10
PHONE	C	13
DISCOUNT	N	2

		131

ITEM DATABASE

ITEM NUMBER	C	5
ITEM DESC	C	25
PRICE	N	5.2
ON HAND	N	5
STOCK LEVEL	N	5
ORDER AMOUNT	N	5
ORDER FLAG	L	1

		51

ORDER DATABASE

ORDER NUMBER	N	5
CUSTOMER NUMBER	N	5
DATE ORDERED	C	8

		18

ORDER ITEMS DATABASE

ORDER NUMBER	N	5
ITEM NUMBER	N	5
QUANTITY	N	3
PRICE	N	5.2

		18

The last step is to determine the storage requirements for the system. Fred estimates the following:

200 Customers in the customer file
300 Items in the item file
500 Orders per month in the order file
 10 Items per order in the order items file

Fred wants to keep the last three month's orders in the order files. The following calculations determine storage requirements:

200 Customers × 131 bytes/
    customer   = 26,200b
300 Items × 51 bytes/item   = 15,300b
500 Orders/month × 18 bytes/
    order × 3 months   = 27,000b

10 Items/order × 500 orders
   /months   = 270,000b
Total Storage
Needed for 3 Months Data   338,500 bytes

Fred has now finished his database design. He calls the local computer stores and each assures him that they have a storage medium that will hold 338,000 bytes. Fred's only problem is that they gave him 338,000 different prices and choices too. Oh, well, if the fish don't byte, Fred will. He makes a firm decision based on his resources and his needs.

In the final section of this book you will see Fred's entire design again, and you will see Fred program his design. Fred's fish are moving closer to the computer age!!!

Section III
Programming Using dBase II

Chapter 18

Reexamining Fred's Fish Market Design

In the first two sections of this book, you saw how to go about producing a business design, a database design, and a programming design. The next step is to begin the actual coding using dBASE II. A good place to start is to examine the final design. In the first two sections, the design was scattered throughout several chapters. In Appendix A of this book, you can find the design of Fred's Fish Market System in its entirety. In Appendix B, you can find all the programs that make up Fred's system.

In this section you will see Fred, as he begins to code his system. Fred will start with the customer system, then do the order system, and conclude by coding the Inventory System menu and additions modules.

You may see some small changes in the final design as presented in this section of the book and in the appendices when you compare it to the design shown in the first two sections. These changes allow a more comprehensive presentation of the commands that are used in dBASE II.

CREATING THE DATABASES

Fred wants to test his programs just as quickly as he writes them. He knows that you can't test the programs without the databases. The first thing Fred wants to do is to create his databases. He can add data to them after he creates the programs that will enable the operator to add data to each module. The databases should be created in *native* dBASE II and not from a command procedure (program).

Fred begins with the customer system. He knows that the customer system is designed to print the mailing labels for his circulars and produce a customer directory so he can look up data such as phone numbers or discounts. The customer database will also be one of the files needed by his order system, which he will code after he finishes the customer system. The customer system seems the most logical place for Fred to start.

Actually the real reason is Fred's brother Frank. After Fred went out and bought a book on how to program and design databases using dBase II, Frank was very upset. Fred spent most of the day reading and writing these strange charts. Instead of cutting through the paperwork each day, Fred was creating this huge computer design. Now Fred wants to go and spend six months' profit on a computer. Frank says, "Fred, since you bought that book, Elsa and Fred Jr. haven't seen you; I haven't seen you; and the lobsters are beginning to wonder. If you can really save us six hours a day, then go buy the machine. But if we don't save that time, you and that computer are going into the ocean." Fred has heard enough. He is already on his way to the bus stop.

Fred quickly sets his machine up and is ready to go. He has been practicing on his friend Myron's computer and is all set to start with the databases. Fred begins by reviewing his customer file design, getting dBASE II working on his machine, and creating his customer database:

CUSTOMER DATABASE

Fieldname	Data Type	Length
CUSTNO	N	5
COMPANY	C	20
FNAME	C	20
LNAME	C	20
ADDRESS	C	25
CITY	C	15
STATE	C	2
ZIP	N	9
PHONE	C	13
DISCOUNT	N	2

Fred's customer database is ready to be typed in. All the fields he has defined in his reports and those needed by other programs, such as the discount field, which is used by the order program, are there. Fred starts dBASE II and creates the customer database by entering the following:

```
. CREATE

ENTER FILENAME: CUSTOMER

ENTER RECORD STRUCTURE AS FOLLOWS:

FIELD    NAME,TYPE,WIDTH,DECIMAL PLACES

  001      CUSTN,N,5
  002      COMP,C,20
  003      FNAME,C,20
  004      LNAME,C,20
  005      ADDR,C,25
  006      CITY,C,15
  007      ST,C,2
  008      ZIP,C,10
  009      PHONE,C,13
  010      DIS,N,2
  011

INPUT DATA NOW?   N
```

After creating the customer file, Fred uses the DISPLAY STRUCTURE command to check his database. Fred uses the abbreviation DISP STRU to save time:

```
. DISP STRU
STRUCTURE FOR FILE:   CUSTOMER.DBF
NUMBER OF RECORDS:      00000
DATE OF LAST UPDATE: 01/02/84
PRIMARY USE DATABASE
FLD       NAME     TYPE WIDTH    DEC
001    CUSTN       N   005
002    COMP        C   020
003    FNAME       C   020
004    LNAME       C   020
005    ADDR        C   025
006    CITY        C   015
007    ST          C   002
008    ZIP         C   010
009    PHONE       C   013
010    DIS         N   002
** TOTAL **            00133
```

Fred notices the total number of characters is 133. He counts his fields again. "133, this is strange!" says Fred. "I know there are only 132 characters, I guess dBASE II doesn't know how to count." Actually the character counter always counts an extra character when responding to the DISPLAY STRUCTURE command. dBASE II keeps an extra character to tell when a record has been deleted. This is known as the delete byte. Note that the creation date and the number of records are also shown. When a database is created, it will have 00000 records.

Fred decides to define the rest of his databases now. He will create the order databases next. He looks up his design for the order databases:

```
              ORDER DATABASE
ORDER NUMBER          N              5
CUSTOMER NUMBER       N              5
DATE ORDERED          C              8

            ORDER ITEMS DATABASE

ORDER NUMBER          N              5
ITEM NUMBER           N              5
QUANTITY              N              3
PRICE                 N              5.2
```

These are Fred's databases for the order program. Just because the order-items database will contain multiple records for each order number does not mean that anything in the creation of the databases is different. They will be created and displayed in exactly the same way as the customer databases:

```
. CREATE
ENTER FILENAME: ORDER
ENTER RECORD STRUCTURE AS FOLLOWS:
FIELD    NAME,TYPE,WIDTH,DECIMAL PLACES
001      ORDRN,N,5
002      CUSTN,N,5
003      DATE,C,8
004

INPUT DATA NOW? N

. DISP STRU
STRUCTURE FOR FILE:    ORDER.DBF
NUMBER OF RECORDS:     00000
DATE OF LAST UPDATE: 01/02/84
PRIMARY USE DATABASE
FLD        NAME      TYPE WIDTH   DEC
001      ORDRN        N    005
```

```
FLD        NAME      TYPE WIDTH   DEC
002        CUSTN       N    005
003        DATE        C    008
** TOTAL **                00019
```

```
. CREATE
ENTER FILENAME: ORDERITM
ENTER RECORD STRUCTURE AS FOLLOWS:
 FIELD  NAME,TYPE,WIDTH,DECIMAL PLACES
 001      ORDRN,N,5
 002      ITEMN,N,5
 003      QTY,N,3
 004      PRICE,N,5,2
 005
INPUT DATA NOW? N

. DISP STRU
STRUCTURE FOR FILE:    ORDERITM.DBF
NUMBER OF RECORDS:     00000
DATE OF LAST UPDATE: 01/02/84
PRIMARY USE DATABASE
FLD        NAME      TYPE WIDTH   DEC
001        ORDRN       N    005
002        ITEMN       N    005
003        QTY         N    003
004        PRICE       N    005   002
** TOTAL **                00019
```

Fred has created the two-order databases. He has called the main database ORDER and the order-items database ORDERITM. He decides to create just one more database at this time. The item database is needed by the order program. Even though he doesn't plan to write the inventory program now, he will need the item database in order to test the order program.

The design for the item database looked like this:

```
              ITEM DATABASE

ITEM NUMBER         C              5
ITEM DESC           C             25
PRICE               N              5.2
ON HAND             N              5
STOCK LEVEL         N              5
ORDER AMOUNT        N              5
ORDER FLAG          L              1
```

Fred decides to create only the fields he needs now. He can modify the database later. He creates and displays the following:

```
.CREATE
ENTER FILENAME: ITEM
ENTER RECORD STRUCTURE AS FOLLOWS:
 FIELD  NAME,TYPE,WIDTH,DECIMAL PLACES
 001     ITEMN,N,5
 002     DESC,C,25
 003     PRICE,N,5,2
 004
INPUT DATA NOW? N

. DISP STRU
STRUCTURE FOR FILE:     ITEM.DBF
NUMBER OF RECORDS:      00000
DATE OF LAST UPDATE: 01/02/84
PRIMARY USE DATABASE
FLD        NAME       TYPE WIDTH     DEC
001      ITEMN        N     005
002      DESC         C     025
003      PRICE        N     005      002
** TOTAL **                 00036
```

INDEXING THE DATABASES

The last thing to do for these databases is to set up the index pointers. There will be one index field in each database. The customer number field will be used in the customer database, the order number field in the order and order-items databases, and the item number field in the item database. Fred decides to give the index the same name as the database. If there is only going to be one index, it is usually a good idea to give the index the same name as the database. Otherwise you may want to give the index the same name as the index field. The index field in the customer database is called CUSTN, in the order and order-item databases, it is called ORDRN, and in the ITEM database, it is called ITEMN. Fred creates the indicies with the following dBASEII commands:

```
. USE CUSTOMER
. INDEX ON CUSTN TO CUSTOMER
. USE ORDER
. INDEX ON ORDRN TO ORDER
```

```
. USE ORDERITM
. INDEX ON ORDRN TO ORDERITM
. USE ITEM
. INDEX ON ITEMN TO ITEM
```

That's all there is to it. Whenever a record is added to the databases, it will automatically be indexed according to the index field as long as the database was USEd with the index. It doesn't matter that there are no records in the database yet, dBASE II only sets up the initial pointers.

The command to use the customer index with the customer database looks like this:

. USE CUSTOMER INDEX CUSTOMER

The same type of command would be used with the other databases. If they are indexed, you will almost always want to USE them with the index. If you don't, errors may occur, especially when you are adding records or PACKing the database after using the DELETE command.

If Fred were to look on his storage media (disk, or tape) he would see eight files:

```
CUSTOMER.DBF
CUSTOMER.NDX
ORDER.DBF
ORDER.NDX
ORDERITM.DBF
ORDERITM.NDX
ITEM.DBF
ITEM.NDX
```

Remember all database files have the extension .DBF, while all indices will have the extension .NDX.

MODIFYING DATABASES

Fred's friend Myron walks in and looks at the design. "Fred why is your design different from what you created for the item file?" Fred explained that he was only going to use the item file to retrieve the description and price. Fred also tells Myron that he didn't want to have to put data in all

the other fields such as ONHAND, STKLVL, OR-
DRAMT, and ORDRFLAG. Myron tells Fred,
"Fred, you don't have to put data in any field you
don't want to unless you are using the field as an
index field. You should always create the database
as it will be. You can always go back and add data
later. dBASE II can store blanks without any
problem."

That costs Fred another lobster and Fred
modifies the database:

```
. USE ITEM INDEX ITEM
. MODIFY STRUCTURE

MODIFY ERASES ALL DATA RECORDS ...

   PROCEED? (Y/N)
                NAME      TYP LEN  DEC
FIELD 01  :ITEMN          N   005  000  :
FIELD 02  :DESC           C   025  000  :
FIELD 03  :PRICE          N   005  002  :
FIELD 04  :                               :
FIELD 05  :                               :
FIELD 06  :                               :
FIELD 07  :                               :
FIELD 08  :                               :
FIELD 09  :                               :
FIELD 10  :                               :
FIELD 11  :                               :
FIELD 12  :                               :
FIELD 13  :                               :
FIELD 14  :                               :
FIELD 15  :                               :
FIELD 16  :                               :
```

The modified database structure looks like this:

```
FIELD 01  :ITEMN      N   005  000  :
FIELD 02  :DESC       C   025  000  :
FIELD 03  :PRICE      N   005  002  :
FIELD 04  :ONHAND     N   005  000  :
FIELD 05  :STKLVL     N   005  000  :
FIELD 06  :ORDAMT     N   005  000  :
FIELD 07  :ORDFLG     L   001  000  :
FIELD 08  :                           :
FIELD 09  :                           :
FIELD 10  :                           :
FIELD 11  :                           :
FIELD 12  :                           :
```

```
FIELD 13  :                  :
FIELD 14  :                  :
FIELD 15  :                  :
FIELD 16  :                  :
```

Fred has modified the database and pressed
CTRL-W to save those changes. He could have
pressed CTRL-Q and not saved the changes, if he
was not satisfied with them. Fred didn't care about
losing all his records because he had none. If Fred
had some records in the file the MODIFY section
would have looked like this:

```
. USE ITEM INDEX ITEM
. COPY TO TEMP
nnnnn RECORDS COPIED
. MODIFY STRUCTURE
MODIFY ERASES ALL DATA RECORDS ...
    PROCEED? (Y/N)
               NAME      TYP LEN  DEC
FIELD 01  :ITEMN         N   005  000  :
FIELD 02  :DESC          C   025  000  :
FIELD 03  :PRICE         N   005  002  :
FIELD 04  :                              :
FIELD 05  :                              :
FIELD 06  :                              :
FIELD 07  :                              :
FIELD 08  :                              :
FIELD 09  :                              :
FIELD 10  :                              :
FIELD 11  :                              :
FIELD 12  :                              :
FIELD 13  :                              :
FIELD 14  :                              :
FIELD 15  :                              :
FIELD 16  :                              :
```

```
FIELD 01  :ITEMN      N   005  000  :
FIELD 02  :DESC       C   025  000  :
FIELD 03  :PRICE      N   005  002  :
FIELD 04  :ONHAND     N   005  000  :
FIELD 05  :STKLVL     N   005  000  :
FIELD 06  :ORDAMT     N   005  000  :
FIELD 07  :ORDFLG     L   001  000  :
FIELD 08  :                           :
FIELD 09  :                           :
FIELD 10  :                           :
FIELD 11  :                           :
FIELD 12  :                           :
```

```
FIELD 13 :                    :
FIELD 14 :                    :
FIELD 15 :                    :
FIELD 16 :                    :

. APPEND FROM TEMP
nnnnn RECORDS ADDED
. DELETE FILE TEMP
FILE DELETED
```

In this example, you can see that before the structure was modified, all the records were copied to a file called TEMP. The database structure for TEMP would be the same as the database structure for ITEM. After you have modified the structure of the item database, the records are copied back to it. Since the records are copied on a field by field basis, it doesn't matter that there are some new fields in the item database. By the same token, if fields had been removed from ITEM, the data in those fields would simply not have been copied when the AP-PEND *FROM* TEMP was performed. After the APPENDIX is done, the TEMP file is deleted.

Fred checks the new ITEM structure:

```
. DISP STRU
STRUCTURE FOR FILE:   ITEM.DBF
NUMBER OF RECORDS:    00000
DATE OF LAST UPDATE: 01/02/84
PRIMARY USE DATABASE
FLD     NAME      TYPE WIDTH    DEC
001    ITEMN      N    005
002    DESC       C    025
003    PRICE      N    005      002
004    ONHAND     N    005
005    STKLVL     N    005
006    ORDAMT     N    005
007    ORDFLG     L    001
** TOTAL **             00052
```

He decided that it is satisfactory.

Chapter 19

dBASE II Programming Commands

Fred has finished creating the database structures. He is now ready to begin programming. Fred will review his design to remind himself what there is to program. This is where his design techniques are put to the test. How long it will take to code and test the programs will depend on how good his screen designs and pseudocode are.

There are many new commands that you will need contained in the programs in the following chapters. In order to make the explanations easier, this section will briefly review the commands, mostly out of context. You will see them put to the ultimate test in the programs themselves.

ASSIGNMENT STATEMENTS

The only command used in the following examples to assign values to variables will be the STORE command. The statements using the STORE command simply allow the "storage" of the values of literals, variables, or expressions in another variable:

```
STORE 25 TO QTY
STORE 'JOE SMITH' TO NAME
STORE QTY TO NEWQTY
STORE QTY*100/NEWQTY TO PCTCHANGE
```

In the first example you can see the number 25 being put into the variable QTY. The second example shows the character literal "JOE SMITH" being placed in the variable NAME. The third shows the value of one variable being assigned to another variable. Here whatever is in the variable QTY is put into NEWQTY. QTY stays the same. It doesn't matter if QTY is a character string or a number; dBASE II adjusts for either. The final example shows an expression QTY*100/NEWQTY being calculated and the value placed into the new variable PCTCHANGE.

SCREEN AND PRINTER OUTPUT COMMANDS

The following set of commands enable you to display material on the screen and to print it on paper. By using the various commands you can precisely determine how the material will look.

?

This command is used to write literals and variables to the screen or printer. Remember, literals are constants such as titles, while variables are those fields which receive data:

Order Number: 203

In this example, Order Number: is a literal, and 203 is a value that has been assigned to a variable.

The ? command is used at the beginning of a line and writes the line to the device previously specified (more about that later). The ? command that produced the example shown above looked like this:

```
?  '          Order Number:  ' + ORDRN
```

The phrase Order Number: is enclosed in single quotes to show that it is a literal. Because the ORDRN field is a variable, it is not enclosed in quotes. The value of ORDRN is printed as shown above.

The line is printed wherever the screen cursor or printer head is at that moment. Subsequent lines are printed following the original line.

You will notice a + between the literal and the variable in the command. The + is a connector between literals and variables that allows them to be *concatenated*. Concatenation is a term that means putting strings together. In math, 1+1=2, in concatenation 1+1=11. There is also another symbol for concatenation. The − concatenates fields but eliminates any blanks between the fields. The following example shows the difference:

Command	Result
? 'Order Number:' + ORDRN	Order Number: 231
? 'Order Number:' − ORDRN	Order Number:231

There is no limit to the number of concatenations on a line. You can combine many variables and literals:

```
? 'Dear ' + NAME
```

```
? 'On ' + DATE + 'You bought' + AMT + 'Widgets'
```

Set Print On, Set Print Off

The SET PRINT ON command must be used before the ? command if you want the output to go to the printer. The SET PRINT OFF command follows the printing.

You can use the ? command is to control the printer. Any printer code you might wish to send can be sent with the ? command. For example:

```
. SET PRINT ON
. ? CHR(15)
. ? 'This would be compressed print'
. ? CHR(27) + CHR(69)
. ? 'This would be emphasized print'
. SET PRINT OFF
```

@ line, column SAY xxxxxxxx

This command allows literals or variables to be positioned at a precise spot on the screen or paper. The @ command signals that the literal or variable following the SAY should be displayed on the screen or printed at the exact location indicated by the values for the line and the column. The "line" and "column" can be numbers or variables. The "line" can be a number from 1 to 24 for screens or 1 to the maximum number of lines per page allowed by your printer. The "column" can be 1 to 80 for eighty column screens, and 1 to the maximum number of columns allowed by your printer.

Programmers depend on this command because of its ability to put any output at any location of the screen or paper. Whether you are programming menus or screens of any kind, or printed reports you will need to use the @SAY command.

Some examples of the use of this command follow:

```
@ 5,15 SAY 'Dear'
@ 5,20 SAY NAME
@ 6,15 SAY 'On'
@ 6,18 SAY DATE
@ 6,27 SAY 'You bought'
@ 6,37 SAY AMT
@ 6,42 SAY 'Widgets';
```

Though this command requires more effort than the ? command, there are times when the ? cannot precisely position your output for you. You can also use the two together if you wish:

```
@ 5,15 SAY 'Dear'
@ 5,20 SAY NAME
? 'On + DATE + ' You bought ' + AMT +
   'Widgets'
```

The commands above allow the exact positioning of the first two words. The first line of the text follows them because the ? command is used.

There is also an advanced form of the @SAY command called the @ SAY USING command. It allows you to determine what the value of a variable will look like when it is output. This form of the command is usually used with numeric variables to form an *edit mask*. Special *digit selectors* or *edit mask characters* are used to determine the form in which the values will be printed.

The edit mask characters and their functions are as follows.

\# next number will be output
9 next number will be output
X next character will be output
A next character will be output
\$ a number or \$ will be output instead of leading zeros
* a number or * will be output instead of leading zeros

The #, 9, \$, and * are used for numbers while the X, and A are used for characters. Any other characters in the edit mask, such as (,), −, or any others, will be printed but will not be used as digit selectors. Some examples follow:

```
      STORE 12345 TO XYZ
1.    @ 5,10 SAY XYZ USING  '99999'
2.    @ 5,10 SAY XYZ USING  '$$$,$$$.99'
3.    @ 5,10 SAY XYZ * 50 USING '**$,$$$,$99'
4.    @ 5,10 SAY XYZ * 50 USING '999'
5.    STORE 2035557463 TO PHONE
      @ 1,5 SAY PHONE USING '(999)999-9999

1.            12345
2.            $12,345.00
3.            **$617,250
4.            250

5.   (203)555-7463
```

As indicated in examples 3 and 4, you can use expressions in the @ SAY command. Any mathematical expression may appear here.

As can be seen the same number looks very different when different edit masks are used. Be very careful not to specify an edit mask that does not contain enough digit selectors such as $#,9,X,A,\$$, or *. If there are not enough, the number will be shortened from left to right as in example number 4.

Set Format to Print, Set Format to Screen

The SET FORMAT TO PRINT command must be used before the @SAY command if you want your output to go to the printer. The SET FORMAT TO SCREEN redirects all @SAY commands to the screen after you are done printing. The initial default is to the screen, if no SET FORMAT TO command is used.

Remember the Last Line

When using any type of output command be very, very careful to remember the last line. When you print a line in dBASE II, you actually only send it to an internal buffer or storage area. Only when the next line is output, is the preceding line printed out. In order to print the last line, you should always print one extra blank line. With the ? commands, this means printing a line such as ? '   '. With the @ SAY command, you would print @ line+1,1 SAY '   '

ERASE

The ERASE command will clear the screen and reposition the cursor at position 1,1.

EJECT

The EJECT command will advance the paper to the top of the next form on the printer and set the line and column count to 1,1.

SCREEN INPUT COMMANDS

The following commands allow you to enter information into the system.

@ line,column GET variable

READ

This command allows input to be read from the screen directly into the named variable. The screen location for the input may be exactly determined with the @line,column GET command. The @GET command signals that there should be an area set up and defined by colons (: :) with a length equal to the variable length. The variable can be predefined as a new program variable, or it can be a field from a database. If the field name exists as a program variable, that is, a variable created with a STORE command outside of a database, and also exists as a field in an open database, the length of the database field will be used. Normally the area between the colons will be blank unless the variable presently has data in it. If the program variable or database field has data in it, the data will be displayed between the colons. In both cases, the cursor will be

positioned to the beginning of the field ready to receive input. If there are more than one field to be input, the cursor will be positioned to the first one.

dBASE II will not stop to "read" all the GETs until a READ command is issued. This causes dBASE II to stop and look for all pending GETs. If there is no READ command, there will be no input from the screen.

The exact location at which the input will appear depends on the values for the line and column. The line and column values can be numbers or variables. The line value can be a number from 1 to 24, while the column value can be from 1 to 80 for eighty column screens.

Generally the @GET command is preceded by a @SAY command. An example of the use of these commands follows:

```
STORE '          ' TO NAME
@5,15 SAY 'Enter Your Name'
@5,31 GET NAME
READ
```

Enter Your Name :   :

Figure 19-1 shows a more extensive example.

In this example, you can see multiple @SAY and @GET commands. The first four fields already have data in them, and new data can now be entered. The last field is blank as no data is present. Notice the @SAY and GET are on the same line. You will also notice there is no line and column specification for the GET command. If they are on the same line, the GET is assumed to be one character to the right of where the @SAY ends.

There is also an advanced form of the @GET command called the @GET PICTURE command. With this command, you can determine what a variable will look like when it is input. The @GET PICTURE command is used with numeric variables to form an edit mask for the input just as the @SAY

```
          STORE 0 TO QTY
          STORE '            ' TO BIRTH
          STORE '              ' TO PARTNO
          STORE '                ' TO PHONE
        @  5,15 SAY 'Enter Your Changes:'
        @  7,10 SAY 'QUANTITY  'GET QTY PICTURE '999'
        @  8,10 SAY 'BIRTHDATE 'GET BIRTH PICTURE '99/99/99'
        @  9,10 SAY 'PARTNO    ' ;
             GET PARTNO PICTURE 'AAA-XX-999'
        @ 10,10 SAY 'PHONE NO. ' ;
             GET PHONE PICTURE '(999)999-9999'
        READ

               Enter Your Changes

          QUANTITY  :    :
          BIRTHDATE :  /  / :
          PARTNO    :    -  -    :
          PHONE NO. :(   )  -    :
```

Fig. 19-1. Example of the Multiple @ GET Command.

USING command can be used to form an edit mask for the output. The edit mask characters used and their effects are

\# only digits 0-9, and +, −, ., and spaces can be input

9 only digits 0-9, and +, −, ., and spaces can be input

X any character can be input

A only alpha characters (A-Z) can be input

The #, and 9 are used for numbers, while the X, and A are used for characters. Any other characters in the edit mask, such as (,), −, or any others will appear but will not be used as digit selectors.

Figure 19-2 shows how the edit masks specified in the GETs commands allow special characters to be inserted in the fields. The quantity field is straight forward and allows up to three numbers to be inserted. The birthdate field will accept six

numbers with each set of two being separated by slashes. The part number field uses some of the more interesting digit selectors for GET commands; it is an eight character field. The first three places can contain alphabetic characters only (A-Z); the next two places can contain any character or number; and the last three must contain numbers (0-9). The phone number field is a ten character field in which all characters must be numeric. Parentheses and a dash are included in the field.

When these fields are saved, they will be saved with the special characters. The birthdate field will grow to eight characters, the part number field to ten, and the phone number field to thirteen. All these fields, except the quantity field, must be defined as character fields because of the use of special characters. You may enter a − sign in front of quantity to show a negative value or a . to show decimal places. These characters will also take up room. If decimals are to be stored, the database field must be defined as having decimals.

```
          STORE 'CAROL ZARSKY      ' TO NAME
          STORE '212 Auburn Rd.    'TO ADDR
          STORE 'Springfield, MA   ' TO LOCATION
          STORE '05774' TO ZIP
          STORE '          ' TO BIRTH
          @  5,15 SAY 'Enter Your Changes:'
          @  7,10 SAY 'NAME       'GET NAME
          @  8,10 SAY 'ADDRESS    'GET ADDR
          @  9,10 SAY 'LOCATION   'GET LOCATION
          @ 10,10 SAY 'ZIP CODE   'GET ZIP
          @ 11,10 SAY 'BIRTHDATE 'GET BIRTH
          READ


             Enter Your Changes

          NAME       :CAROL ZARSKY      :
          ADDRESS    :212 Auburn Rd.    :
          LOCATION   :Springfield, MA   :
          ZIP CODE   :05774:
          BIRTHDATE  :          :
```

Fig. 19-2. Examples of Input Edit Masks.

The final two examples in Fig. 19-2 show the @ SAY and GET on separate lines. This is allowed as long as the @ SAY line ends with a semicolon, (;).

A final note about inputting numbers: when you enter numbers into the system they will sometimes not look correct. This is because the system stores numbers right-justified but you are entering them left-justified:

QUANTITY: 0: (before anything is typed)
QUANTITY:23 0: (after 23 is typed)
QUANTITY: 23: (after the enter key is pressed)

QUANTITY: 205: (before anything is typed)
QUANTITY:2135: (after 213 is typed)
QUANTITY: 213: (after the enter key is pressed)

When you specify a certain number of charac-ters in your edit mask, make sure that the field itself is set up for at least the same number of characters. Though the edit mask will decrease the number of spaces allowed for input, it will not lengthen the input field itself. A three character input field with a five digit mask will still only accept three charac-ters.

CLEAR GETS

The CLEAR GETS command is a seldom un-derstood or used command, but it has great poten-tial as a shortcut. You usually hear about this com-mand only because of a limitation in dBASE II. When using GET commands you must either ERASE the screen or CLEAR GETS after every sixty-four GETS. Normally this never needs to be done as a good program erases the screen con-stantly. If you have a lot of input fields on a screen and will execute them a number of times without using the ERASE command, then you should have a CLEAR GETS after each READ.

The CLEAR GETS command can also be used when data is to be retrieved from a database for the purposes of display only. Consider the following examples; the first one does not use the CLEAR GETS command. The second one does.

```
@ 5,10 SAY 'Persons Name:'
@ 5,25 SAY NAME
@ 7,10 SAY 'Address:'
@ 7,25 SAY ADDR
@ 8,10 SAY 'City:'
@ 8,25 SAY CITY
@ 9,10 SAY 'Zipcode:'
@ 9,25 SAY ZIP
```

```
@ 5,10 SAY 'Persons Name:   '  ' GET NAME
@ 7,10 SAY 'Address:        '  ' GET ADDR
@ 8,10 SAY 'City:           '  ' GET CITY
@ 9,10 SAY 'Zipcode:        '  ' GET ZIP
CLEAR GETS
```

Since the @SAY command cannot display both literals and variables at the same time, you must use many @SAY commands, as shown in the first example. In the second example, there are fewer statements. Notice the absence of the READ command and the inclusion of the CLEAR GETS command. These two examples are equivalent.

CHARACTER, STRING, AND NUMERIC COMMANDS

There are many commands that allow the use of character strings as numbers and numbers as character strings. There are also commands to put characters in the uppercase, trim blanks from the end of a field, and use only part of a field. There are also several numeric commands that should be known.

STR

The STR command allows a numeric value to be used as a character string. Normally numbers are defined as numeric. There are many times you

will want to use a number and place it in a field that has been defined a character field. To do this you must use the STR command:

```
STORE 765 TO X
STORE STR(X,3) TO CHARX

STORE STR(633*265,4) TO CHARX
```

The first example changes the number 765 to the character string 765. The ,3 indicates the number of characters to be transferred to the variable CHARX. The second example calculates the value of the expression 633×265 as 167745, and then transfers only the first four characters to the variable CHARX, which now has the character value 1677. The variable CHARX can now be used in any character string expression.

VAL

The opposite of the STR function is the VAL function. This translates character strings that contain legitimate numerical characters into numbers of any length. The only characters that are considered legitimate are the digits 0-9, one decimal point, and a negative (−) sign at the beginning of the number. A legitimate use of the VAL command is

```
STORE '765' TO X
STORE VAL(X) TO NUMX
```

TRIM

The TRIM command removes final blanks from character fields. This is especially useful when you are concatenating fields with ? commands. The TRIM command works on character fields only. This is how the TRIM command functions:

```
STORE 'BILL       '  ' TO FIRST
STORE 'SMITH      '  ' TO LAST

? FIRST + LAST
? FIRST − LAST
? TRIM(FIRST) + ' ' + LAST
```

```
BILL                    SMITH
BILLSMITH
BILL SMITH
```

$

The $ command is called the substring command. It allows you to use only part of a character string. To use the substring function, you must specify the variable or literal, the starting character, and the length.

```
STORE 'BILL          ' TO FIRST
STORE 'SMITH         ' TO LAST

? FIRST + LAST
? $(FIRST,1,1) + '. ' + LAST
? $('ABCDEFG',3,4)

BILL                    SMITH
B. SMITH
CDEF
```

INT

The INT command is the integer command. It allows you to take only the whole number part of a numeric field. It eliminates all decimals. It is especially useful for rounding numbers and for determining common dividers. Three uses of the command are illustrated below.

```
        STORE 123.456 TO NUMBER
        STORE 75.6 TO ROUNDTST
        STORE 56 TO DIVTEST1
        STORE 66 TO DIVTEST2

   1)   ? NUMBER
        ? INT(NUMBER)

   2)   ? INT(NUMBER+.5)
        ? INT(ROUNDTST+.5)

   3)   ? DIVTEST1/7-INT(DIVTEST1/7)
        ? DIVTEST2/7-INT(DIVTEST2/7)

   1)   123.456
        123

   2)   123
        76

   3)   0
        .42857
```

The first example simply shows the number 123.456 before and after the use of the INT command. The INT command simply removes the decimal portion of the number.

The second example shows the use of the INT command as part of the rounding procedure. Because there is no rounding function in dBASE II, you have to make one. This is done by taking onehalf of the value that you wish to round to, adding that to the original value, and taking the integer of the total. Simply put, to round to a whole number, add .5 to the original value and take the integer. To round to two decimal places add .005, multiply by 100, take the integer, and divide by 100. To round to five decimal places, add .000005, multiply by 100000, take the integer, and divide by 100000.

The final example shows how you can determine whether or not two numbers can be divided evenly by the same number. Does seven go into fifty-six evenly? Yes. Does it go into sixty-six evenly? No, when the integer of the result of the division is subtracted from the complete result, the answer is greater than zero. Therefore 66 cannot be evenly divided by 7.

!

The ! is the uppercase function. This changes a value into uppercase characters or evaluates a value as uppercase characters:

```
        STORE 'abcde' TO X
        STORE !(X) TO Y
        STORE 'y' TO CHECK

   1) ? 'X = ' X
      ? 'Y = ' Y

   2) IF !(X) = 'ABCDE'
            ? 'OK'
      ELSE
            ? 'NOT OK'
      ENDIF
      ? 'X = ' X

   1) X = abcde
      Y = ABCDE
```

```
2) OK
   X = abcde
```

In the first example, the ! command is used to physically change the characters abcde to the characters ABCDE. The ! in the second example allows you to check to see if the uppercase version of the variable is the same as a given literal, in this case, its uppercase equivalent—and it is.

COMPARISON OPERATORS AND LOGICAL CONNECTORS

There are several groups of comparison operators and logical operators that are used in dBASE II. The major groups are *arithmetic operators, comparison operators,* and *logical connectors.*

The arithmetic operators are

+ addition
− subtraction
* multiplication
/ division

The comparison operators are

= Equal to
Not Equal to
< Less Than
> Greater Than
<= Less Than or Equal to
>= Greater Than or Equal to

The logical connectors are

.AND.
.OR.
.NOT.
.T.
.F.

LOGICAL CONSTRUCTS USED IN dBASE II

The logical constructs explained in detail in Section I are written according to various rules of *syntax* (computer grammar) in dBASE II. The basic constructs, which are the IF-THEN-ELSE statement, the loop construction, the subroutines call, and the CASE statement are shown here.

IF-THEN-ELSE . . . ENDIF

The IF-THEN-ELSE logical construct allows a decision between two courses of action to be made. The action following the IF clause is followed if the expression in the IF clause is true. If it is not, and there is an ELSE clause, control passes to the ELSE clause.

There is no actual THEN clause in dBASE II. It is implied that everything after the IF clause is part of the THEN clause until the ELSE clause is reached. Notice that all IF-THEN-ELSE statements end with an ENDIF.

```
1)   STORE 'DEF' TO X
     IF X = 'ABC'
          ? 'THEN CLAUSE'
     ENDIF


     NO OUTPUT

2)   STORE 'ABC' TO X
     IF X = 'ABC'
          ? 'THEN CLAUSE'
     ELSE
          ? 'ELSE CLAUSE'
     ENDIF

     THEN CLAUSE

3)   STORE 'DEF' TO X
     IF X = 'ABC'
          ? 'THEN CLAUSE'
     ELSE
          ? 'ELSE CLAUSE'
     ENDIF

     ELSE CLAUSE
```

In the first example, there is only an IF-THEN clause. Since the condition X="ABC" is false, there is no output and control passes out of the IF-THEN construct.

The condition in the second example is true and the then clause is executed. The condition in the final example is false and control passes to the ELSE clause.

DO WHILE . . . ENDDO

Looping is accomplished through a command known as DO WHILE. The DO WHILE loop is performed over and over again until the condition is no longer true.

```
STORE 1 TO COUNTER
DO WHILE COUNTER <= 5
   @ COUNTER,COUNTER SAY COUNTER
   STORE COUNTER + 1 TO COUNTER
ENDDO


  1
   2
    3
     4
      5
```

In this example, a variable COUNTER is set to one. The loop is entered, and the condition COUNTER <= 5 is checked to see if it is true. Since it is true, the loop continues. Each pass through the loop adds one to the variable COUNTER and outputs the value of counter at screen location COUNTER,COUNTER. The first pass puts it at 1,1, the next at 2,2, the third pass at 3,3 and so on all the way to 5,5. Notice the diagonal pattern that is created.

Any expression can be put in a DO WHILE loop. It can be a simple comparison or a complex conditional expression. You can even make the loop last forever (an *infinite loop*) if you never make the condition being tested false. Each DO WHILE ends with an ENDDO.

A complex loop is shown below. The SKIP command shows that you are moving through an indexed database.

```
DO WHILE CUSTNO='00001' .AND. DATE = '05/45/83'
   @ 5,10 SAY AMOUNT
   SKIP
ENDDO
```

An infinite loop caused by not incrementing the variable X is shown below.

```
STORE 1 TO X
DO WHILE X < 5
   @ 1,1 SAY 'HELLO'
ENDDO
```

LOOP

The LOOP command is used to exit a DO WHILE construct regardless of what is between the LOOP and the ENDDO. For example

```
WITHOUT "LOOP"

STORE 1 TO X
DO WHILE X <= 5
   STORE X+6 TO Y
   @ X,X SAY 'HELLO'
   @ X,Y SAY 'THERE
ENDDO
@ X,20 SAY X



HELLO THERE
 HELLO THERE
  HELLO THERE
   HELLO THERE
    HELLO THERE     5




WITH "LOOP"

STORE 1 TO X
   DO WHILE X <= 5
   STORE X+6 TO Y
   @ X,X SAY 'HELLO'
   IF X = 3
     LOOP
   ENDIF
   @ X,Y SAY 'THERE'
ENDDO
@ X,20 SAY X


HELLO THERE
 HELLO THERE
  HELLO     3
```

In the first example, the DO WHILE construct is performed five times as specified in the DO WHILE condition. The phrase HELLO and THERE are repeated 5 times. The second example contains a LOOP command. This tells the program that when X = 3, it should go immediately to the statement following the ENDDO without performing any of the other statements in the DO WHILE. As you can see, the statement following the ENDDO prints the value of X. In the second example X is 3. The LOOP command caused a premature and immediate end to the DO WHILE loop.

The main use for the LOOP command is as a quick way out when an error condition occurs. If you are performing a series of IF statements and an error condition occurs, it is usually faster to use a LOOP statement than a series of ELSE statements. The LOOP statement should be used sparingly, however, as it is not the most stable statement, and has been known to cause the loss of the end of a loop.

DO . . . RETURN

The subroutine call procedure is another form of the DO command. It requires no ENDDO. Instead of performing a series of statements over and over again, it calls another program.

```
MAIN.PRG

HOUSEKEEPING
READ COMMANDS
DO SUB1
DO SUB2

SUB1.PRG

SOME STATEMENTS
MORE STATEMENTS
RETURN

SUB2.PRG

SOME STATEMENTS
MORE STATEMENTS
RETURN
```

In the example above, the command procedure

(program) MAIN.PRG or MAIN.CMD for CP/M machines calls the subprocedures SUB1.PRG and SUB2.PRG. These subprocedures can be programs by themselves, but it is likely that they share options and data with the main program. A subprocedure can call another subprocedure. The RETURN statement is dBASE IIs way of keeping track of where it is. The RETURN statement immediately returns control to the statement that follows the DO statement that called the subprocedure. In the case of the RETURN statement in SUB1.PRG, control is returned to the DO SUB2 command. The RETURN in SUB2.PRG returns control to the statement after the DO SUB2 in the main program.

QUIT

The QUIT command causes an immediate exit from dBASE II and a return to the operating system. All loops are ended; all files are closed; no further statements are processed.

DO CASE . . . ENDCASE

The last logical construct is the CASE statement. This statement is used when an IF-THEN-ELSE statement is not sufficient to handle the situation. The IF-THEN-ELSE condition allows only two paths—one for true and one for false. The CASE construct allows an infinite number of paths along with an OTHERWISE clause:

```
READ AN ANSWER
DO CASE
   CASE ANS = 1
      DO SOMETHING
   CASE ANS = 2
      DO SOMETHING
   CASE ANS > 2 .AND. ANS <= 10
      DO SOMETHING
   OTHERWISE
      DO SOMETHING
ENDCASE
```

This DO CASE statement allows four different courses of action. If the answer was a 1 the first path is followed; 2 causes something else to be performed; an answer between 2 and 10 causes a third path to be followed, while anything else will follow the instructions in the OTHERWISE clause. These CASE statements are often used in selection menus. All DO CASE statements will end with an ENDCASE statement. If there is no OTHERWISE clause and none of the CASE statements are true, none of the commands within the CASE structure will be performed. The DO CASE construct is not a loop of any kind. It is performed only once unless it is inside a DO WHILE loop. Many IF-THEN-ELSE statements can be used instead of a CASE construct, but the procedure will not be as easy to use or understand.

DATABASE COMMANDS USED IN PROGRAMMING

There are many database commands that can be used in programming. Some commands have already been talked about and will be reviewed. Others are new and are only used in programming in dBASE II. They would have no value outside of a program.

For the next few commands let's assume a database with the following structure:

```
NAME    Character
AGE     Numeric
SEX     Character
PHONE   Character
```

REPLACE

The REPLACE command is used to add or change fields in a database. For the REPLACE command to be used, the database must be open. When the REPLACE command is issued, the current contents of the specified fields are REPLACEd by the contents for those fields specified in the REPLACE command. If you wish to place a numeric field into character fields or vice-versa the STR or VAL command must also be used. Here are two examples of the REPLACE command.

```
USE DATABASE

STORE 'FRED SMITH' TO MYNAME
STORE 'M' TO GENDER
REPLACE NAME WITH MYNAME,SEX WITH GENDER

STORE '35' TO MYAGE
STORE 2347767 TO PHONENO
STORE 'BILL SMITH TO MYNAME
REPLACE AGE WITH VAL(MYAGE),PHONE WITH
    STR(MYPHONE,7), NAME WITH MYNAME
```

The first example shows a simple REPLACE on two fields of the database. Usually the values come from screen input, not from a direct assignment statement. The second example shows the method of converting from numeric data to character data using the STR command and from character data to numeric data using the VAL command. These conversions are only necessary when the data types are incompatible.

The ; at the end of the first line of the REPLACE command in the second example is a *continuation* character and is needed by dBASE II to indicate that there is more to the line. All the fields in a database need not be referenced within the REPLACE command; reference only those you wish to change.

APPEND BLANK

While the REPLACE command lets you change existing fields, the APPEND BLANK command is needed to add fields. This command adds a totally blank record to the end of the database. The APPEND BLANK command is usually followed by a REPLACE command as shown below.

```
READ IN A NAME, AGE, SEX, and PHONE
IF NAME # '           '
    APPEND BLANK
    REPLACE NAME WITH NAME, AGE WITH AGE, ;
        SEX WITH SEX, PHONE WITH PHONE
    ELSE @ 5,10 SAY 'ERROR - NO NAME FOUND'
ENDIF
```

The indexes of an indexed database will automatically be updated by either command. If an APPEND

BLANK command is performed and no REPLACE command ever follows it, there will be a blank record in the file. Therefore the APPEND BLANK command should not be used unless a REPLACE will immediately follow it. You should do all your error checking first, and then use the APPEND BLANK and REPLACE commands.

FIND, #, SKIP, EOF

These four commands are used together to search databases for records. The FIND command works only on indexed databases. The FIND command allows a database to be searched very quickly. Almost any record can be found in under two seconds. Use of the LOCATE statement should be avoided if at all possible. (See Chapter 14).

The FIND command is used with a *memory variable*. A memory variable is a variable outside of a database. If you have a database field called NAME and you wish to search another database for that name, you must STORE the database variable to a memory variable. This is done with a normal store command. The memory variable is then used with a & preceding it.

```
STORE NAME TO NAME

FIND &NAME
```

Here, the memory variable NAME is stored separately from the database field NAME. The memory variable can now be changed without affecting the database field. When using the FIND command, the memory variable, or macro as it is sometimes called, must be a character variable. If it is a number you can use the STR command to change it as shown below.

```
FIND STR(&PHONE,7)
```

The FIND command will search the database for the first occurrence of the *key* being searched for. You can tell if it is found because the *record counter* will be set to that record number. The record counter is represented by the # symbol. You can check the # symbol. If it is zero, the key was not found; if it is greater than zero, it was found.

The SKIP command will not cause the search to continue. The SKIP command simply moves to the next record in the database. You must check each record to see if it is also equal to the key. Another item you must check for is *end-of-file*.

"End-of-file" means the last record of the file has been retrieved, and an attempt was made to retrieve another record. A variable called EOF is set to true. If you don't check for EOF, and you continue to use the SKIP command, your record pointer will just sit at the bottom of the file. The use of the four search commands is shown below.

```
USE NAMES INDEX NAMES
STORE 'BILL SMITH' TO NAME
FIND &NAME
IF # # 0
  DO WHILE NAME='BILL SMITH' .AND. .NOT. EOF
    WRITE A RECORD
    SKIP
  ENDDO
ENDIF
```

This example shows the use of a database called NAMES, and the STORing of the name "BILL SMITH" to a memory variable called NAME. The database is then searched with the search key of BILL SMITH. Remember, the key field is not necessarily the first field on the database. The key field is determined when the INDEX is initially set up with the INDEX command. If the record number (#) is not equal (also the # sign) to zero, the record is found. Only if the record is found will the statements inside the IF condition be performed.

If the record is found the DO WHILE loop is performed. As long as the NAME is "BILL SMITH" and the end-of-file has not been reached (".NOT. EOF"), the loop will continue. The SKIP command will move the record pointer to the next record in the indexed database.

DELETE, PACK, *

The final group of commands are used when records are being deleted or have been deleted. Whenever a record is no longer wanted, the DELETE command is used. This will not physically remove the record but will mark it for removal.

In order to remove the record, you must use the PACK command. The PACK command copies the entire file except for the marked records to a new database and then gives the new database the same name as the old database had. The old database with the marked records is then deleted. If the old file was indexed, the new file is indexed using the same key fields.

One problem you can have is that after you DELETE records, they can still be found when search commands are used. The * command can be used to see if any of the records found are marked for deletion and are just "hanging around" until the PACK command is given. The following is an example of the use of these commands using both pseudocode and dBASE II code:

```
ASK FOR A RECORD TO BE DELETED
DO WHILE MORE RECORDS
  FIND THE RECORD
  IF # # 0 .AND. .NOT. *
    DELETE
  ENDIF
ENDDO
PACK
```

The .NOT. * phrase checks to see that the record has not already been deleted. This is especially useful when PACKs are done infrequently and searches of a database yield deleted records. This in effect makes them invisible. A new version of dBASE II v2.4 has solved this problem with the SET DELETED ON command, which makes deleted records invisible.

The DELETE command marks the current record in the database for deletion. At the end of the DO WHILE loop, after the ENDO command, the database is finally PACKed.

Since PACKing a database means copying all the records, it can take some time. Use a PACK command only when you have to, not every time you delete a single record.

RELEASE

When using memory variables, you must be very careful not to exceed the dBASE II maximum of 64 memory variables. If you reach this maximum, you will get an error message. To avoid this problem use the RELEASE command. This will eliminate memory variables that are no longer needed:

```
MAIN.PRG

SET SOME VARIABLES
DO SUB1.PRG

. . .
MORE STATEMENTS

SUB1.PRG

STORE 'ABC' TO X
STORE 'DEF' TO Y
STORE 'GHI' TO Z
STORE 12345 TO NUM

. . .
MORE STATEMENTS

. . .
RELEASE X,Y,Z,NUM
```

SUMMARY

This chapter has presented the new programming commands in dBASE II. For another look at the database statements that are used outside of the programming system of dBASE II, see Section II. The statements in this chapter are all used in the programs in the next several chapters. You may want to use this chapter for reference as you analyze Fred's coding efforts.

Chapter 20

Coding Selection Menus

The following chapters will show you how Fred went about coding his system. Each program will be built from the middle outward. The body or sequence part of a program will be built first; then any IF conditions and error checking routines will be coded, and finally the loops will be added. As new code is added, the new lines will be set in darker type to make them easier to find.

Fred is now ready to code. He has learned how to use all the dBASE II programming statements that he learned about in the programming section. He now knows some interesting techniques and is ready to code.

SETTING THE ENVIRONMENT

Before Fred starts the coding of the main body of the menu he must set his *environment*. The environment consists of global parameters that will affect the rest of the program. The most important ones are

SET ECHO OFF. This command turns off the display of the commands in the command file. When the echo is on, the actual commands themselves will show up on the screen. The echo is used only as a testing tool when all else fails.

SET TALK OFF. This command turns off the display of database command results. When a database command such as DELETE is given, the message 000001 DELETION appears on the screen. The SET TALK OFF command eliminates the display of such messages.

SET EXACT ON. This command assures that only exact matches are found when searches are performed. Without this command the computer will not detect the difference between BILL SMITH and BILL SMITH JONES.

SET BELL OFF. This command turns off the warning bell that sounds every time the end of a field is reached. One of the defaults established in dBASE II is to sound the alarm each time the last character of a field is entered. The alarm is used as a warning to tell you that you can't type anymore. It is also most annoying if most of your entries will reach the end of the field.

SET CONFIRM OFF. When you are entering information that fills the entire space allowed for the field, this command will automatically enter the input when the end of the field is reached. This keeps you from having to press the enter key every time a field is completed. Again, this works only at the end of a field.

SET INTENSITY OFF. dBASE II displays input in reverse video. This is a white background with black characters. If you don't like this, set the intensity off.

The other major SET commands either are not often used or are defaults that you would want in the programming mode.

The beginning of Fred's program is shown in Fig. 20-1. Notice that Fred has not forgotten to document his program. Each module is clearly marked with the module name and purpose, along with the system name. Fred decides to call his main menu MAIN. It will be MAIN.PRG on MS-DOS systems or MAIN.CMD on CP/M systems.

Fred has defined his environment and is now ready to continue coding.

CODING THE SELECTION MENUS

First, Fred looks at the system hierarchy chart shown in Fig. 20-2. He sees that there are four main subsystems: the customer system, the employee system, the order system, and the inventory system.

The Main Menu

Fred looks at the design screen, shown in Fig. 20-3, and pseudocode for the main system menu:

```
MAIN MENU

SET EXIT TO "N"
DO WHILE NOT EXIT
   READ SELECTION
   CASE
      WHEN SELECTION = "1"
         PERFORM CUSTOMER SYSTEM
      WHEN SELECTION = "2"
         PERFORM EMPLOYEE SYSTEM
```

```
*****************************************
*                                       *
*                MAIN                   *
*            FREDS FISH MARKET          *
*               MAIN MENU               *
*               MAIN.PRG                *
*                                       *
*****************************************
SET ECHO OFF
SET EXACT ON
SET TALK OFF
SET BELL OFF
SET CONFIRM OFF
SET INTENSITY OFF
```

Fig. 20-1. The main program—setting the environment.

164

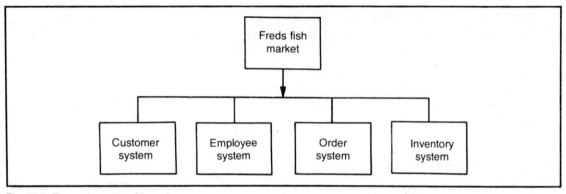

Fig. 20-2. The main system hierarchy.

WHEN SELECTION = "3"
    PERFORM ORDER SYSTEM
WHEN SELECTION = "4"
    PERFORM INVENTORY SYSTEM
WHEN SELECTION = "X"
    SET EXIT TO "Y"
OTHERWISE
    WRITE "INVALID OPTION"
    ENDCASE
  ENDCASE
ENDDO

He realizes that he forgot to put DISPLAY

SCREEN in his pseudocode. It would have gone before the READ SELECTION. "The screen is a good place to start," says Fred. He codes the body of the screen display:

```
@  1,20 SAY 'FREDS FRIENDLY FISH MARKET'
@  3,20 SAY '        MAIN MENU          '
@  7,19 SAY '  ENTER SELECTION  ===>    '
@ 10,22 SAY ' 1 - CUSTOMER SYSTEM       '
@ 11,22 SAY ' 2 - EMPLOYEE SYSTEM       '
@ 12,22 SAY ' 3 - ORDER SYSTEM          '
@ 13,22 SAY ' 4 - INVENTORY SYSTEM      '
@ 15,22 SAY ' X - EXIT SYSTEM           '
```

Fred uses the @ SAY commands. He prefers

Fig. 20-3. The main system menu.

these commands to the ? commands. If he wants to add changes later, it will just be a matter of changing the line and column specifications. This code will produce the screen design shown in Fig. 20-3.

The next part of the pseudocode indicates that the ability to get the selection from the screen must be coded. Fred adds the necessary commands to read the input:

```
STORE ' ' TO OPTION

@   1,20 SAY 'FREDS FRIENDLY FISH MARKET'
@   3,20 SAY '              MAIN MENU          ',
@   7,19 SAY '  ENTER SELECTION  ===>     ';

GET OPTION

@ 10,22 SAY ' 1 - CUSTOMER SYSTEM        ',
@ 11,22 SAY ' 2 - EMPLOYEE SYSTEM        ',
@ 12,22 SAY ' 3 - ORDER SYSTEM           ',
@ 13,22 SAY ' 4 - INVENTORY SYSTEM       ',
@ 15,22 SAY ' X - EXIT SYSTEM            ',

READ
```

He added three lines. First the STORE command was necessary to allow a "field" for the entry of the option. Next he added the ; to the end of the "ENTER SELECTION ===>" line to indicate that the line continued. Then he added the GET OPTION command on the next line. The READ at the end will allow the selection to be read into the variable OPTION.

Now the program will display the menu and read the selection. But, what is it to do after it reads the selection? The next step is to process the selection. As shown in the pseudocode on the preceding page, the next step is to code the CASE statement that will process the selection:

```
DO CASE
   CASE OPTION = '1'
      DO CUSTOMER
   CASE OPTION = '2'
      DO EMPLOYEE
   CASE OPTION = '3'
      DO ORDER
```

```
   CASE OPTION = '4'
      DO INVENTRY
   CASE !(OPTION) = 'X'
      QUIT
   OTHERWISE
      ? CHR(7)
      @ 5,18 SAY '*** INVALID ENTRY-TRY
         AGAIN ***'
ENDCASE
```

The CASE statement was easy to code. Each option contains a DO statement, which calls a subroutine. These subroutines are to be written later.

If OPTION = 'X', control will go to the operating system, just as the menu selection says. Notice the ! before the option clause. This means that the response should be evaluated as an upper-case letter when it is compared to the literal "X". Without the !, an entry of "x" would not be equated with "X". Any time you use character strings in comparisons, you should translate the response to uppercase letters instead of comparing the response to both the lowercase and the uppercase versions of the expected response.

The OTHERWISE clause displays the error message. If the operator does not type one of the listed responses, the system will write an error message to the screen after issuing an alarm (a beep or a sound from the speaker on hardware so equipped).

This might be the completed menu program, thought Fred. But when he compared it to the pseudocode, he saw he had forgotten the main loop. Without the loop, this menu would only be displayed once. If an improper response was entered, the error message would have been displayed but, the program would not have allowed a reentry of the option. Fred adds the loop and reexamines the complete menu program, which is shown in Fig. 20-4.

The DO WHILE EXIT = 'F' is actually an infinite loop because nowhere will the value of EXIT ever be changed. However there is no need to ever exit the loop in the normal fashion because the

```
SET ECHO OFF
SET EXACT ON
SET TALK OFF
SET BELL OFF
SET CONFIRM OFF
SET INTENSITY OFF
STORE 'F' TO EXIT
STORE ' ' TO OPTION
DO WHILE EXIT = 'F'
   @  1,20 SAY 'FREDS FRIENDLY FISH MARKET'
   @  3,20 SAY '           MAIN MENU             '
   @  7,19 SAY '   ENTER SELECTION  ===>    ';
           GET OPTION
   @ 10,22 SAY ' 1 - CUSTOMER SYSTEM         '
   @ 11,22 SAY ' 2 - EMPLOYEE SYSTEM         '
   @ 12,22 SAY ' 3 - ORDER SYSTEM            '
   @ 13,22 SAY ' 4 - INVENTORY SYSTEM        '
   @ 15,22 SAY ' X - EXIT SYSTEM             '
   READ
   DO CASE
      CASE OPTION = '1'
        DO CUSTOMER
      CASE OPTION = '2'
        DO EMPLOYEE
      CASE OPTION = '3'
        DO ORDER
      CASE OPTION = '4'
        DO INVENTRY
      CASE !(OPTION) = 'X'
        QUIT
      OTHERWISE
        ? CHR(7)
        @ 5,18 SAY '*** INVALID ENTRY-TRY AGAIN ***'
   ENDCASE
ENDDO
```

Fig. 20-4. The main system dBASE II code.

QUIT option allows an exit from the loop.

Fred decides it is time to test the code. He starts by typing DBASE MAIN because his program is called MAIN. Immediately the main menu appeared just as it was supposed to. "So far, so good," thought Fred. "Now since I don't have any of the other programs working yet, I'll just try making an incorrect entry." Fred types in a D and observes the results shown in Fig. 20-5.

Now, Fred wonders, "Why is that D still there? Wow! my first bug." It is time for Fred to begin debugging. Some people will spend hours writing great pseudocode, and after typing in their code, they will check it for hours before running it. Others will type in what they want, run the program, find one error, and change the program over and over again. Though this takes less thinking time, it will take you hours longer to code the program.

Fred quickly realizes the problem. He is not clearing out the OPTION field after an error. He adds the line STORE '' to OPTION after the END-CASE statement, retests the program and voila! It is done! After a final look at the program, Fred is ready to move on.

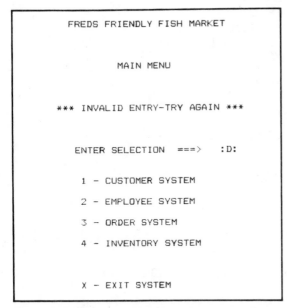

```
          FREDS FRIENDLY FISH MARKET



                    MAIN MENU



     *** INVALID ENTRY-TRY AGAIN ***



     ENTER SELECTION  ===>    :D:



       1 - CUSTOMER SYSTEM

       2 - EMPLOYEE SYSTEM

       3 - ORDER SYSTEM

       4 - INVENTORY SYSTEM



       X - EXIT SYSTEM
```

Fig. 20-5. The main system screen with an error code.

The Customer System Menu

The next system to code is the customer subsystem. Fred looks at the hierarchy chart, shown in Fig. 20-7, to determine which module to begin with.

Fred realizes that the main customer menu should be the first part of the system to be coded.

```
***************************************
*                MAIN                 *
*         FREDS FISH MARKET           *
*            MAIN MENU                *
*             MAIN.PRG                *
***************************************
SET ECHO OFF
SET EXACT ON
SET TALK OFF
SET BELL OFF
SET CONFIRM OFF
SET INTENSITY OFF
STORE 'F' TO EXIT
STORE ' ' TO OPTION
ERASE
DO WHILE EXIT = 'F'
   @  1,20 SAY 'FREDS FRIENDLY FISH MARKET'
   @  3,20 SAY '          MAIN MENU         '
   @  7,19 SAY '  ENTER SELECTION  ===>    ';
            GET OPTION
   @ 10,22 SAY ' 1 - CUSTOMER SYSTEM       '
   @ 11,22 SAY ' 2 - EMPLOYEE SYSTEM       '
   @ 12,22 SAY ' 3 - ORDER SYSTEM          '
   @ 13,22 SAY ' 4 - INVENTORY SYSTEM      '
   @ 15,22 SAY ' X - EXIT SYSTEM           '
   READ
   DO CASE
      CASE OPTION = '1'
         DO CUSTOMER
      CASE OPTION = '2'
         DO EMPLOYEE
      CASE OPTION = '3'
         DO ORDER
      CASE OPTION = '4'
         DO INVENTRY
      CASE !(OPTION) = 'X'
         QUIT
      OTHERWISE
         ? CHR(7)
         @ 5,18 SAY '*** INVALID ENTRY-TRY AGAIN
   ***' ENDCASE
      STORE ' ' TO OPTION
ENDDO
```

Fig. 20-6. The main system dBASE II Code—the final version.

After his success with the main menu, he figures this should be easy. He starts by looking at the menu and pseudocode for the customer system menu shown in Fig. 20-8.

Something immediately strikes Fred as being strange. How do you return to the main menu from the customer menu? There should be a RETURN option in the menu. Fred will remember to add one in.

Fred knows he can use his main menu program over again and just change some words and lines.

Fig. 20-7. Customer System Hierarchy Chart.

He makes a copy of the program using his word processor—that's right, his word processor. The MODIFY COMMAND commands (that is, the set of commands used to change program lines) of dBASE II are difficult to use. You are much better off to use a fullscreen word processor to enter and modify your programs.

Fred makes a copy and makes a few changes and produces the code shown in Fig. 20-9.

It is now time to test again. Fred starts up dBASE II enters the main menu and types a "1". What he sees is shown in Fig. 20-10.

Fred tries the error message routine by typing a blank entry. This too works. Great, says Fred. "I plagiarized a whole module; programming is easy! Now I'll make sure the RETURN function works, and I am done."

Fred types an "R" and—Oh-Oh! There seems to be a problem. Part of the customer menu appears at the bottom of the main menu, shown in Fig. 20-11. Fred reviews the code of the main menu. "Nothing wrong here," he thinks. Fred looks again at the customer menu and finds nothing wrong

again. Fred has a nice bowl of Elsa's chowder and comes back later.

Now Fred is really wondering. There is nothing wrong with the main menu, and there is nothing wrong with the customer menu, but the program is not working. Maybe something is wrong going between menus. Fred is about to discover that when you redisplay menus it is a good idea to use an ERASE command. ERASE would go before RETURN in the customer menu. Fred adds this and his problem is solved.

Fred takes a final look at his program, shown in Fig. 20-12.

SUMMARY

In this chapter, you have seen how to create, test, and debug selection menus. Selection menus are the cornerstones of any interactive system. They play the role of the traffic cop, enabling the operator to determine what road to take and when to return.

Now that the selection menus are coded it is time to move on to the data entry menus.

```
---------------------------------------------------
|                                                 |
|         FRED'S FRIENDLY FISH MARKET             |
|           CUSTOMER SYSTEM MENU                  |
|                                                 |
|                                                 |
|                                                 |
|         ENTER SELECTION ===>  __                |
|                                                 |
|            1 - ADD CUSTOMER                     |
|            2 - CHANGE CUSTOMER                  |
|            3 - REMOVE CUSTOMER                  |
|            4 - DISPLAY CUSTOMER                 |
|                                                 |
|            5 - PRINT MAILING LABELS             |
|            6 - PRINT DIRECTORY                  |
|                                                 |
|            X - EXIT SYSTEM                      |
|                                                 |
---------------------------------------------------
```

```
SET EXIT TO "N"
DISPLAY MENU SCREEN
DO WHILE EXIT = "N"
   READ OPTION
   CASE
      WHEN OPTION = 1 PERFORM "ADD CUSTOMER"
      WHEN OPTION = 2 PERFORM "CHANGE CUSTOMER"
      WHEN OPTION = 3 PERFORM "REMOVE CUSTOMER"
      WHEN OPTION = 4 PERFORM "DISPLAY CUSTOMER"
      WHEN OPTION = 5 PERFORM "PRINT MAILING LABELS"
      WHEN OPTION = 6 PERFORM "PRINT DIRECTORY"
      WHEN OPTION = X SET EXIT TO "Y"
      OTHERWISE WRITE "INVALID OPTION"
   ENDCASE
ENDDO
```

Fig. 20-8. The customer system menu screen and pseudocode.

```
STORE 'F' TO CUSTEXIT
STORE ' ' TO OPTION
ERASE
DO WHILE CUSTEXIT = 'F'
   @  1,20 SAY 'FREDS FRIENDLY FISH MARKET'
   @  3,20 SAY '   CUSTOMER SYSTEM MENU      '
   @  7,19 SAY '  ENTER SELECTION  ===>    ';
           GET OPTION
   @ 10,21 SAY ' 1 - ADD CUSTOMER          '
   @ 11,21 SAY ' 2 - CHANGE CUSTOMER       '
   @ 12,21 SAY ' 3 - REMOVE CUSTOMER       '
   @ 13,21 SAY ' 4 - DISPLAY CUSTOMER      '
   @ 15,21 SAY ' 5 - PRINT MAILING LABELS '
   @ 16,21 SAY ' 6 - PRINT DIRECTORY       '
   @ 18,21 SAY ' R - RETURN TO MAIN MENU   '
   @ 19,21 SAY ' X - EXIT SYSTEM           '
   READ
   DO CASE
      CASE OPTION = '1'
        DO CUSTADD
      CASE OPTION = '2'
        DO CUSTCHG
      CASE OPTION = '3'
        DO CUSTREM
      CASE OPTION = '4'
        DO CUSTDIS
      CASE OPTION = '5'
        DO CUSTLBL
      CASE OPTION = '6'
        DO CUSTDIR
      CASE !(OPTION) = 'R'
        RETURN
      CASE !(OPTION) = 'X'
        QUIT
      OTHERWISE
        ? CHR(7)
        @ 5,20 SAY '*** INVALID ENTRY -TRY AGAIN ***'
   ENDCASE
   STORE ' ' TO OPTION
ENDDO
```

Fig. 20-9. The customer system menu code.

```
FREDS FRIENDLY FISH MARKET

  CUSTOMER SYSTEM MENU



ENTER SELECTION  ===>   : :



1 - ADD CUSTOMER
2 - CHANGE CUSTOMER
3 - REMOVE CUSTOMER
4 - DISPLAY CUSTOMER

5 - PRINT MAILING LABELS
6 - PRINT DIRECTORY

R - RETURN TO MAIN MENU
X - EXIT SYSTEM
```

Fig. 20-10. The customer system menu screen.

```
FREDS FRIENDLY FISH MARKET

      MAIN MENU


ENTER SELECTION   ===>   : :


1 - CUSTOMER SYSTEM
2 - EMPLOYEE SYSTEM
3 - ORDER SYSTEM
4 - INVENTORY SYSTEM

X - EXIT SYSTEM
6 - PRINT DIRECTORY

R - RETURN TO MAIN MENU
X - EXIT SYSTEM
```

Fig. 20-11. The main menu and the customer menu shown together.

```
**************************************
*                                    *
*                1                   *
*         FREDS FISH MARKET          *
*          CUSTOMER MENU             *
*          CUSTOMER.PRG              *
*                                    *
**************************************

STORE 'F' TO CUSTEXIT
STORE ' ' TO OPTION
ERASE
DO WHILE CUSTEXIT = 'F'

  @  1,20 SAY 'FREDS FRIENDLY FISH MARKET'
  @  3,20 SAY '   CUSTOMER SYSTEM MENU      '
  @  7,19 SAY '  ENTER SELECTION  ===>     ';
         GET OPTION
  @ 10,21 SAY ' 1 - ADD CUSTOMER           '
  @ 11,21 SAY ' 2 - CHANGE CUSTOMER        '
  @ 12,21 SAY ' 3 - REMOVE CUSTOMER        '
  @ 13,21 SAY ' 4 - DISPLAY CUSTOMER       '
  @ 15,21 SAY ' 5 - PRINT MAILING LABELS   '
  @ 16,21 SAY ' 6 - PRINT DIRECTORY        '
  @ 18,21 SAY ' R - RETURN TO MAIN MENU    '
  @ 19,21 SAY ' X - EXIT SYSTEM            '

  READ
  DO CASE
     CASE OPTION = '1'
        DO CUSTADD
     CASE OPTION = '2'

        DO CUSTCHG
     CASE OPTION = '3'
        DO CUSTREM
     CASE OPTION = '4'
        DO CUSTDIS
     CASE OPTION = '5'
        DO CUSTLBL
     CASE OPTION = '6'
        DO CUSTDIR
     CASE !(OPTION) = 'R'
        ERASE
        RETURN
     CASE !(OPTION) = 'X'
        QUIT
     OTHERWISE
        ? CHR(7)
        @ 5,20 SAY '*** INVALID ENTRY -TRY
          AGAIN ***'
  ENDCASE
  STORE ' ' TO OPTION
ENDDO
```

Fig. 20-12. The customer menu screen code.

172

Chapter 21

Coding Data Entry Screens

The next step is to code the data entry screens for the customer system. The first subsystem to code is the ADD CUSTOMERS module. Fred begins by looking at the screen design and pseudocode for the system, both of which are shown in Fig. 21-1.

Fred decides to approach the problem by creating the screen display first. He starts coding the body of the data entry screen:

```
@  1,20 SAY 'FREDS FRIENDLY FISH MARKET'
@  3,20 SAY '  CUSTOMER ADDITIONS MENU '
@  7,18 SAY 'CUSTOMER NUMBER: '
@  9,15 SAY 'COMPANY:         '
@ 10,15 SAY 'LAST NAME:    '
@ 11,15 SAY 'FIRST NAME: '
@ 13,15 SAY 'ADDRESS: '
@ 14,15 SAY 'CITY:        '
@ 16,15 SAY 'STATE:       '
@ 16,30 SAY 'ZIP: '
@ 18,15 SAY 'PHONE NUMBER: '
@ 20,15 SAY 'DISCOUNT: '
```

That was easy, thought Fred, "Now to add the commands to get the data from the screen." Fred

remembers to use the initialization commands for the fields that are used in the GET commands. Figure 21-2 shows the results of his efforts.

Fred has defined the input section of his customer additions screen. He began by listing the field names needed for the GET and defining their lengths with a series of blanks. The lengths of the fields correspond to the lengths of the matching fields in the database.

As explained earlier in this section, it is better to initialize these variables in this manner than by using the APPEND BLANK command and then reading the lengths of the fields from the database. If you use the fields from the database, and you decide not to use the blank record, you must then take the extra step of deleting the blank record and packing the database.

In his last three fields, Fred has used the PICTURE clause to change how the input data will look. The special characters such as the dashes and

```
------------------------------------------------
|                                                |
|         FRED'S FRIENDLY FISH MARKET            |
|             CUSTOMER ADDITIONS                 |
|                                                |
|                                                |
|     CUSTOMER NUMBER: CUSTN                      |
|                                                |
|     COMPANY:       COMPANY-------------X       |
|     LAST NAME:     LNAME---------------X       |
|     FIRST NAME:    FNAME---------------X       |
|                                                |
|     ADDRESS: ADDRESS----------------X          |
|     CITY:       CITY----------X                |
|                                                |
|     STATE: ST    ZIP: ZIP-----X                |
|                                                |
|     PHONE NUMBER: PHONE-------X                 |
|                                                |
|     DISCOUNT: DS                               |
|                                                |
------------------------------------------------

    ADD A CUSTOMER

        ACCESS CUSTOMER FILE
        SET CUSTOMER NUMBER TO NOT BLANK
        DO WHILE CUSTOMER NUMBER NOT BLANK
           DISPLAY SCREEN
           ENTER DATA
           VERIFY CUSTOMER NUMBER
           IF NEW NUMBER
             THEN
                ADD CUSTOMER DATA
                CLEAR DATA FIELDS
             ELSE
                WRITE "NUMBER ALREADY ON FILE"
           ENDIF
        ENDDO
```

Fig. 21-1. The customer additions screen and pseudocode.

parentheses will be stored along with the data in the database. Fred also used the PICTURE clause in the first field to make sure that no data other than numbers could be entered into that field. In dBASE II the PICTURE clause is used a lot when data is entered into fields. It provides an easy way to reformat the data as you read it into the program.

Notice that the @ SAY clause and the @ GET

```
STORE '      ' TO CSN
STORE '              ' TO CMP
STORE '              ' TO LNM
STORE '              ' TO FNM
STORE '                  ' TO ADR
STORE '              ' TO CTY
STORE '    ' TO STT
STORE '          ' TO ZP
STORE '            ' TO PHN
STORE 0 TO DS
   @  1,20 SAY 'FREDS FRIENDLY FISH MARKET'
   @  3,20 SAY '  CUSTOMER ADDITIONS MENU  '
   @  7,18 SAY 'CUSTOMER NUMBER: ' GET CSN   PICTURE '#####'
   @  9,15 SAY 'COMPANY:       '   GET CMP
   @ 10,15 SAY 'LAST NAME:   '     GET LNM
   @ 11,15 SAY 'FIRST NAME: '      GET FNM
   @ 13,15 SAY 'ADDRESS: '         GET ADR
   @ 14,15 SAY 'CITY:       '      GET CTY
   @ 16,15 SAY 'STATE:      '      GET STT
   @ 16,30 SAY 'ZIP: '             GET ZP    PICTURE '#####-####'
   @ 18,15 SAY 'PHONE NUMBER: '    GET PHN   PICTURE '(###)###-####'
   @ 20,15 SAY 'DISCOUNT: '        GET DS    PICTURE '##'
   READ
```

Fig. 21-2. The customer additions program—the main body and GETS.

clause are on the same line. As explained earlier in this section, this is an important way to save some work in coding. The input space will appear one space to the right of the end of the @ SAY line.

The discount input variable, DS, is set to 0, but the PICTURE clause will use two characters. The number is actually assumed to be eight digits long until it is set into the database.

According to the pseudocode, the next step is to verify the customer number to make sure it doesn't already exist and then to add the customer data to the database. The pseudocode also says to clear the data fields if the record is added to the database. An error message should be displayed if the customer number already exists. Fred writes the following:

```
FIND &CSN
IF # = 0
    APPEND BLANK
    REPLACE CUSTN WITH VAL (CSN);
       COMP WITH CMP, LNAME WITH LNM;
       FNAME WITH FNM, ADDR WITH ADR;
       CITY WITH CTY, ST WITH STT;
       ZIP WITH ZP, PHONE WITH PHN;
       DIS WITH DS
@5,15 SAY ' *** CUSTOMER ADDED ***
    STORE '      ' TO CSN
    STORE '              ' TO CMP
    STORE '              ' TO LNM
    STORE '              ' TO FNM
    STORE '                  ' TO ADR
    STORE '              ' TO CTY
```

```
          STORE ' ' TO STT
          STORE '          ' TO ZP
          STORE '               ' TO PHN
          STORE 0 TO DS
ELSE
  ? CHR (7)
  @ 5,15 SAY '*** CUSTOMER NUMBER
          ALREADY ON FILE ***'
ENDIF
```

This section of code would come directly after the READ command in the previous section. Fred begins by using the FIND command to check the open database for the key CSN. This should be the customer number that was typed in. There is a single IF-THEN-ELSE construction that handles the FIND. If the record number (#) equals zero, there is no existing record with the current customer number and the record should be added. The APPEND BLANK command will create a blank record, while the REPLACE command will fill the fields of the record. A message is printed on the screen saying that the customer was added. All the fields are then cleared so that when the menu is

```
STORE 'T' TO MORECUST
DO WHILE MORECUST = 'T'
  IF CSN = '        '
       ERASE
       RETURN
    ELSE
      FIND &CSN
      IF # = 0
          APPEND BLANK
          REPLACE CUSTN WITH VAL(CSN),COMP WITH CMP,LNAME WITH LNM;
            FNAME WITH FNM,ADDR WITH ADR,CITY WITH CTY,ST WITH STT;
            ZIP WITH ZP,PHONE WITH PHN,DIS WITH DS
          @ 5,15 SAY '       *** CUSTOMER ADDED   *** '
          STORE '     ' TO CSN
          STORE '                    ' TO CMP
          STORE '                  ' TO LNM
          STORE '                  ' TO FNM
          STORE '                    ' TO ADR
          STORE '                ' TO CTY
          STORE '   ' TO STT
          STORE '           ' TO ZP
          STORE '              ' TO PHN
          STORE 0 TO DS
        ELSE
          ? CHR(7)
          @ 5,15 SAY '*** CUSTOMER NUMBER ALREADY ON FILE ***'
      ENDIF
  ENDIF
ENDDO
```

Fig. 21-3. The customer additions program—the DO WHILE and more customers Loops.

redisplayed, the data fields will again be empty.

If the result of the FIND was that the current customer number already existed the error message saying CUSTOMER ALREADY ON FILE would be displayed. The fields are not cleared as it is possible that only the customer number need be entered again.

The screen should now be redisplayed so that any new customers can be entered or any errors corrected. Fred needs to add the DO WHILE loop. He also must remember to add a check to see whether or not there are more customers to be added. If the operator does not have any more customers to add, he will press the enter key, without typing a customer number, and the CSN field will be blank. Fred adds the appropriate loop to the action section as shown in Fig. 21-3.

To show the loop and the IF condition better the code for the screen has been removed. An IF condition that checked to see if customer number was blank was added. If it is blank, the RETURN statement will cause the system to go to the customer menu so that all the customer functions can be redisplayed. The main part of the action statements were moved under an ELSE condition. This is the process known as *nesting*. You can put as many IF-THEN-ELSE expressions within each other as you wish.

The use of indentation can be seen in this code. The process of indenting your code does nothing for the performance of the computer, but it does everything for you when you are testing and debugging your code. Remember to match each IF with its ENDIF, each DO with its ENDDO, and each CASE with its ENDCASE. This will save you many hours later on.

Again, as in the selection menus, the loop is actually an infinite loop that you are exiting from with the RETURN statement. Some people would say this is not correct. They would say that instead of having the RETURN where it is, the RETURN

should be after the ENDDO, and the current location of the RETURN should contain the condition that makes the loop false—STORE "F" TO MORECUST. The program will work either way. dBASE II does allow you to leave a loop quickly as Fred did. If the method works, use it.

Fred is ready to add the final touches and test the program. He adds the USE filename command to open the data file at the beginning of the program and the file close command (USE alone) in the RETURN procedure. Fred also adds an ERASE at the beginning to clear the screen. The resulting program is shown in Fig. 21-4.

The USE CUSTOMER INDEX CUSTOMER that has been added to the top of the program illustrates the first step in most programs that deal with data files: the opening of the database. By the same token, one of the last things done is the closing of the file. The USE command with no parameters closes the active file. Since there is only one file open, the customer file is closed.

Realistically, there would probably be some bugs in this code. With good design techniques and previously written *clean* code, you can minimize your errors almost totally. Fred decides to test his screen.

He starts dBASE II. After he gets the main menu, he types a 1 to get to the customer menu. Again he types a 1 to use the add customer function. This function is known as 1.1, because it was called by typing a one followed by a one. This information appears in the documentation. The main program doesn't really have a name and is called MAIN. The customer menu is called 1 and each function of the customer menu is called 1, choice number. The add customers function is 1.1, the change customer function is 1.2 and so on.

After the pair of ones are typed, the screen in Fig. 21-5 is shown. The operator can now type in the input for any or all fields. The only field that must be filled is the customer number. If this is blank, the program will return to the main customer menu.

Figure 21-6 shows a completed customer record. The screen has been filled in and the record is ready to be entered into the database. When the last field is filled in, the blank data-entry screen is displayed again ready for the information for the next record to be entered. A message indicates that

```
**************************************
*                                    *
*               1.1                  *
*         FREDS FISH MARKET          *
*     CUSTOMER ADDITIONS PROGRAM     *
*            CUSTADD.PRG             *
*                                    *
**************************************
ERASE
USE CUSTOMER INDEX CUSTOMER
STORE T TO MORECUST
STORE '        ' TO CSN
STORE '                         ' TO CMP
STORE '                        ' TO LNM
STORE '                        ' TO FNM
STORE '                          ' TO ADR
STORE '                  ' TO CTY
STORE '   ' TO STT
STORE '          ' TO ZP
STORE '                 ' TO PHN
STORE 0 TO DS
DO WHILE MORECUST = 'T'
   @  1,20 SAY 'FREDS FRIENDLY FISH MARKET'
   @  3,20 SAY '  CUSTOMER ADDITIONS MENU  '
   @  7,18 SAY 'CUSTOMER NUMBER: ' GET CSN      PICTURE '#####'
   @  9,15 SAY 'COMPANY:       '   GET CMP
   @ 10,15 SAY 'LAST NAME:  '      GET LNM
   @ 11,15 SAY 'FIRST NAME: '      GET FNM
   @ 13,15 SAY 'ADDRESS: '         GET ADR
   @ 14,15 SAY 'CITY:      '       GET CTY
   @ 16,15 SAY 'STATE:    '        GET STT
   @ 16,30 SAY 'ZIP: '             GET ZP       PICTURE '#####-####'
   @ 18,15 SAY 'PHONE NUMBER: '    GET PHN      PICTURE '(###)###-####'
   @ 20,15 SAY 'DISCOUNT: '        GET DS       PICTURE '##'
   READ
   IF CSN = '      '
        ERASE
        USE
```

```
        RETURN
    ELSE
        FIND &CSN
        IF # = 0
            APPEND BLANK
            REPLACE CUSTN WITH VAL(CSN),COMP WITH CMP,LNAME WITH LNM;
                FNAME WITH FNM,ADDR WITH ADR,CITY WITH CTY,ST WITH STT;
                ZIP WITH ZP,PHONE WITH PHN,DIS WITH DS
            @ 5,15 SAY '        *** CUSTOMER ADDED   *** '
            STORE '       ' TO CSN
            STORE '                        ' TO CMP
            STORE '                      ' TO LNM
            STORE '                     ' TO FNM
            STORE '                         ' TO ADR
            STORE '                  ' TO CTY
            STORE '   ' TO STT
            STORE '           ' TO ZP
            STORE '              ' TO PHN
            STORE 0 TO DS
        ELSE
            ? CHR(7)
            @ 5,15 SAY '*** CUSTOMER NUMBER ALREADY ON FILE ***'
        ENDIF
    ENDIF
ENDDO
```

Fig. 21-4. The customer Additions dBase II code—final version.

the previous customer record has been successfully added. Figure 21-7 shows the results of attempting to assign an existing customer number to a new customer. Although all the data the operator has entered is different, the customer number has already been used. The operator is alerted by the error message. Only the customer number has to be changed; the rest of the data is good. The operator has two choices: He can change the customer number to a nonexisting one, and the record will be added, or he can blank out the number and return to the customer menu without adding the record. The data fields that were typed in will be lost if the operator chooses the second option. Fred decides

to change the customer number and the record is added to the file. Figure 21-8 shows the result.

There seems to be a small problem. Part of the old message is still there. dBASE II doesn't totally clear a display line just because you write to it. It only clears as much of the line as is required for the new text. Since the old message is longer than the new message, the longer portion isn't erased. A solution for this is to code the statement @ 5,1 before the CUSTOMER ADDED message. The @ 5,1 command means that line 5 will be totally cleared. This is the only change that has to be made to this module.

Fred's last test is to test the return to the main

```
            FREDS FRIENDLY FISH MARKET

              CUSTOMER ADDITIONS MENU

          CUSTOMER NUMBER: :        :

      COMPANY:        :                    :
      LAST NAME:      :                    :
      FIRST NAME: :                        :

      ADDRESS: :                          :
      CITY:       :                  :

      STATE:    :  :   ZIP: :      —      :

      PHONE NUMBER: : (    )   —      :

      DISCOUNT: : O:
```

Fig. 21-5. The customer additions screen ready for input.

```
            FREDS FRIENDLY FISH MARKET

              CUSTOMER ADDITIONS MENU


          CUSTOMER NUMBER: :200   :

      COMPANY:       :LEE SIDE FISHERIES   :
      LAST NAME:   :KAY                    :
      FIRST NAME: :LEE JAY                 :

      ADDRESS: :151 FARMINGTON AVE        :
      CITY:       :NORTH HAVEN      :

      STATE:    :CA:   ZIP: :88667—2443:

      PHONE NUMBER: : (968)555—1424:

      DISCOUNT: :10:
```

Fig. 21-6. The filled-in customer additions screen.

```
            FREDS FRIENDLY FISH MARKET

              CUSTOMER ADDITIONS MENU

     *** CUSTOMER NUMBER ALREADY ON FILE ***

          CUSTOMER NUMBER: :200  :

     COMPANY:     :SAMS LOX HAVEN      :
     LAST NAME:   :BURTON              :
     FIRST NAME:  :SAMUEL              :

     ADDRESS: :18465 TRAIL STREET      :
     CITY:    :BOCA DELRAY     :

     STATE:   :MO:  ZIP: :88673-2227:
     PHONE NUMBER: :(564)555-1525:

     DISCOUNT: : 0:
```

Fig. 21-7. The customer additions screen error message.

```
            FREDS FRIENDLY FISH MARKET

              CUSTOMER ADDITIONS MENU

        *** CUSTOMER ADDED  ***  FILE ***

          CUSTOMER NUMBER: :       :

     COMPANY:     :                 :
     LAST NAME:   :                 :
     FIRST NAME:  :                 :

     ADDRESS: :                     :
     CITY:    :                :

     STATE:   : :  ZIP: :      -     :

     PHONE NUMBER: :(   )    -     :

     DISCOUNT: : 0:
```

Fig. 21-8. The customer additions screen message problem.

customer menu. Fred enters a blank line for a customer number and the customer system menu is correctly displayed.

Fred is done with the ADD CUSTOMER function. Next he will turn his sights to the CHANGE CUSTOMER function.

CHANGING RECORDS

To start, Fred looks at the screens and pseudocode for the CHANGE CUSTOMER function. These are shown in Fig. 21-9. He sees remarkable similarities between the add screen and the change screen. The biggest difference is in the looping. First, it appears that there will be two READ statements. The first will get the customer number to be retrieved from the file; the second, which will be used if the customer number is found, will enter any changes.

```
┌──────────────────────────────────────────────┐
│         FRED'S FRIENDLY FISH MARKET           │
│            CUSTOMER CHANGES                    │
│                                               │
│                                               │
│      CUSTOMER NUMBER: CUSTN                    │
│                                               │
│                                               │
│                                               │
│                                               │
│                                               │
└──────────────────────────────────────────────┘

┌──────────────────────────────────────────────┐
│         FRED'S FRIENDLY FISH MARKET           │
│            CUSTOMER CHANGES                    │
│                                               │
│                                               │
│      CUSTOMER NUMBER: CUSTN                    │
│                                               │
│      COMPANY:    COMPANY------------X         │
│      LAST NAME:  LNAME--------------X         │
│      FIRST NAME: FNAME--------------X         │
│                                               │
│      ADDRESS: ADDRESS----------------X        │
│      CITY:    CITY----------X                 │
│                                               │
│      STATE: ST    ZIP: ZIP-----X              │
│                                               │
│      PHONE NUMBER: PHONE--------X             │
│                                               │
│      DISCOUNT: DS                             │
└──────────────────────────────────────────────┘
```

```
CHANGE A CUSTOMER

      ACCESS CUSTOMER FILE
      SET CUSTOMER NUMBER TO NOT BLANK
      DO WHILE CUSTOMER NUMBER NOT BLANK
         DISPLAY SCREEN
         ENTER CUSTOMER NUMBER
         VERIFY CUSTOMER NUMBER
      IF FOUND
         THEN
            RETRIEVE CUSTOMER DATA
            CHANGE DESIRED FIELDS
            UPDATE RECORD
            CLEAR DATA FIELDS
         ELSE
            WRITE "NUMBER NOT ON FILE"
      ENDIF
      ENDDO
```

Fig. 21-9. The customer change data entry screen, pseudocode and preliminary screen code.

There does not need to be any defining and clearing of the variables in this module. Fred notices that the database field names themselves can be used. He begins with the first part of the code, the preliminary screen:

```
@  1,20 SAY 'FREDS FRIENDLY FISH MARKET'
@  3,20 SAY '    CUSTOMER CHANGES    ,
@  7,18 SAY 'CUSTOMER NUMBER: ' GET CSN;
         PICTURE '#####'
READ
```

This part will display the top part of the screen and allow the input of the customer number for the retrieval process.

Fred then codes the retrieve and display section as shown in Fig. 21-10. This code begins by checking the customer number for a nonblank entry. If it is blank, the usual RETURN is performed, and the system returns to the main customer menu. If there is a customer number entered, the system checks to make sure it exists. If the customer number does not exist, an error message is displayed, the preliminary screen is redisplayed, and the opportunity to enter another customer number is given.

After the customer number is found, the record pointer in the database would be pointing at the found record. When the @ GET commands are issued and the field names match the field names in the database, the data from the database is automatically put into the fields in the menu program.

The IF # # 0 command is different from the IF

```
IF CSN = '        '
    USE
    ERASE
    RETURN
  ELSE

    FIND &CSN
    IF # # 0
        @  9,15 SAY 'COMPANY:      '   GET COMP
        @ 10,15 SAY 'LAST NAME:   '    GET LNAME
        @ 11,15 SAY 'FIRST NAME:  '    GET FNAME
        @ 13,15 SAY 'ADDRESS: '        GET ADDR
        @ 14,15 SAY 'CITY:         '   GET CITY
        @ 16,15 SAY 'STATE: '          GET ST
        @ 16,30 SAY 'ZIP: '            GET ZIP     PICTURE '#####-####'
        @ 18,15 SAY 'PHONE NUMBER: '   GET PHONE   PICTURE '(###)###-####'
        @ 20,15 SAY 'DISCOUNT: '       GET DIS     PICTURE '##'
        READ
        ERASE
        @ 5,1
        @ 5,15 SAY '     *** CUSTOMER CHANGED   ***            '
        STORE '        ' TO CSN
      ELSE
        ? CHR(7)
        ERASE
        @ 5,15 SAY '*** CUSTOMER NUMBER NOT FOUND ***'
    ENDIF
ENDIF
```

Fig. 21-10. The customer changes main screen code.

= 0 command used for the CUSTOMER ADDI-
TIONS screen because opposite outcome is desired. The IF # = 0 is checking to make sure a
record with that customer number does not exist as
you wish to add the record with that number. In the
CHANGE function, you are hoping the customer
number exists. IF # # 0 means that the record
counter is not equal to zero, and therefore the
record has been found.

When the record is found the data is displayed
on the screen and any fields except the customer
number can be changed. As soon as the cursor

passes the last field, the record is entered into the
file.

Notice that there is no REPLACE command.
This is because you are updating the database by
the direct method. Since you are using the fields
directly, there is no need to use a REPLACE command. The fields are updated when the READ
command is performed.

All Fred needs to add now is the USE file
command to open the data file and the main loop.
These procedures are the same as the ones used in
the CUSTOMER screen. Fred adds these state-

```
*************************************
*              1.2                  *
*        FREDS FISH MARKET          *
*    CUSTOMER CHANGE PROGRAM        *
*          CUSTCHG.PRG              *
*************************************
USE CUSTOMER INDEX CUSTOMER
STORE 'T' TO MORECUST
STORE '      ' TO CSN
ERASE
DO WHILE MORECUST = 'T'
  @  1,20 SAY 'FREDS FRIENDLY FISH MARKET'
  @  3,20 SAY '    CUSTOMER CHANGES          '
  @  7,18 SAY 'CUSTOMER NUMBER: ' GET CSN PICTURE '#####'
  READ
  IF CSN = '      '
      USE
      ERASE
      RETURN
    ELSE
      FIND &CSN
      IF # # 0
          @  9,15 SAY 'COMPANY:        '      GET COMP
          @ 10,15 SAY 'LAST NAME:  '          GET LNAME
          @ 11,15 SAY 'FIRST NAME: '          GET FNAME
          @ 13,15 SAY 'ADDRESS: '             GET ADDR
          @ 14,15 SAY 'CITY:       '          GET CITY
          @ 16,15 SAY 'STATE: '               GET ST
          @ 16,30 SAY 'ZIP: '                 GET ZIP; PICTURE
                                                   '#####-####'
          @ 18,15 SAY 'PHONE NUMBER: '        GET PHONE;PICTURE '
                                                   (###)###-####'
          @ 20,15 SAY 'DISCOUNT: '            GET DIS; PICTURE '##'
        READ
        ERASE
        @ 5,1
        @ 5,15 SAY '     *** CUSTOMER CHANGED   ***          '
        STORE '      ' TO CSN
      ELSE
        ? CHR(7)
        ERASE
        @ 5,15 SAY '*** CUSTOMER NUMBER NOT FOUND ***'
    ENDIF
  ENDIF
ENDDO
```

Fig. 21-11. The customer changes dBase II code—final version.

ments and looks at the final results as shown in Fig. 21-11.

REMOVING RECORDS

Fred thinks, "It is amazing how similar each program is to the next. All I have to do is code the basic screen layout for one module, and the rest of the modules just fall into place. I think I'll code the other two functions, REMOVE CUSTOMERS and DISPLAY CUSTOMERS before I test the system.

Fred looks at the design for the REMOVE CUSTOMER function, which is shown in Fig. 21-12.

He thinks to himself, "I must be getting lazy. I forgot to design the preliminary screen. Oh well, I'm getting good at this. The CUSTOMER REMOVAL screen should be easy. Its the same in the beginning, except there is no READ for the rest of the data, just a retrieve. Then instead of updating the database, I will ask for a confirmation of the removal. If it is confirmed, I'll delete the record; otherwise I'll leave it alone."

Fred should not be getting lazy, a good and complete design is important no matter what. Fred codes the program as shown in Fig. 21-13.

There are a few things that are different in this program than they are in the CUSTOMER CHANGE program. The first difference is in the display section. After the @ GETs, there is a new command called CLEAR GETs. This makes the GETs useless. This is a programming shortcut to quickly display fields from a database. The CLEAR GETs simply makes it so the cursor will not go to the fields and therefore no changes can be made.

There are differences in the display portion of the data fields. There are no PICTURE phrases associated with the @ GETs because there will be no input taking place.

As you can see, following the CLEAR GETs command is the section of code for the DELETE CONFIRMATION. This portion starts with the display of the confirmation message. Notice the same line is always used for error messages, informational messages, and input. Prior to the display of the confirmation message is a line of code that sets up a one character field called DELCON. You must always set up a field and space for an entry before using a field name. The READ will allow the entering of the confirmation. The uppercase command is used in case the operator types a lowercase d. If the delete is confirmed, the record is deleted. If the operator types anything other than a D, the record is not deleted. Either way a message is output telling what happened.

The final difference is found in the line of code before the RETURN command. It is the PACK command. As explained earlier, the PACK command physically deletes the records after they are marked for deletion by the DELETE command.

DISPLAYING RECORDS

The next step is to code the CUSTOMER DISPLAY module. There are very few differences between the CUSTOMER REMOVAL module and the CUSTOMER DISPLAY module. Instead of the delete confirmation message, there is an opportunity to pause before the display clears itself and gets ready for the next customer record to be displayed.

Fred looks at the design and makes the necessary changes: the screen design and pseudocode are in Fig. 21-14. The final code is shown in Fig. 21-15.

There are only two differences between the two modules. The first is the line SET COLON OFF at the top of the display lines. This command turns off the display of the colons (: :) that normally appear around input data. This is used for two reasons. First, because Fred is using the @ GET, there are colons around the data even though the data is only being displayed. There is no need to have these field size delimiters if no data is being read into the file.

```
-------------------------------------------------
|                                               |
|        FRED'S FRIENDLY FISH MARKET            |
|             CUSTOMER DELETION                 |
|                                               |
|  ENTER "D" TO CONFIRM DELETE ===>  __         |
|                                               |
|     CUSTOMER NUMBER: CUSTN                     |
|                                               |
|     COMPANY:      COMPANY------------X         |
|     LAST NAME:    LNAME-------------X          |
|     FIRST NAME:   FNAME------------X           |
|                                               |
|     ADDRESS:  ADDRESS-----------------X        |
|     CITY:     CITY----------X                  |
|                                               |
|     STATE: ST    ZIP: ZIP-----X                |
|                                               |
|     PHONE NUMBER: PHONE-------X                |
|                                               |
|     DISCOUNT: DS                               |
|                                               |
-------------------------------------------------

        ACCESS CUSTOMER FILE
        SET CUSTOMER NUMBER TO NOT BLANK
        DO WHILE CUSTOMER NUMBER NOT BLANK
           DISPLAY SCREEN
           ENTER CUSTOMER NUMBER
           VERIFY CUSTOMER NUMBER
           IF FOUND
             THEN
                RETRIEVE CUSTOMER DATA
                ENTER DELETE CONFIRMATION
                IF CONFIRM = "D"
                   THEN
                      DELETE RECORD
                      CLEAR DATA FIELDS
                ENDIF
             ELSE
                WRITE "NUMBER NOT ON FILE"
           ENDIF
        ENDDO
```

Fig. 21-12. The customer removal screen and pseudocode.

```
*************************************
*                                   *
*              1.3                  *
*         FREDS FISH MARKET         *
*    CUSTOMER REMOVAL PROGRAM       *
*            CUSTREM.PRG            *
*                                   *
*************************************
USE CUSTOMER INDEX CUSTOMER
STORE 'T' TO MORECUST
STORE '      ' TO CSN
ERASE
DO WHILE MORECUST = 'T'
   @  1,20 SAY 'FREDS FRIENDLY FISH MARKET'
   @  3,20 SAY '     CUSTOMER REMOVAL         '
   @  7,18 SAY 'CUSTOMER NUMBER: ' GET CSN PICTURE '#####'
   READ
   IF CSN = '      '
        PACK
        USE
        ERASE
        RETURN
      ELSE
        FIND &CSN
        IF # # 0
            @  9,15 SAY 'COMPANY:        '  GET COMP
            @ 10,15 SAY 'LAST NAME:      '  GET LNAME
            @ 11,15 SAY 'FIRST NAME:     '  GET FNAME
            @ 13,15 SAY 'ADDRESS:        '  GET ADDR
            @ 14,15 SAY 'CITY:           '  GET CITY
            @ 16,15 SAY 'STATE:          '  GET ST
            @ 16,35 SAY 'ZIP: '            GET ZIP
            @ 18,15 SAY 'PHONE NUMBER: '   GET PHONE
            @ 20,15 SAY 'DISCOUNT:       '  GET DIS
            CLEAR GETS
            STORE ' ' TO DELCON
            @ 5,15 SAY 'ENTER "D" TO CONFIRM DELETE ===> ' GET DEL
            READ
            IF !(DELCON) = 'D'
                DELETE
                ERASE
                @ 5,1
                @ 5,15 SAY '     *** CUSTOMER DELETED ***'
              ELSE
                ERASE
                @ 5,1
                @ 5,15 SAY '   *** CUSTOMER NOT DELETED ***'
            ENDIF
            STORE '      ' TO CSN
          ELSE
            ? CHR(7)
            ERASE
            @ 5,15 SAY '*** CUSTOMER NUMBER NOT FOUND ***'
        ENDIF
    ENDIF
ENDDO
```

Fig. 21-13. The customer removal dBase code—final version.

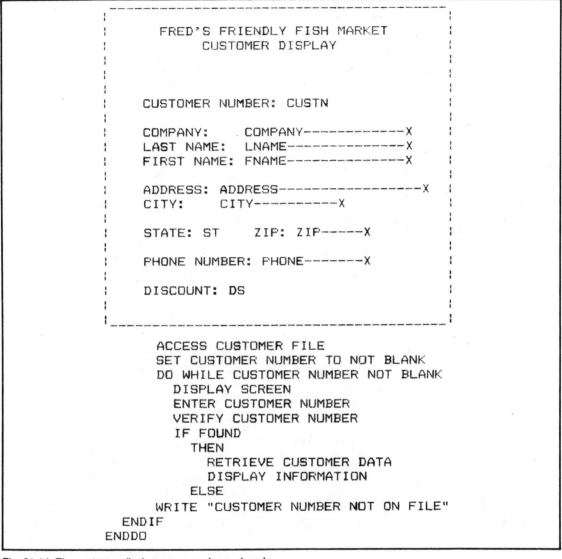

```
                FRED'S FRIENDLY FISH MARKET
                     CUSTOMER DISPLAY



        CUSTOMER NUMBER: CUSTN

        COMPANY:    . COMPANY--------------X
        LAST NAME:    LNAME---------------X
        FIRST NAME:   FNAME---------------X

        ADDRESS:  ADDRESS------------------X
        CITY:       CITY---------X

        STATE: ST    ZIP: ZIP-----X

        PHONE NUMBER: PHONE-------X

        DISCOUNT: DS
```

```
        ACCESS CUSTOMER FILE
        SET CUSTOMER NUMBER TO NOT BLANK
        DO WHILE CUSTOMER NUMBER NOT BLANK
           DISPLAY SCREEN
           ENTER CUSTOMER NUMBER
           VERIFY CUSTOMER NUMBER
           IF FOUND
              THEN
                 RETRIEVE CUSTOMER DATA
                 DISPLAY INFORMATION
              ELSE
           WRITE "CUSTOMER NUMBER NOT ON FILE"
        ENDIF
   ENDDO
```

Fig. 21-14. The customer display screen and pseudocode.

The second reason for using the SET COLON OFF command involves the lines of code following the CLEAR GETS command. These lines form an example of the use of a *pause code*. Because the colon has been set to off, there is no entry line shown—just the words ENTER ANY KEY TO CONTINUE. The display appears to pause until the operator presses any key. The READ command enables the program to continue, and then the SET COLON ON command is given so that when the

```
**************************************
*                                    *
*              1.4                   *
*         FREDS FISH MARKET          *
*     CUSTOMER DISPLAY PROGRAM       *
*           CUSTDIS.PRG              *
*                                    *
**************************************
USE CUSTOMER INDEX CUSTOMER
STORE 'T' TO MORECUST
STORE '     ' TO CSN
ERASE
DO WHILE MORECUST = 'T'
  @  1,20 SAY 'FREDS FRIENDLY FISH MARKET'
  @  3,20 SAY '    CUSTOMER DISPLAY       '
  @  7,18 SAY 'CUSTOMER NUMBER: ' GET CSN PICTURE '#####'
  READ
  @ 5,1
  IF CSN = '      '
      USE
      ERASE
      RETURN
    ELSE
      FIND &CSN
      IF # # 0
          SET COLON OFF
          @  9,15 SAY 'COMPANY:      '   GET COMP
          @ 10,15 SAY 'LAST NAME:    '   GET LNAME
          @ 11,15 SAY 'FIRST NAME:   '   GET FNAME
          @ 13,15 SAY 'ADDRESS:      '   GET ADDR
          @ 14,15 SAY 'CITY:         '   GET CITY
          @ 16,15 SAY 'STATE:        '   GET ST
          @ 16,35 SAY 'ZIP: '            GET ZIP
          @ 18,15 SAY 'PHONE NUMBER: '   GET PHONE
          @ 20,15 SAY 'DISCOUNT:     '   GET DIS
          STORE ' ' TO RESP
          CLEAR GETS
          @ 5,20 SAY 'ENTER ANY KEY TO CONTINUE'  GET RESP
          READ
          SET COLON ON
          STORE '     ' TO CSN
          ERASE
        ELSE
          ? CHR(7)
          ERASE
          @ 5,15 SAY '*** CUSTOMER NUMBER NOT FOUND ***'
      ENDIF
  ENDIF
ENDDO
```

Fig. 21-15. The customer display dBase code—final version.

next customer number is input, it will be surrounded by colons.

It is now time for Fred to test the modules he has built. Usually you should test the module as it is completed, but Fred has put testing the CHANGE CUSTOMER module until now. Fred first displays the CUSTOMER CHANGE screen. He can then enter the customer number for the record he wishes to change. He enters customer number 100 and presses the enter key. Figure 21-16 shows the display that he sees. He can now make any changes he wants. So far, the system is working. He makes his changes and the screen changes to

FREDS FRIENDLY FISH MARKET

CUSTOMER CHANGES

*** CUSTOMER CHANGED ***

CUSTOMER NUMBER: :   :

To test the error condition, Fred tries to enter a customer number that does not exist:

FREDS FRIENDLY FISH MARKET

CUSTOMER CHANGES

*** CUSTOMER NUMBER NOT FOUND ***

CUSTOMER NUMBER: :5000 :

So far, so good—no errors so far. After Fred enters a blank customer number, the system returns to the main customer menu screen. Fred enters a 3 to test the CUSTOMER REMOVAL program. He enters customer number 300 and presses the enter key. The resulting display is shown in Fig. 21-17. Fred can now see the record to make sure it is the one he wishes to delete. Fred decides to leave it on the file. He just presses the enter key, and the next screen appears.

```
          FREDS FRIENDLY FISH MARKET

               CUSTOMER CHANGES



          CUSTOMER NUMBER: :100  :

     COMPANY:     :KARENS CHOWDER POT  :
     LAST NAME:   :HAYDEN              :
     FIRST NAME:  :KAREN               :

     ADDRESS: :46 OBERLAND PARK           :
     CITY:     :WHEAT FIELD    :

     STATE: :KY:    ZIP: :35546-2223:

     PHONE NUMBER:  :(454)555-1626:

     DISCOUNT: :15:
```

Fig. 21-16. The customer change screen.

```
          FREDS FRIENDLY FISH MARKET

            CUSTOMER REMOVAL

  ENTER "D" TO CONFIRM DELETE ===> : :

     CUSTOMER NUMBER: :300  :

  COMPANY:        :SAMS LOX HAVEN     :
  LAST NAME:      :BURTON             :
  FIRST NAME:     :SAMUEL             :

  ADDRESS:        :18465 TRAIL STREET      :
  CITY:           :BOCA DELRAY     :

  STATE: :MO:    ZIP: :35546-2223:

  PHONE NUMBER: :(564)555-1525:

  DISCOUNT:      : 0:
```

Fig. 21-17. The customer removal screen with a confirmation message.

```
          FREDS FRIENDLY FISH MARKET

            CUSTOMER DISPLAY

          ENTER ANY KEY TO CONTINUE

     CUSTOMER NUMBER: :200  :

  COMPANY:        LEE SIDE FISHERIES
  LAST NAME:      KAY
  FIRST NAME:     LEE JAY

  ADDRESS:        151 FARMINGTON AVE
  CITY:           NORTH HAVEN

  STATE:          CA    ZIP:  88667-2443

  PHONE NUMBER:  (968)555-1424

  DISCOUNT:       10
```

Fig. 21-18. The preliminary customer display screen.

```
FREDS FRIENDLY FISH MARKET

        CUSTOMER REMOVAL

 *** CUSTOMER NOT DELETED ***

 CUSTOMER NUMBER:   :    :
```

The final module to be tested is the CUS-TOMER DISPLAY program. Fred returns to the main customer menu and enters a 4 for the customer display. He decides to display customer number 200. The resulting display is shown in Fig. 21-18.

Fred once again has had a clean test. Actually these screens and programs took Fred over two days to develop. Considering it was his first experience, it wasn't bad. With the exception of the initial additions program, Fred has had very little trouble with the programs so far. Once he learned to test his pseudocode over and over again, he was able to program much more effectively.

As Fred has seen, the most important part of coding the programs is the correct coding of the original module. When using standard add, change, remove, and display record modules, most of the code can be reused.

Chapter 22

Customizing and Printing Reports

There are two programs left for Fred to write in the customer system. Both involve printing reports. Fred decides to start with the customer label program.

A MAILING LABEL PROGRAM

When coding reports, there is usually very little screen work and a lot of printer work. This program is no different. Fred decides to tackle the mailing label program by breaking it into several smaller modules. He first examines the screen he must code, along with the mailing label format, and the pseudocode for the main part of the printing routine, as shown in Fig. 22-1.

Fred decides that since this is a new type of module for him, he will start with the main part of the screen.

```
STORE ' ' TO OPTION
   @  1,20 SAY 'FREDS FRIENDLY;
      FISH MARKET'
```

```
@  3,20 SAY ' CUSTOMER MAILING;
   LABELS'
@  7,18 SAY 'ENTER "A" FOR;
   ALIGNMENT PRINT,'
@  8,18 SAY '         "X" TO EXIT;
   PRINT,'
@  9,18 SAY '    OR <cr> TO BEGIN;
   PRINT'
@ 11,18 SAY '         ====> ' GET
   OPTION
READ
```

This code is straight forward. The first six lines simply set up the option field and display the body of the menu. The next line contains the GET command, which will allow the entry of the option field.

The next step is to put in the loop and IF condition. For some reason Fred has used multiple IF statements instead of a CASE statement. Either way the program will work. The resulting code is shown in Fig. 22-2.

This code forms the basis for the coding of the

```
------------------------------------------------------
¦                                                    ¦
¦          FRED'S FRIENDLY FISH MARKET               ¦
¦             MAILING LABEL PRINT                     ¦
¦         ENTER "A" FOR ALIGNMENT PRINT,             ¦
¦             "X" TO EXIT PRINT,                      ¦
¦           OR <cr> TO BEGIN PRINT                    ¦
¦                                                    ¦
¦                ====>  ___                           ¦
¦                                                    ¦
------------------------------------------------------

X------COMPANY------X
X------FNAME-------X  X------LNAME-------X
X------ADDRESS----------X

    PRINT MAILING LABELS

        STORE " " TO CHOICE
        DO WHILE CHOICE NOT "X"
           DISPLAY SCREEN
           READ CHOICE
           IF CHOICE = "X"
              THEN EXIT
           ENDIF
           IF CHOICE = "A"
              THEN PERFORM "ALIGNMENT PRINT"
           ENDIF
           IF CHOICE = "<cr>"
              ACCESS CUSTOMER FILE
              READ A CUSTOMER RECORD
              INITIALIZE RECORD COUNTER
              DO WHILE MORE RECORDS
                 PERFORM "FORMAT FOR PRINT"
                 IF LABEL COUNTER = 3
                    THEN
                       PRINT A ROW OF LABELS
                       RESET LABEL COUNTER
                 ENDIF
                 READ NEXT RECORD
              ENDDO
              IF LABEL COUNTER # 0
                 THEN PRINT PARTIAL ROW
              ENDIF
           ENDIF
        ENDDO
```

Fig. 22-1. The customer mailing label print screen, layout, and pseudocode.

```
STORE 'T' TO MOREANS
STORE ' ' TO OPTION
DO WHILE MOREANS = 'T'
   ERASE
   @  1,20 SAY 'FREDS FRIENDLY FISH MARKET'
   @  3,20 SAY ' CUSTOMER MAILING LABELS'
   @  7,18 SAY 'ENTER "A" FOR ALIGNMENT PRINT,'
   @  8,18 SAY '       "X" TO EXIT PRINT,'
   @  9,18 SAY '    OR <cr> TO BEGIN PRINT'
   @ 11,18 SAY '          ====> ' GET OPTION
   READ
   IF !(OPTION) = 'X'
   ENDIF
   IF !(OPTION) = 'A'
   ENDIF
   IF !(OPTION) # 'A' .AND. !(OPTION) # 'X'
   ENDIF
   STORE ' ' TO OPTION
ENDDO
```

Fig. 22-2. The customer mailing label program main body code and subroutine stubs.

```
STORE 'T' TO MOREANS
STORE ' ' TO OPTION
DO WHILE MOREANS = 'T'
   ERASE
   @  1,20 SAY 'FREDS FRIENDLY FISH MARKET'
   @  3,20 SAY ' CUSTOMER MAILING LABELS'
   @  7,18 SAY 'ENTER "A" FOR ALIGNMENT PRINT,'
   @  8,18 SAY '       "X" TO EXIT PRINT,'
   @  9,18 SAY '    OR <cr> TO BEGIN PRINT'
   @ 11,18 SAY '          ====> ' GET OPTION
   READ
   IF !(OPTION) = 'X'
     USE
     ERASE
     RETURN
   ENDIF
   IF !(OPTION) = 'A'
     DO CUSTLBLA
   ENDIF
   IF !(OPTION) # 'A' .AND. !(OPTION) # 'X'
   ENDIF
   STORE ' ' TO OPTION
ENDDO
```

Fig. 22-3. The customer mailing label program main body code.

options. The first option is X, to exit the program. Fred uses the usual commands in this routine: USE, ERASE, and RETURN. The A command will call another subroutine. Fred codes the subroutine call. Fred looks over his new code which is shown in Fig. 22-3.

Fred is now ready to land the big one. He will code the routine to print the labels. He has coded the beginning of this routine using the compound expression IF OPTION # "A" . AND. OPTION # "X". This means that anything other than an A or X will cause the labels to be printed. The A routine is used only if Fred wishes to have some dummy labels printed so he can make sure that the printer is printing on the labels and not between them.

The pseudocode can be followed almost literally. The pseudocode directs Fred to ACCESS CUSTOMER FILE, which Fred translates into the USE CUSTOMER INDEX CUSTOMER command. Since Fred must read all the customer records, he must start another loop. Fred develops the following program:

```
USE CUSTOMER INDEX CUSTOMER
DO WHILE .NOT. EOF
   STORE 0 TO LBLCNT
   DO CUSTLBLF
   SKIP
ENDDO
```

The CUSTLBLF is a subroutine of the CUSTOMER LABEL PRINT subroutine. On the hierarchy chart, this subroutine is shown on the third level. Before Fred can code any more in the main program, he must code this subroutine.

The point of the subroutine is to take a record and format it on the label. It takes three records to fill the width of the label sheet because there are three labels across. The format subroutine will store the required fields until there are three labels. Fred writes the codes shown in Fig. 22-4.

Fred divides the labels into labels one, two,

and three. He also divides the fields into A through D. Depending upon which label is being formatted, the appropriate code will be used.

Notice the use of the different concatenation symbols. The labels will be in the form of

```
X------COMPANY------X
I. X------LNAME-------X
X------ADDRESS----------X
X----CITY-----X ST XZIPX
```

Fred will use only the first initial of the first name. He will use only the first five characters of the zip code because he discovered he couldn't fit any more on the labels. The same reasoning explains his use of the first initial. Even though he had designed his program for the full name, when he went to look at his labels, he realized he could not get forty characters (the maximum length of two twenty-character fields) on a label.

Knowing how the labels will be formatted allows Fred to start to finish the print label routine as shown in Fig. 22-5.

The SET PRINT ON phrase redirects the output from the ? commands to the printer. At the end of the printing, the SET PRINT OFF phrase directs the output back to the screen.

The DO WHILE .NOT. EOF loop will read records and process them from the first record to the last. After each set of three records the formatting will be complete, and a set of labels can be printed. After counting the spaces Fred decided it was easier to use the ? commands than the @ SAY commands. The code inside the IF statement prints a full set of labels. The label counter is reset to 0 to get ready for the next set. When the end-of-file is reached, there may be only one or two records left to print. After the ENDDO, some code must be added to account for this. Fred adds the following code:

```
IF LBLCNT = 1
  ? A1
```

```
? B1
? C1
? D1
?
ENDIF
IF LBLCNT = 2
  ? A1,'          ',A2
  ? B1,'     ',B2
  ? C1,' ',C2
  ? D1,' ',D2
  ?
ENDIF
```

This takes care of any labels left over at the end of the program if there were not a number exactly divisible by three. There is a different routine used for one remaining label than for two remaining labels. When there is one label, there will be two empty labels, while when there are two labels to be printed, there will be only one empty label.

Fred has now coded everything but the alignment routine. He has the program shown in Fig. 22-6.

A few lines have been added. In the X option, a RELEASE command was added. When you are using a great number of memory variables and you are done with them, you should dispose of them.

```
*************************************
*                                   *
*         1.5.CUSTLBLF              *
*         FREDS FISH MARKET         *
*   CUSTOMER MAILING LABEL FORMAT   *
*            CUSTLBLF.PRG           *
*                                   *
*************************************
STORE LBLCNT + 1 TO LBLCNT
IF LBLCNT = 1
  STORE COMP TO A1
  STORE $(FNAME,1,1)-'. '+LNAME TO B1
  STORE ADDR TO C1
  STORE CITY+'  '+ST+' '+$(ZIP,1,5) TO D1
ENDIF
IF LBLCNT = 2
  STORE COMP TO A2
  STORE $(FNAME,1,1)-'. '+LNAME TO B2
  STORE ADDR TO C2
  STORE CITY+'  '+ST+' '+$(ZIP,1,5) TO D2
ENDIF
IF LBLCNT = 3
  STORE COMP TO A3
  STORE $(FNAME,1,1)-'. '+LNAME TO B3
  STORE ADDR TO C3
  STORE CITY+'  '+ST+' '+$(ZIP,1,5) TO D3
ENDIF
RETURN
```

Fig. 22-4. The customer mailing label format-labels code.

198

```
IF !(OPTION) # 'A' .AND. !
 (OPTION) # 'X'
  USE CUSTOMER INDEX CUSTOMER
  STORE 0 TO LBLCNT
  DO WHILE .NOT. EOF
    DO CUSTLBLF
    IF LBLCNT = 3
      SET PRINT ON
      ? A1,'        ',A2,'      ',A3
      ? B1,'     ',B2,'      ',B3
      ? C1,' ',C2,' ',C3
      ? D1,' ',D2,' ',D3
      ?
      STORE 0 TO LBLCNT
    ENDIF
    SKIP
  ENDDO
  SET PRINT OFF
ENDIF
```

Fig. 22-5. The customer mailing label print code.

Since you can only have sixty-four at a time, the more you can release the better.

The final coding for this module is the label alignment program. This code is shown in Fig. 22-7.

This code will print three sets of dummy labels with Xs where the fields normally go. This is done using a simple DO WHILE loop and a few ? commands.

Did you notice the extra ? ' ' at the end of the printing routine? This is to prevent the last line from remaining in the internal print buffer. In the main program, the extra ? ' ' is there for the same reason. In this program, the extra line also serves to separate the labels from each other.

A DIRECTORY PROGRAM

The final program Fred must code for the customer system is the CUSTOMER DIRECTORY program. Fred again starts by looking at the design, which is shown in Fig. 22-8.

```
***********************************
*            1.5               *
*      FREDS FISH MARKET       *
*   CUSTOMER MAILING LABEL PRINT  *
*         CUSTLBL.PRG          *
*                              *
***********************************
USE CUSTOMER INDEX CUSTOMER
STORE 'T' TO MOREANS
STORE ' ' TO OPTION
DO WHILE MOREANS = 'T'
  ERASE
  @  1,20 SAY 'FREDS FRIENDLY FISH MARKET'
  @  3,20 SAY ' CUSTOMER MAILING LABELS'
  @  7,18 SAY 'ENTER "A" FOR ALIGNMENT PRINT,'
  @  8,18 SAY '      "X" TO EXIT PRINT,'
  @  9,18 SAY '    OR <cr> TO BEGIN PRINT'
  @ 11,18 SAY '        ====> ' GET OPTION
  READ
  IF !(OPTION) = 'X'
    USE
    RELEASE A1,A2,A3,B1,B2,B3,C1,C2,C3,D1,D2,D3
    RETURN
  ENDIF
```

```
                        IF !(OPTION) = 'A'
                           DO CUSTLBLA
                        ENDIF
                        IF !(OPTION) # 'A' .AND. !(OPTION) # 'X'
                           USE CUSTOMER INDEX CUSTOMER
                           STORE 0 TO LBLCNT
                           DO WHILE .NOT. EOF
                             DO CUSTLBLF
                             IF LBLCNT = 3
                               SET PRINT ON
                               ? A1,'        ',A2,'        ',A3
                               ? B1,'     ',B2,'     ',B3
                               ? C1,' ',C2,' ',C3
                               ? D1,' ',D2,' ',D3
                               ?
                               STORE 0 TO LBLCNT
                             ENDIF
                             SKIP
                           ENDDO
                           IF LBLCNT = 1
                             ? A1
                             ? B1
                             ? C1
                             ? D1
                             ?
                           ENDIF
                           IF LBLCNT = 2
                             ? A1,'        ',A2
                             ? B1,'     ',B2
                             ? C1,' ',C2
                             ? D1,' ',D2
                             ?
                           ENDIF
                           SET PRINT OFF
                        ENDIF
                        STORE ' ' TO OPTION
                        ENDDO
```

Fig. 22-6. The customer mailing label print code—final version.

Fred decides to try to use the same rough skeleton from his last printing module. After all, if it works for add, change, and delete, it may work for printing too. Fred plagiarizes the code shown in Fig. 22-9.

"Not bad," decides Fred. All that's left is the actual printing format commands and some type of paging routine. Everything will come between the DO WHILE and ENDDO. Fred adds the appropriate code, and his program, shown in Fig. 22-10, is complete.

Fred decided to use all @SAY commands. He has used a line counter variable called LINECNT instead of directly specifying the vertical placement of each line. This was necessary in order to print multiple records on the same page. Within each record, the line counter is updated several times. Fred has found that he can fit only four records on a page. Each time he prints a line, he updates the line counter. At the bottom of the loop Fred used the SKIP command to read another record and continue processing.

```
**************************************
*                                    *
*         1.5.CUSTLBLA               *
*        FREDS FISH MARKET           *
*    CUSTOMER LABEL ALIGNMENT        *
*         CUSTLBLA.PRG               *
*                                    *
**************************************
    SET COLON OFF
    STORE ' ' TO ANS
    @ 7,13 SAY 'ALIGN PRINTER AND HIT ANY KEY TO CONTINUE' GET ANS
    @ 8,1
    @ 9,8  SAY 'THIS WILL PRINT THREE ROWS OF LABEL ALIGNMENT DATA'
    @ 11,1
    READ
    SET PRINT ON
    STORE 1 TO COUNT
    DO WHILE COUNT <= 3
       STORE COUNT + 1 TO COUNT
       ? 'XXXXXXXXXXXXXXXXXXXX    XXXXXXXXXXXXXXXXXXXX    XXXXXXXXXXXXXXXXXXXX'
       ? 'X. XXXXXXXXXXXXXXXXXXX   X. XXXXXXXXXXXXXXXXXXX   X. XXXXXXXXXXXXXXXXXXX
       ? 'XXXXXXXXXXXXXXXXXXXXXXXX XXXXXXXXXXXXXXXXXXXXXXXX XXXXXXXXXXXXXXXXXXXXXXXX
       ? 'XXXXXXXXXXXXXXX, XX XXXXX XXXXXXXXXXXXXX, XX XXXXX XXXXXXXXXXXXXX, XX XX
       ? ' '
    ENDDO
    SET PRINT OFF
    RETURN
```

Fig. 22-7. The customer label alignment code—final version.

Fred used another new command in his output, the TRIM command. This is used to eliminate trailing blanks from the end of a field. This command is necessary when you are concatenating two fields in which the value does not fill the full size of the first field. In this case, the LNAME must be trimmed so that it will be followed immediately by a comma and the first name.

At the beginning of the DO WHILE loop Fred has added a *header* routine:

```
IF LINECNT = 1 .OR. LINECNT = 56
   @ 1,30 SAY '    FREDS FISH;
       MARKET'
   @ 2,30 SAY 'CUSTOMER DIRECTORY;
       PRINT'
   STORE 4 TO LINECNT
ENDIF
```

A header routine is a block of code that should only be performed at the top of a page. In this program, the routine will be performed at the top of the first page, because that is the only time LINECNT will be 1 and whenever LINECNT reaches 56 (after the printing of the fourth customer record on a page). The line count of 56 was determined by counting printed lines. When LINECNT is 56 and there are more customers, LINECNT is set back to 4, so the topmost customer record will always start in the same spot on each page.

There is a SET FORMAT TO PRINT in this code. When it is time to direct all output to the printer, you will use this code. When printing is through, you will use the SET FORMAT TO SCREEN command to redirect output to the screen. Fred has remembered the last line. He has added the command @ LINECNT+1,1. This will release the last line in the print buffer. Remember,

```
 -----------------------------------------------
:                                               :
:        FRED'S FRIENDLY FISH MARKET            :
:        CUSTOMER DIRECTORY PRINT               :
:                                               :
:                                               :
:        ENTER <cr> TO BEGIN PRINT              :
:        OR "X" TO EXIT PRINT                   :
:                                               :
:            ====> ___                          :
:                                               :
:                                               :
:                                               :
:                                               :
:                                               :
:                                               :
 -----------------------------------------------
```

Customer Number: CUSTN

X------COMPANY------X
X-------LNAME-------X,

X-------FNAME-------X
X-------ADDRESS----------X
X-----CITY-----X, ST X--ZIP--X

Phone: (AAA)NNN-NNNN

Discount: XX%

PRINT MAILING LIST

```
    READ CHOICE
    IF CHOICE = 'X'
       THEN EXIT
    ENDIF
    IF CHOICE = "<cr>"
       THEN
         ACCESS CUSTOMER FILE
         READ CUSTOMER RECORD
         SET LINECOUNT TO 1
         DO WHILE MORE RECORDS
            IF LINECOUNT = 1 OR = 56
              THEN
                PRINT HEADER
                SET LINECOUNT TO 4
            ENDIF
            PRINT DIRECTORY ENTRY
            UPDATE LINECOUNT
            READ NEXT RECORD
         ENDDO
    ENDIF
```

Fig. 22-8. The customer directory print screen, layout, and pseudocode.

202

```
USE CUSTOMER INDEX CUSTOMER
STORE 'T' TO MOREANS
STORE ' ' TO OPTION
DO WHILE MOREANS = 'T'
  ERASE
  @  1,20 SAY 'FREDS FRIENDLY FISH MARKET'
  @  3,20 SAY ' CUSTOMER DIRECTORY PRINT '
  @  7,20 SAY 'ENTER "X" TO EXIT PRINT,'
  @  8,18 SAY '   OR <cr> TO BEGIN PRINT'
  @ 10,18 SAY '          ====> ' GET OPTION
  READ
  IF !(OPTION) = 'X'
    USE
    STORE ' ' TO OPTION
    RETURN
  ENDIF
  USE CUSTOMER INDEX CUSTOMER
  DO WHILE .NOT. EOF
     SKIP
   ENDDO
   STORE ' ' TO OPTION
ENDDO
```

Fig. 22-9. The beginnings of the customer directory program.

```
*************************************
*              1.6               *
*        FREDS FISH MARKET       *
*     CUSTOMER DIRECTORY PRINT   *
*          CUSTDIR.PRG           *
*************************************
USE CUSTOMER INDEX CUSTOMER
STORE 'T' TO MOREANS
STORE ' ' TO OPTION
DO WHILE MOREANS = 'T'
  ERASE
  @  1,20 SAY 'FREDS FRIENDLY FISH MARKET'
  @  3,20 SAY ' CUSTOMER DIRECTORY PRINT '
  @  7,20 SAY 'ENTER "X" TO EXIT PRINT,'
  @  8,18 SAY '   OR <cr> TO BEGIN PRINT'
  @ 10,18 SAY '          ====> ' GET OPTION
  READ
  IF !(OPTION) = 'X'
    USE
    STORE ' ' TO OPTION
     RETURN
```

```
              ENDIF
              USE CUSTOMER INDEX CUSTOMER
              STORE 1 TO LINECNT
              SET FORMAT TO PRINT
              DO WHILE .NOT. EOF
                 IF LINECNT = 1 .OR. LINECNT = 56
                    @ 1,30 SAY '    FREDS FISH MARKET'
                    @ 2,30 SAY 'CUSTOMER DIRECTORY PRINT'
                    STORE 4 TO LINECNT
                 ENDIF
                 STORE LINECNT + 4 TO LINECNT
                 @ LINECNT,1 SAY 'Customer Number:'
                 @ LINECNT,18 SAY CUSTN
                 STORE LINECNT + 2 TO LINECNT
                 @ LINECNT,1 SAY COMP
                 STORE LINECNT + 1 TO LINECNT
                 @ LINECNT,1 SAY TRIM(LNAME)+', '+FNAME
                 STORE LINECNT + 1 TO LINECNT
                 @ LINECNT,15 SAY ADDR

                 STORE LINECNT + 1 TO LINECNT
                 @ LINECNT,15 SAY TRIM(CITY)+', '+ST+' '+ZIP
                 STORE LINECNT + 2 TO LINECNT
                 @ LINECNT,15 SAY 'Phone: '+PHONE
                 STORE LINECNT + 2 TO LINECNT
                 @ LINECNT,15 SAY 'Discount: '
                 @ LINECNT,25 SAY DIS
                 @ LINECNT,27 SAY '%'
                 SKIP
              ENDDO
              @ LINECNT+1,1
              SET FORMAT TO SCREEN
              STORE ' ' TO OPTION
           ENDDO
```

Fig. 22-10. The customer directory program code—final version.

dBASE II is always one line behind—if you print only one line, you will never see it. The blank line at the end of a program will print the last line of output.

SUMMARY

Printing routines are simple but time consuming to write. Many a program has been written in just thirty minutes to produce a report that then took three hours to format correctly on the page. The best way to work fast is to use graph paper. There is special paper for computers that is 60 rows by 132 columns, the size of large computer paper. You can use any part of that to layout your output design. This is also very handy for screen design. You can usually buy a version that is 24 rows by 80 columns. The use of this technique can save you a lot of time at the keyboard.

Chapter 23

Adding Records in a Two-File System

Fred is really moving now. In the last two chapters of this book you will see Fred code two different type of modules. This chapter will explain how Fred coded the additions module of the order program. The final chapter will discuss a report that Fred did that does some calculating and totaling. The complete design for all programs in Fred's system can be found in Appendix A. The dBASE II code for the customer and order systems, in their entirety are found in Appendix B.

THE MAIN RECORD

Fred designed his order system using a two-file approach. As explained before, the order file is actually made up of two files, the main records file, and the item records file. In the main file there will only be one record for each order number. In the order-item file there will be as many records for each order as there are items.

This is very typical of relational database sys-

tems. Each record in the order-item file represents one item in the total order. This way there are no limits to the number of items that can appear on an order.

Fred starts by coding the main order program. This is a simple program that closely follows Fred's work in the customer system. Figure 23-1 shows the screen displays.

Fred designed this program in two parts. First he would read in the order number and customer number. Then he would verify both—the order number to make sure it didn't already exist, and the customer number to make sure that it did exist. If either field had an error, the error was to be displayed. If the data was correct, the customer name was to be displayed to show the operator which customer the number belonged to, just in case he had made a mistake. The operator could then enter the date of the order.

Once the order is created, the items can be

```
,------------------------------------------------------------------,
;                                                                  ;
;              FRED'S FRIENDLY FISH MARKET                         ;
;                    ORDER ADDITIONS                               ;
;                                                                  ;
;        ORDER NUMBER:        ORDRN                                ;
;                                                                  ;
;        CUSTOMER NUMBER:   CUSTN                                  ;
;                                                                  ;
'------------------------------------------------------------------'
   ,------------------------------------------------------------------,
   ;                                                                  ;
   ;              FRED'S FRIENDLY FISH MARKET                         ;
   ;                    ORDER ADDITIONS                               ;
   ;                                                                  ;
   ;                                                                  ;
   ;        ORDER NUMBER:        ORDRN                                ;
   ;                                                                  ;
   ;        CUSTOMER NUMBER:   CUSTN                                  ;
   ;                                                                  ;
   ;        COMPANY:       COMPANY--------------X                     ;
   ;        LAST  NAME:  LNAME---------------X                        ;
   ;        FIRST NAME:  FNAME---------------X                        ;
   ;                                                                  ;
   ;                                                                  ;
   ;        DATE ORDERED: MM/DD/YY                                    ;
   ;                                                                  ;
   '------------------------------------------------------------------'
```

Fig. 23-1. The order additions screens.

entered. This program will use the two-file system. The SELECT PRIMARY, and SELECT SECONDARY commands enable Fred to use two files at once. He will use one file as the main or primary file, and use the secondary file to access any other needed records. The primary file is sometimes the anchor file. While the secondary file is often changed, the primary file is usually set to the file being written to.

Fred looks at the pseudocode that he developed earlier, which is shown in Fig. 23-2. He starts his coding with the first entry screen.

The result is shown in Fig. 23-3. This is easy so far, thought Fred. Nothing new to be seen here. The screen is presented, and the operator can enter an order number and a customer number.

The next step is to add the error checks. The resulting code is shown in Fig. 23-4.

The first section Fred coded were the two IF-THEN-ELSE conditions. The first one checks to see if there was an order number entered. If not, control is passed to the main order menu. Before the RETURN statement are the commands that close the open files. In the two-file system, you must close both the primary and secondary files. Notice the file is selected and then the USE command performed. The last "select" is to the primary file. Always make sure the primary file is selected last. If you do not, the next time you open a file, the system will think it is a secondary file, and you will have problems.

If there is a valid order number entered, the

```
ADD AN ORDER

  ACCESS ORDER FILE
  SET ORDER NUMBER TO NOT BLANK
  DO WHILE ORDER NUMBER NOT BLANK
    DISPLAY SCREEN
    ENTER ORDER NUMBER AND CUSTOMER NUMBER
    IF ORDER NUMBER NOT BLANK
      VERIFY ORDER NUMBER
      IF NEW NUMBER
        THEN
          ACCESS CUSTOMER FILE
          VERIFY CUSTOMER NUMBER
          IF FOUND
            THEN
              DISPLAY CUSTOMER DATA
              ENTER DATE FIELD
              ADD TO ORDER FILE
              PERFORM "ADD ITEMS"
            ELSE
              WRITE "CUSTOMER NUMBER NOT FOUND"
          ENDIF
        ELSE
          WRITE "ORDER NUMBER ALREADY ON FILE"
      ENDIF
    ENDIF
  ENDDO
```

Fig. 23-2. The order additions pseudocode.

order number is checked to see that it does not exist. If it does, an error message is generated and the preliminary screen is redisplayed. The customer file is then searched for the customer number. An error is produced if the customer number cannot be found.

The customer file becomes the secondary file. This is so the main order file can remain open. By

```
  STORE '     ' TO ORN
  STORE '     ' TO CSN
    @  1,20 SAY 'FREDS FRIENDLY FISH MARKET'
    @  3,20 SAY '   ORDER ADDITIONS MENU   '
    @  7,15 SAY 'ORDER NUMBER:    ' GET ORN    PICTURE '#####'
    @  9,15 SAY 'CUSTOMER NUMBER: ' GET CSN    PICTURE '#####'
  READ
```

Fig. 23-3. The code for the order additions system initial screen.

```
    STORE '      '  TO ORN
    STORE '      '  TO CSN
      @  1,20 SAY 'FREDS FRIENDLY FISH MARKET'
      @  3,20 SAY '  ORDER ADDITIONS MENU  '
      @  7,15 SAY 'ORDER NUMBER:     ' GET ORN    PICTURE '#####'
      @  9,15 SAY 'CUSTOMER NUMBER: ' GET CSN    PICTURE '#####'
      READ
    IF ORN = '       '
        SELECT PRIMARY
        USE
        SELECT SECONDARY
        USE
        SELECT PRIMARY
        ERASE
        RETURN
    ELSE
        SELECT PRIMARY
        FIND &ORN
        IF # = 0
            SELECT SECONDARY
            USE CUSTOMER INDEX CUSTOMER
            FIND &CSN
            IF # # 0
              ELSE
                 ? CHR(7)
                 ERASE
                 @ 5,15 SAY '  *** CUSTOMER NUMBER NOT ON FILE   *
            ENDIF
          ELSE
            ? CHR(7)
            ERASE
            @ 5,15 SAY '*** ORDER NUMBER ALREADY ON FILE ***'
        ENDIF
    ENDIF
```

Fig. 23-4. The order additions system display screen code.

selecting the primary and secondary files, you can switch between any two files.

Once the data is found, the customer information should be displayed so the operator can be sure that the right customer will get the order. The date can then be entered, and the record can be written to the main order file.

The final step is the call to the order-items program to add the items. The resulting code is shown in Fig. 23-5.

Unlike other modules you have seen in this book, most of the work is done after the order

```
*************************************
*                                   *
*              3.1                  *
*        FREDS FISH MARKET          *
*     ORDER ADDITIONS PROGRAM       *
*           ORDRADD.PRG             *
*                                   *
*************************************
ERASE
USE ORDER INDEX ORDER
STORE T TO MOREORDR
STORE '     ' TO ORN
STORE '     ' TO CSN
STORE '        ' TO DTO
DO WHILE MOREORDR = 'T'
  @  1,20 SAY 'FREDS FRIENDLY FISH MARKET'
  @  3,20 SAY '  ORDER ADDITIONS MENU  '
  @  7,15 SAY 'ORDER NUMBER:    ' GET ORN    PICTURE '#####'
  @  9,15 SAY 'CUSTOMER NUMBER: ' GET CSN    PICTURE '#####'
  READ
  @ 5,1
  IF ORN = '     '
      SELECT PRIMARY
      USE
      SELECT SECONDARY
      USE
      ERASE
      RETURN
    ELSE
      SELECT PRIMARY
      FIND &ORN
      IF # = 0
          SELECT SECONDARY
          USE CUSTOMER INDEX CUSTOMER
          FIND &CSN
          IF # # 0
           @ 11,15 SAY 'COMPANY: '
           @ 11,32 SAY COMP
           @ 12,15 SAY 'LAST NAME:'
           @ 12,32 SAY LNAME
           @ 13,15 SAY 'FIRST NAME: '
           @ 13,32 SAY FNAME
           @ 15,15 SAY 'DATE ORDERED: ' GET DTO PICTURE '##/##/##'
          READ
          STORE COMP TO COMP
          STORE LNAME TO LNAME
          STORE FNAME TO FNAME
```

```
              SELECT PRIMARY
              APPEND BLANK
              REPLACE ORDRN WITH VAL(ORN),CUSTN WITH VAL(CSN),DATE WITH
              DO ORDRADIT
              ERASE
              @ 5,20 SAY '  *** ORDER ADDED  *** '
              SELECT PRIMARY
              USE ORDER INDEX ORDER
              STORE '       ' TO ORN
              STORE '       ' TO CSN
              STORE '         ' TO DTO
           ELSE
              ? CHR(7)
              ERASE
              @ 5,15 SAY '  *** CUSTOMER NUMBER NOT ON FILE  ***'
           ENDIF
        ELSE
           ? CHR(7)
           ERASE
           @ 5,15 SAY '*** ORDER NUMBER ALREADY ON FILE ***'
        ENDIF
     ENDIF
  ENDDO
```

Fig. 23-5. The order additions system main module code.

number and customer number are verified. The customer information is displayed, and then the date is entered. After the READ statement for the date, the customer information is saved in memory variables. This is so the customer information can be displayed on the order-items screen without having to be retrieved again.

After the date is read, the file is set back to primary and the data is entered into the main file. Fred remembered that both order number and customer number are really numbers and had to be converted to numerics data with the VAL statement before they could be added to the file.

The main file is updated and the order-items program is called. The items can then be entered, and then control returns to the main module. The primary file is then restored to the main order file. (In the order-item program, the order-item file became the primary file.)

THE SUBSIDIARY RECORDS

The next program to code is the order-items module. Fred first looks over his design, which is shown in Fig. 23-6. The screen displays a lot, but only one line at a time is active for input. Fred codes the basic display section of the program:

```
ERASE
@  1,20 SAY 'FREDS FRIENDLY FISH MARKET'
@  3,20 SAY 'ORDER ITEM ADDITIONS MENU'
@  7,20 SAY 'ORDER NUMBER:     '
@  7,37 SAY ORN
@  9,20 SAY 'COMPANY:'
@  9,37 SAY COMP
@ 10,20 SAY 'LAST NAME:'
@ 10,37 SAY LNAME
@ 11,20 SAY 'FIRST NAME:'
@ 11,37 SAY FNAME
@ 13,15 SAY '#'
@ 13,20 SAY 'QUANTITY'
@ 13,35 SAY 'ITEM NUMBER'
```

```
-------------------------------------------------
:                                               :
:         FRED'S FRIENDLY FISH MARKET           :
:            ORDER ITEM ADDITIONS               :
:                                               :
:                                               :
:      ORDER NUMBER:        ORDRN               :
:                                               :
:      COMPANY:        COMPANY-------------X    :
:      LAST   NAME:  LNAME---------------X      :
:      FIRST NAME:  FNAME----------------X      :
:                                               :
:         #   QUANTITY   ITEM NUMBER            :
:                                               :
:         1      QTY        ITEMN               :
:         2      QTY        ITEMN               :
:         3      QTY        ITEMN               :
:        ...     QTY        ITEMN               :
:        10      QTY        ITEMN               :
:                                               :
-------------------------------------------------
   ADD ITEMS

        ACCESS ORDER FILE
        ACCESS ORDER ITEM FILE
        SET ITEMCOUNT TO 1
        SET QUANTITY TO NOT BLANK
        DO WHILE QUANTITY NOT BLANK
           DISPLAY SCREEN AND EXISTING ITEM NUMBERS
           ENTER QUANTITY AND ITEM NUMBER
           IF QUANTITY NOT BLANK
             VERIFY ITEM NUMBER
             IF FOUND
               THEN
                  RETRIEVE PRICE
                  WRITE RECORD TO ORDER ITEM FILE
                  INCREMENT ITEMCOUNT BY 1
               ELSE
                  WRITE "ITEM NUMBER NOT ON FILE"
             ENDIF
           ENDIF
           IF ITEMCOUNT IS A MULTIPLE OF 10
             THEN REDISPLAY ITEM SCREEN
           ENDIF
        ENDDO
```

Fig. 23-6. The order items additions screen and pseudocode.

```
         SELECT PRIMARY
         USE ORDERITM INDEX ORDERITM
         SELECT SECONDARY
         USE ITEM INDEX ITEM
         STORE T TO MOREORDI
         ERASE
         @  1,20 SAY 'FREDS FRIENDLY FISH MARKET'
         @  3,20 SAY 'ORDER ITEM ADDITIONS MENU'
         @  7,20 SAY 'ORDER NUMBER:        '
         @  7,37 SAY ORN
         @  9,20 SAY 'COMPANY:'
         @  9,37 SAY COMP
         @ 10,20 SAY 'LAST NAME:'
         @ 10,37 SAY LNAME
         @ 11,20 SAY 'FIRST NAME:'
         @ 11,37 SAY FNAME
         @ 13,15 SAY '#'
         @ 13,20 SAY 'QUANTITY'
         @ 13,35 SAY 'ITEM NUMBER'
         STORE 15 TO LINECNT
         STORE 1 TO CNT
         STORE '   ' TO QT
         STORE '     ' TO ITN
         DO WHILE MOREORDI = 'T'
            @ LINECNT,14 SAY CNT USING '99'
            @ LINECNT,22 GET QT PICTURE '###'
            @ LINECNT,38 GET ITN PICTURE '#####'
            READ
            @ 5,1
            IF QT = '     '
               RETURN
             ELSE
               SELECT SECONDARY
               FIND &ITN
               IF # # 0
                 ELSE
                    ? CHR(7)
                    @ 5,15 SAY '*** ITEM NUMBER NOT ON FILE ***'
               ENDIF
            ENDIF
         ENDDO
```

Fig. 23-7. The order additions code.

212

```
STORE S.PRICE TO PRI
SELECT PRIMARY
APPEND BLANK
REPLACE ORDRN WITH VAL(ORN),QTY WITH VAL(QT) ;
   ITEMN WITH VAL(ITN),PRICE WITH PRI
@ 5,20 SAY '  *** ORDER ADDED  *** '
STORE '    ' TO QT
STORE '       ' TO ITN
STORE CNT + 1 TO CNT
STORE LINECNT + 1 TO LINECNT
IF LINECNT = 25
   STORE 15 TO LINECNT
   STORE 15 TO ERASER
   DO WHILE ERASER < 25
     @ ERASER,1
     STORE ERASER + 1 TO ERASER
   ENDDO
ENDIF
```

Fig. 23-8. The order additions code—adding to the database.

```
*************************************
*                                   *
*            3.1.ORDRADIT           *
*          FREDS FISH MARKET        *
*   ORDER ITEM ADDITIONS PROGRAM    *
*            ORDRADIT.PRG           *
*                                   *
*************************************
SELECT PRIMARY
USE ORDERITM INDEX ORDERITM
SELECT SECONDARY
USE ITEM INDEX ITEM
STORE T TO MOREORDI
ERASE
@  1,20 SAY 'FREDS FRIENDLY FISH MARKET'
@  3,20 SAY 'ORDER ITEM ADDITIONS MENU'
@  7,20 SAY 'ORDER NUMBER:      '
@  7,37 SAY ORN
@  9,20 SAY 'COMPANY:'
@  9,37 SAY COMP
@ 10,20 SAY 'LAST NAME:'
@ 10,37 SAY LNAME
@ 11,20 SAY 'FIRST NAME:'
```

```
      @ 11,37 SAY FNAME
      @ 13,15 SAY '#'
      @ 13,20 SAY 'QUANTITY'
      @ 13,35 SAY 'ITEM NUMBER'
      STORE 15 TO LINECNT
      STORE 1 TO CNT
      STORE '   ' TO QT
      STORE '     ' TO ITN
      DO WHILE MOREORDI = 'T'
         @ LINECNT,14 SAY CNT USING '99'
         @ LINECNT,22 GET QT PICTURE '###'
         @ LINECNT,38 GET ITN PICTURE '#####'
         READ
         @ 5,1
         IF QT = '   '
             RETURN
           ELSE
             SELECT SECONDARY
             FIND &ITN
             IF # # 0
                 STORE S.PRICE TO PRI
                 SELECT PRIMARY
                 APPEND BLANK
                 REPLACE ORDRN WITH VAL(ORN),QTY WITH VAL(QT) ;

                    ITEMN WITH VAL(ITN),PRICE WITH PRI
                 @ 5,20 SAY '  *** ORDER ADDED  *** '
                 STORE '   ' TO QT
                 STORE '     ' TO ITN
                 STORE CNT + 1 TO CNT
                 STORE LINECNT + 1 TO LINECNT
                 IF LINECNT = 25
                    STORE 15 TO LINECNT
                    STORE 15 TO ERASER
                    DO WHILE ERASER < 25
                       @ ERASER,1
                       STORE ERASER + 1 TO ERASER
                    ENDDO
                 ENDIF
               ELSE
                 ? CHR(7)
                 @ 5,15 SAY '*** ITEM NUMBER NOT ON FILE ***'
             ENDIF
         ENDIF
      ENDDO
```

Fig. 23-9. The order item additions code—final version.

This section simply displays the main part of the screen. The @ SAY commands produce the screen and set up the headers for the record number, quantity, and item-number fields.

The next section to add is the section that allows entry of the quantity and the item number. Fred writes the following codes:

```
STORE 15 TO LINECNT
STORE 1 TO CNT
STORE '   ' TO QT
STORE '     ' TO ITN
    @ LINECNT,14 SAY CNT USING '99'
    @ LINECNT,22 GET QT PICTURE '###'
    @ LINECNT,38 GET ITN PICTURE '#####'
    READ
```

This section will permit the entry of each quantity and item number. The CNT field is just a number from one to ten that tells you how many records have been entered on each screen.

Next Fred adds the error loops and the verification of the item number, and produces the code shown in Fig. 23-7.

"There is nothing hard here," said Fred. Fred is right, so far. The last section is the toughest. Fred has to code the section to retrieve the price from the item file, and add the record to the order-item file. Fred must also code the section to clear the screen after each set of 10 records. Figure 23-8 shows the resulting code.

This section completes the code for the order-items section. After the item file is accessed and the item number is found, the price must be retrieved. It is retrieved as S.PRICE because both the primary and secondary files have a field called PRICE. After retrieving the price from the item file, the program switches back to the primary file so the data can be entered into the order-item file.

The order is added, and the fields are cleared for another entry. The DO WHILE loop that uses a field called ERASER is used when ten records have been entered. This loop simply clears lines fifteen through twenty-four.

Fred redisplays the final program as shown in Fig. 23-9.

Chapter 24

Producing Reports in a Multifile System

The final chapter in this book will show how Fred produces a report using the order file, the order-item file, the customer file, and the item file. Not all the files are used at once, but in order to produce this report, data is needed from all four files. The program is a good example of the use of multiple files. The complete report is shown in Fig. 24-1.

MULTIPLE FILES

Data comes from all four files to make up this report. The order file is the main driver for this report. It is accessed for a specific order number. This order-record will contain the customer number through which the customer information is retrieved. The order number then will point to the order-item file records where the quantity, item numbers, and prices are found. The descriptions for the items are found in the item file.

A report of this type is actually made up of four separate parts. The first part is the screen that simply allows the alignment of the paper and the confirmation to print. The second part prints the customer information on the top of the report. Part three prints the item records, while the last part prints the total amount and discount.

Fred uses his pseudocode shown in Fig. 24-2 and begins with the first part of the report. The code is shown in Fig. 24-3.

This code forms the basis of the program. Fred starts by clearing the screen and opening the order database. Since that is the main file that will drive the other files, it becomes the primary file.

The main loop is set up, as well as the preliminary screen which will read and search for the order number, and if it is found, will begin the print. Since the ENTER <cr> TO CONTINUE is only a confirmation request, the colons are turned off.

The next section of code, shown in Fig. 24-4, turns on the print and prints everything up to the items themselves:

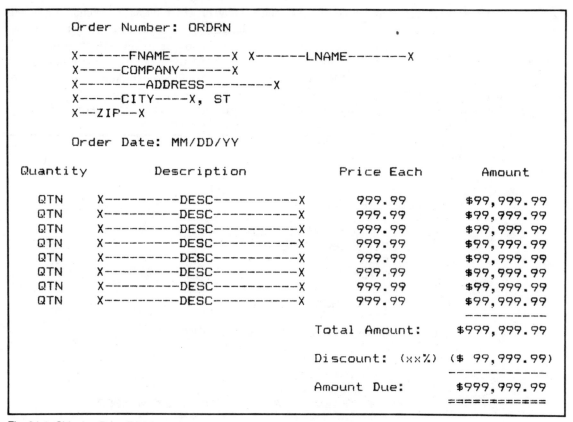

```
       Order Number: ORDRN                        .

       X-------FNAME-------X X------LNAME-------X
       X-----COMPANY------X
       X--------ADDRESS--------X
       X-----CITY----X, ST
       X--ZIP--X

       Order Date: MM/DD/YY

Quantity            Description              Price Each         Amount

   QTN      X---------DESC----------X          999.99        $99,999.99
   QTN      X---------DESC----------X          999.99        $99,999.99
   QTN      X---------DESC----------X          999.99        $99,999.99
   QTN      X---------DESC----------X          999.99        $99,999.99
   QTN      X---------DESC----------X          999.99        $99,999.99
   QTN      X---------DESC----------X          999.99        $99,999.99
   QTN      X---------DESC----------X          999.99        $99,999.99
   QTN      X---------DESC----------X          999.99        $99,999.99
                                                             ----------
                                      Total Amount:        $999,999.99

                                      Discount: (xx%)     ($ 99,999.99)
                                                             ----------
                                      Amount Due:          $999,999.99
                                                           ============
```

Fig. 24-1. Shipping Form Print Layout.

This code contains no loops or IF conditions. It retrieves and prints the customer information, main order information, and headers for the items.

First the output is directed to the printer with the SET FORMAT TO PRINT commands. There is only one other file needed in this section, the customer file. The SELECT SECONDARY command is given, and the customer file opened.

Since the customer number is stored on the order file as a numeric field, and to use it in the FIND command requires it to be a character field, the STR command is used for conversion purposes.

Next the customer number is found. Notice that there is no way to verify the number. How can this be? Good programming will generate good data. There is no way that an illegal customer number can get into the order file because the customer file is checked before the customer number is added to the order file. The customer number has already been verified and there is no reason to verify it again.

With the two necessary files open, you can see that the code simply prints each line after retrieving any information needed from the open customer and order files. After the customer information is retrieved, the primary order file is selected to retrieve the date.

The last print command in this part produces

the headers for the item information. Four @SAY commands take care of these.

The next portion of code, shown in Fig. 24-5, prints any and all items.

This section begins by defining the files needed for this section of the report. The two files needed are the order-item file and the item file. It doesn't matter which file is the primary or secondary file, as long as you reference them correctly.

The next step is to retrieve the first order-item record with the appropriate order number and set the total amount owed bucket, TOTAL, to zero. As long as the value of the original order number you entered is the same as the order number in the

```
PRINT SHIPPING FORMS

        STORE BLANK TO ORDER NUMBER
        DO WHILE ORDER NUMBER NOT BLANK
           DISPLAY SCREEN
           ENTER ORDER NUMBER
           IF ORDER NUMBER NOT BLANK
              ACCESS ORDER FILE
              VERIFY ORDER NUMBER
              IF FOUND
                 THEN
                    PRINT HEADER OF ORDER
                    ACCESS CUSTOMER FILE
                    RETRIEVE CUSTOMER INFORMATION
                    PRINT ORDER INFORMATION
                    ACCESS ORDER ITEM FILE
                    SET TOTAL TO 0
                    DO WHILE MORE RECORDS
                       RETRIEVE QUANTITY AND ITEM NUMBER
                       ACCESS ITEM FILE
                       RETRIEVE DESCRIPTION AND PRICE
                       AMOUNT = QUANTITY X PRICE
                       ADD AMOUNT TO TOTAL
                       PRINT RECORD
                    ENDDO
                    WRITE TOTAL
                    DISCOUNT AMOUNT = DISCOUNT/100 X TOTAL
                    WRITE DISCOUNT
                    SUBTRACT DISCOUNT FROM TOTAL
                    WRITE AMOUNT DUE
                 ELSE
                    WRITE "ORDER NUMBER NOT ON FILE"
              ENDIF
           ENDIF
        ENDDO
```

Fig. 24-2. Order Shipping Forms Pseudocode.

```
ERASE
USE ORDER INDEX ORDER
STORE T TO MOREORDR
STORE '     ' TO ORN
DO WHILE MOREORDR = 'T'
   @ 1,20 SAY 'FREDS FRIENDLY FISH MARKET'
   @ 3,20 SAY 'SHIPPING FORMS PRINT MENU  '
   @ 7,19 SAY 'ORDER NUMBER:    ' GET ORN    PICTURE '#####'
   READ
   @ 5,1
   IF ORN = '     '
       RETURN
     ELSE
       SELECT PRIMARY
       FIND &ORN
       IF # # O  .AND. .NOT. *
           SET COLON OFF
           STORE ' ' TO ANS
           @ 5,1
           @ 5,23 SAY 'ENTER <cr> TO PRINT' GET ANS
           READ
           SET COLON ON
```

Fig. 24-3. The order shipping forms code, part one.

```
SET FORMAT TO PRINT
SELECT SECONDARY
USE CUSTOMER INDEX CUSTOMER
STORE STR(CUSTN,5) TO CSN
FIND &CSN
```

BUSINESS PROGRAMMING USING dBASE II

```
@ 1,25 SAY 'FREDS FRIENDLY FISH MARKET'
@ 3,25 SAY '       SHIPPING FORM         '
@ 6,15 SAY 'Order Number: '
@ 6,29 SAY ORN PICTURE '99999'
@ 8,15 SAY TRIM(FNAME)+' '+LNAME
@ 9,15 SAY COMP
@ 10,15 SAY ADDR
@ 11,15 SAY TRIM(CITY)+', '+ST
@ 12,15 SAY ZIP
STORE DIS TO DISCOUNT
SELECT PRIMARY
@ 14,15 SAY 'Order Date: '
@ 14,28 SAY DATE
@ 16,10 SAY 'Quantity'
@ 16,30 SAY 'Description'
@ 16,50 SAY 'Price Each'
@ 16,70 SAY 'Amount'
```

Fig. 24-4. The order shipping forms code, part two.

```
PRINTING FROM SEVERAL FILES

    STORE 18 TO LINECNT
    SELECT SECONDARY
    USE ORDERITM INDEX ORDERITM
    SELECT PRIMARY
    USE ITEM INDEX ITEM
    SELECT SECONDARY
    FIND &ORN
    STORE 0 TO TOTAL
    DO WHILE VAL(ORN)=S.ORDRN .AND. .NOT. EOF
      IF .NOT. *
        @ LINECNT,13 SAY S.QTY USING '999'
        STORE STR(S.ITEMN,5) TO ITN
        SELECT PRIMARY
        FIND &ITN
        @ LINECNT,25 SAY DESC
        SELECT SECONDARY
        @ LINECNT,52 SAY S.PRICE USING '99.99'
        @ LINECNT,67 SAY S.QTY*S.PRICE USING '$99,999.99'
        STORE TOTAL + S.QTY*S.PRICE TO TOTAL
        STORE LINECNT+1 TO LINECNT
      ENDIF
      SKIP
    ENDDO
```

Fig. 24-5. The order shipping forms code, part three.

order-item file, this loop will be processed for more items. The end-of-file marker is also checked in case the order number is the last one in the file. Another check inside the loop is IF .NOT. *. If the record has been marked for deletion and the file has not yet been packed, you don't want the record to appear.

Inside the loop, the quantity and the item number are printed, the item file is searched for the item; and the description is printed. Finally the price is printed, and the amount owed is calculated using S.QTY*S.PRICE, printed, and then added to the total for the order. The line STORE TOTAL + S.QTY*S.PRICE TO TOTAL means to take the previous total, add the new amount to it, and store it back in the total bucket. Finally the linecount is

increased by one so the next line prints below the present one.

At the end of the loop is the SKIP command, which is used to advance to the next record.

CALCULATING AND TOTALING

The final section will print the total, calculate and print the discount, and print the total amount due. The code is shown in Fig. 24-6.

Fred is almost done. He has been coding this procedure for almost a week. He starts by underlining the last column. "Just like the accounts," he mumbles. He has already calculated the total. He prints it with the USING specification and adds dollar signs and commas to the number. Fred then prints the discount line using the formula DIS-

220

```
@ LINECNT,68 SAY '----------'
@ LINECNT+1,50 SAY 'Total Amount:'
@ LINECNT+1,66 SAY TOTAL USING '$999,999.99'
@ LINECNT+3,50 SAY 'Discount:('
@ LINECNT+3,60 SAY DISCOUNT USING '99'
@ LINECNT+3,62 SAY '%)'
@ LINECNT+3,65 SAY '('
STORE TOTAL*(DISCOUNT/100) TO DISC
@ LINECNT+3,66 SAY DISC USING '$999,999.99'
@ LINECNT+3,77 SAY ')'
@ LINECNT+4,66 SAY '------------'
@ LINECNT+5,50 SAY 'Amount Due: '
@ LINECNT+5,66 SAY TOTAL-DISC USING '$999,999.99'
@ LINECNT+6,66 SAY '============'
@ LINECNT+7,1

SELECT PRIMARY
USE ORDER INDEX ORDER
SET FORMAT TO SCREEN
ERASE
STORE '     ' TO ORN
```

Fig. 24-6. The order shipping forms code, part four.

```
*************************************
*                                   *
*              3.6                  *
*         FREDS FISH MARKET         *
*     ORDER SHIPPING FORMS PRINT    *
*           ORDRSHP.PRG             *
*                                   *
*************************************
      ERASE
      USE ORDER INDEX ORDER
      STORE T TO MOREORDR
      STORE '     ' TO ORN

DO WHILE MOREORDR = 'T'
   @ 1,20 SAY 'FREDS FRIENDLY FISH MARKET'
   @ 3,20 SAY 'SHIPPING FORMS PRINT MENU '
   @ 7,19 SAY 'ORDER NUMBER:    ' GET ORN    PICTURE '#####'
   READ
   @ 5,1
   IF ORN = '     '
      ERASE
      SELECT SECONDARY
```

```
                    USE
                  SELECT PRIMARY
                  USE
                  RETURN
                ELSE
                  SELECT PRIMARY
                  FIND &ORN
                  IF # # 0  .AND. .NOT. *
                      SET COLON OFF
                      STORE ' ' TO ANS
                      @ 5,1
                      @ 5,23 SAY 'ENTER <cr> TO PRINT' GET ANS
                      READ
                      SET COLON ON
                      SET FORMAT TO PRINT
                      SELECT SECONDARY
                      USE CUSTOMER INDEX CUSTOMER
                      STORE STR(CUSTN,5) TO CSN
                      FIND &CSN
                      @ 1,25 SAY 'FREDS FRIENDLY FISH MARKET'
                      @ 3,25 SAY '      SHIPPING FORM      '
                      @ 6,15 SAY 'Order Number: '
                      @ 6,29 SAY ORN PICTURE '99999'
                      @ 8,15 SAY TRIM(FNAME)+' '+LNAME
                      @ 9,15 SAY COMP
                      @ 10,15 SAY ADDR
                      @ 11,15 SAY TRIM(CITY)+', '+ST
                      @ 12,15 SAY ZIP
                      STORE DIS TO DISCOUNT
                      SELECT PRIMARY
                      @ 14,15 SAY 'Order Date: '
                      @ 14,28 SAY DATE
                      @ 16,10 SAY 'Quantity'
                      @ 16,30 SAY 'Description'
                      @ 16,50 SAY 'Price Each'
                      @ 16,70 SAY 'Amount'
                      STORE 18 TO LINECNT
                      SELECT SECONDARY
                      USE ORDERITM INDEX ORDERITM
                      SELECT PRIMARY
                      USE ITEM INDEX ITEM
                      SELECT SECONDARY
                      FIND &ORN
                      STORE 0 TO TOTAL
                      DO WHILE VAL(ORN)=S.ORDRN .AND. .NOT. EOF
                         IF .NOT. *
                            @ LINECNT,13 SAY S.QTY USING '999'
                            STORE STR(S.ITEMN,5) TO ITN
                            SELECT PRIMARY
                         FIND &ITN
                         @ LINECNT,25 SAY DESC
                         SELECT SECONDARY
                         @ LINECNT,52 SAY S.PRICE USING '99.99'
                         @ LINECNT,67 SAY S.QTY*S.PRICE USING '$99,999.99'
                         STORE TOTAL + S.QTY*S.PRICE TO TOTAL
```

```
                 STORE LINECNT+1 TO LINECNT
          ENDIF
          SKIP
      ENDDO
      @ LINECNT,68 SAY '----------'
      @ LINECNT+1,50 SAY 'Total Amount:'
      @ LINECNT+1,66 SAY TOTAL USING '$999,999.99'
      @ LINECNT+3,50 SAY 'Discount:('
      @ LINECNT+3,60 SAY DISCOUNT USING '99'
      @ LINECNT+3,62 SAY '%)'
      @ LINECNT+3,65 SAY '('
      STORE TOTAL*(DISCOUNT/100) TO DISC
      @ LINECNT+3,66 SAY DISC USING '$999,999.99'
      @ LINECNT+3,77 SAY ')'
      @ LINECNT+4,66 SAY '------------'
      @ LINECNT+5,50 SAY 'Amount Due: '
      @ LINECNT+5,66 SAY TOTAL-DISC USING '$999,999.99'
      @ LINECNT+6,66 SAY '============'
      @ LINECNT+7,1
      SELECT PRIMARY
      USE ORDER INDEX ORDER
      SET FORMAT TO SCREEN
      ERASE
      STORE '       ' TO ORN
    ELSE
      ? CHR(7)
      ERASE
      @ 5,17 SAY '*** ORDER NUMBER NOT FOUND ***'
    ENDIF
  ENDIF
ENDDO
```

Fig. 24-7. The order shipping forms code, final version.

COUNT/100. This is used because the discount is stored as a whole number. Twelve really means twelve percent or .12. The number twelve must be divided by one-hundred before it is multiplied by the amount.

Finally the discount is subtracted from the total to yield the amount due. Fred even remembers the last line and adds the "@ LINECNT+7,1" command.

Fred now puts it all together and looks at the final program, which is shown in Fig. 24-7.

SUMMARY

In this book, you have been given the tools to produce basic programs using dBASE II. (That's basic as in simple, not the language BASIC.) Whether you are a novice or a seasoned professional, this book has shown you tricks and techniques for contemporary program design for the eighties.

You may wish to review each section as you begin to code in dBASE II. A complete list of the designs for the CUSTOMER and ORDER systems are found in Appendix A. Complete listings of the programs can be found in Appendix B. Good luck in all your data processing endeavors, and . . . may the Fred be with you.

Appendix A
The System Design

This appendix shows all the steps Fred followed in designing his system.

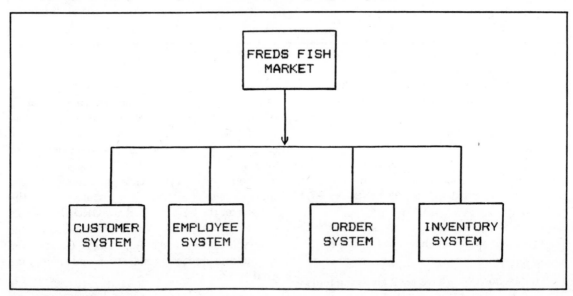

The main system hierarchy.

```
 FRED'S FRIENDLY FISH MARKET
        MAIN MENU



 ENTER SELECTION ===>  __

    1 - CUSTOMER SYSTEM
    2 - EMPLOYEE SYSTEM
    3 - ORDER SYSTEM
    4 - INVENTORY SYSTEM


    X - EXIT SYSTEM
```

The main system menu.

```
MAIN MENU

 SET EXIT TO "N"
 DO WHILE NOT EXIT
   READ SELECTION
   CASE
     WHEN SELECTION = "1"
        PERFORM CUSTOMER SYSTEM
     WHEN SELECTION = "2"
        PERFORM EMPLOYEE SYSTEM
     WHEN SELECTION = "3"
        PERFORM ORDER SYSTEM
     WHEN SELECTION = "4"
        PERFORM INVENTORY SYSTEM
     WHEN SELECTION = "X"
        SET EXIT TO "Y"
     OTHERWISE
        WRITE "INVALID OPTION" ENDCASE
   ENDCASE
 ENDDO
```

The main system pseudocode.

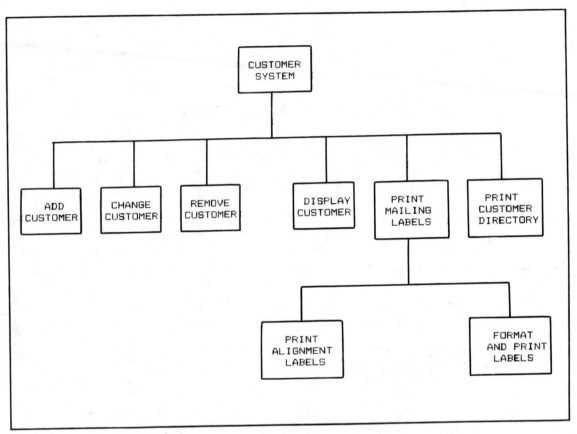

The customer system hierarchy chart.

The customer system menu screen.

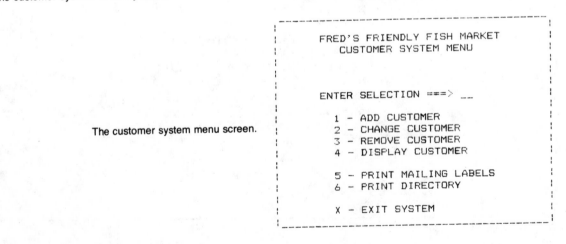

```
-------------------------------------------------
|                                               |
|          FRED'S FRIENDLY FISH MARKET          |
|            CUSTOMER SYSTEM MENU               |
|                                               |
|                                               |
|                                               |
|       ENTER SELECTION ===>  __                |
|                                               |
|          1 - ADD CUSTOMER                     |
|          2 - CHANGE CUSTOMER                  |
|          3 - REMOVE CUSTOMER                  |
|          4 - DISPLAY CUSTOMER                 |
|                                               |
|          5 - PRINT MAILING LABELS             |
|          6 - PRINT DIRECTORY                  |
|                                               |
|          X - EXIT SYSTEM                      |
|                                               |
-------------------------------------------------
```

```
SET EXIT TO "N"
DISPLAY MENU SCREEN
DOWHILE EXIT = "N"
  READ OPTION
  CASE
    WHEN OPTION = 1 PERFORM "ADD CUSTOMER"
    WHEN OPTION = 2 PERFORM "CHANGE CUSTOMER"
    WHEN OPTION = 3 PERFORM "REMOVE CUSTOMER"
    WHEN OPTION = 4 PERFORM "DISPLAY CUSTOMER"
    WHEN OPTION = 5 PERFORM "PRINT MAILING LABELS"
    WHEN OPTION = 6 PERFORM "PRINT DIRECTORY"
    WHEN OPTION = X SET EXIT TO "Y"
    OTHERWISE WRITE "INVALID OPTION"
  ENDCASE
ENDDO
```

The customer system menu pseudocode.

The customer additions screen.

```
FRED'S FRIENDLY FISH MARKET
        CUSTOMER ADDITIONS


CUSTOMER NUMBER: CUSTN

COMPANY:     COMPANY------------X
LAST NAME:   LNAME--------------X
FIRST NAME:  FNAME--------------X

ADDRESS: ADDRESS-----------------X
CITY:    CITY---------X

STATE: ST    ZIP: ZIP-----X

PHONE NUMBER: PHONE-------X

DISCOUNT: DS
```

```
ADD A CUSTOMER

   ACCESS CUSTOMER FILE
   SET CUSTOMER NUMBER TO NOT BLANK
   DO WHILE CUSTOMER NUMBER NOT BLANK
      DISPLAY SCREEN
      ENTER DATA
      VERIFY CUSTOMER NUMBER
      IF NEW NUMBER
         THEN
            ADD CUSTOMER DATA
            CLEAR DATA FIELDS
         ELSE
            WRITE "NUMBER ALREADY ON FILE"
      ENDIF
   ENDDO
```

The customer additions pseudocode.

```
           FRED'S FRIENDLY FISH MARKET
                CUSTOMER CHANGES
         CUSTOMER NUMBER: CUSTN
```

The customer change preliminary screen.

```
           FRED'S FRIENDLY FISH MARKET
                CUSTOMER CHANGES

         CUSTOMER NUMBER: CUSTN

         COMPANY:     COMPANY-------------X
         LAST NAME:   LNAME---------------X
         FIRST NAME:  FNAME---------------X

         ADDRESS: ADDRESS-----------------X
         CITY:      CITY----------X

         STATE: ST    ZIP: ZIP------X

         PHONE NUMBER: PHONE-------X

         DISCOUNT: DS
```

The customer change data entry screen.

228

```
CHANGE A CUSTOMER

        ACCESS CUSTOMER FILE
        SET CUSTOMER NUMBER TO NOT BLANK
        DO WHILE CUSTOMER NUMBER NOT BLANK
          DISPLAY SCREEN
          ENTER CUSTOMER NUMBER
          VERIFY CUSTOMER NUMBER
          IF FOUND
            THEN
               RETRIEVE CUSTOMER DATA
               CHANGE DESIRED FIELDS
               UPDATE RECORD
               CLEAR DATA FIELDS
            ELSE
               WRITE "NUMBER NOT ON FILE"
          ENDIF
        ENDDO
```

The customer change pseudocode.

The customer removal screen.

```
--------------------------------------------------
|                                                |
|        FRED'S FRIENDLY FISH MARKET             |
|              CUSTOMER DELETION                 |
|                                                |
|   ENTER "D" TO CONFIRM DELETE ===> __          |
|                                                |
|     CUSTOMER NUMBER: CUSTN                      |
|                                                |
|     COMPANY:     COMPANY-------------X          |
|     LAST NAME:   LNAME---------------X          |
|     FIRST NAME:  FNAME---------------X          |
|                                                |
|     ADDRESS: ADDRESS-----------------X          |
|     CITY:     CITY----------X                  |
|                                                |
|     STATE: ST     ZIP: ZIP-----X               |
|                                                |
|     PHONE NUMBER: PHONE-------X                |
|                                                |
|     DISCOUNT: DS                               |
|                                                |
--------------------------------------------------
```

```
                ACCESS CUSTOMER FILE
                SET CUSTOMER NUMBER TO NOT BLANK
                DO WHILE CUSTOMER NUMBER NOT BLANK
                  DISPLAY SCREEN
                  ENTER CUSTOMER NUMBER
                  VERIFY CUSTOMER NUMBER
                  IF FOUND
                    THEN
                        RETRIEVE CUSTOMER DATA
                        ENTER DELETE CONFIRMATION
                        IF CONFIRM = "D"
                          THEN
                              DELETE RECORD
                              CLEAR DATA FIELDS
                        ENDIF
                    ELSE
                        WRITE "NUMBER NOT ON FILE"
                  ENDIF
                ENDDO
```

The customer removal pseudocode.

The customer display screen.

```
--------------------------------------------------
|                                                |
|         FRED'S FRIENDLY FISH MARKET            |
|             CUSTOMER DISPLAY                   |
|                                                |
|                                                |
|                                                |
|     CUSTOMER NUMBER: CUSTN                      |
|                                                |
|     COMPANY:    COMPANY-------------X           |
|     LAST NAME:  LNAME---------------X           |
|     FIRST NAME: FNAME---------------X           |
|                                                |
|     ADDRESS: ADDRESS------------------X         |
|     CITY:    CITY----------X                    |
|                                                |
|     STATE: ST   ZIP: ZIP-----X                  |
|                                                |
|     PHONE NUMBER: PHONE-------X                 |
|                                                |
|     DISCOUNT: DS                               |
|                                                |
--------------------------------------------------
```

```
ACCESS CUSTOMER FILE
SET CUSTOMER NUMBER TO NOT BLANK
DO WHILE CUSTOMER NUMBER NOT BLANK
   DISPLAY SCREEN
   ENTER CUSTOMER NUMBER
   VERIFY CUSTOMER NUMBER
   IF FOUND
     THEN
        RETRIEVE CUSTOMER DATA
        DISPLAY INFORMATION
     ELSE
        WRITE "CUSTOMER NUMBER NOT ON FILE"
   ENDIF
ENDDO
```

The customer display pseudocode.

```
         FRED'S FRIENDLY FISH MARKET
             MAILING LABEL PRINT



         ENTER "A" FOR ALIGNMENT PRINT,
               "X" TO EXIT PRINT,
          OR <cr> TO BEGIN PRINT

               ===> __
```

The customer mailing label print.

```
X------COMPANY------X
X------FNAME-------X X------LNAME-------X
X------ADDRESS---------X
X----CITY-----X, ST X--ZIP--X
```

The customer mailing label print layout.

```
                    PRINT MAILING LABELS
                STORE " " TO CHOICE
                DO WHILE CHOICE NOT "X"
                  DISPLAY SCREEN
                  READ CHOICE
                  IF CHOICE = "X"
                    THEN EXIT
                  ENDIF
                  IF CHOICE = "A"
                    THEN PERFORM "ALIGNMENT PRINT"
                  ENDIF
                  IF CHOICE = "<cr>"
                    ACCESS CUSTOMER FILE
                    READ A CUSTOMER RECORD
                    INITIALIZE RECORD COUNTER
                    DOWHILE MORE RECORDS
                      PERFORM "FORMAT FOR PRINT"
                      IF LABEL COUNTER = 3
                        THEN
                          PRINT A ROW OF LABELS
                          RESET LABEL COUNTER
                      ENDIF
                      READ NEXT RECORD
                    ENDDO
                    IF LABEL COUNTER # O
                      THEN PRINT PARTIAL ROW
                    ENDIF
                  ENDIF
                ENDDO
```

The customer mailing label print pseudocode.

```
    ALIGNMENT PRINT
        PRINT ONE ROW OF LABELS WITH X'S FILLING EVERY FIELD
        ADVANCE TO NEXT LABEL
```

The customer mailing label alignment pseudocode.

```
            FORMAT FOR LABELS
            ADD 1 TO LABEL COUNTER
            MOVE CUSTOMER FIELDS TO LABEL 1, 2, OR 3,
                DEPENDING ON LABEL COUNTER
```

The customer mailing label format pseudocode.

The customer directory print screen.

```
-----------------------------------------------------------
:                                                         :
:          FRED'S FRIENDLY FISH MARKET                    :
:          CUSTOMER DIRECTORY PRINT                       :
:                                                         :
:          ENTER <cr> TO BEGIN PRINT                      :
:          OR "X" TO EXIT PRINT                           :
:                                                         :
:          ====> ___                                      :
:                                                         :
-----------------------------------------------------------
```

```
Customer Number: CUSTN

X------COMPANY------X
X------LNAME-------X, X------FNAME-------X
                      X------ADDRESS----------X
                      X----CITY-----X, ST X--ZIP--X
                      Phone: (AAA)NNN-NNNN
                      Discount: XX%
```

The customer directory print layout.

```
PRINT MAILING LIST
    READ CHOICE
    IF CHOICE = 'X'
       THEN EXIT
    ENDIF
    IF CHOICE = "<cr>"
       THEN
          ACCESS CUSTOMER FILE
          READ CUSTOMER RECORD
          SET LINECOUNT TO 1
          DO WHILE MORE RECORDS
             IF LINECOUNT = 1 OR = 56
                THEN
                   PRINT HEADER
                   SET LINECOUNT TO 4
             ENDIF
             PRINT DIRECTORY ENTRY
             UPDATE LINECOUNT
             READ NEXT RECORD
          ENDDO
    ENDIF
```

The customer directory print pseudocode.

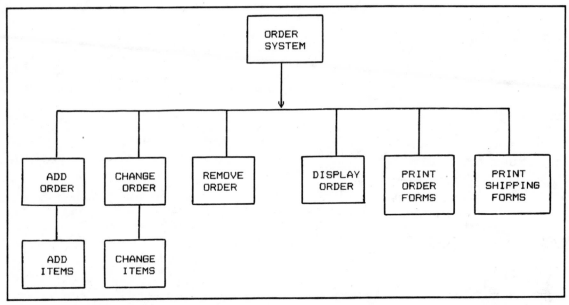

The order system hierarchy chart.

The order system menu screen.

```
FRED'S FRIENDLY FISH MARKET
      ORDER SYSTEM MENU



ENTER SELECTION ===> __

  1 - ADD ORDERS
  2 - CHANGE ORDER
  3 - REMOVE ORDER
  4 - DISPLAY ORDER

  5 - PRINT ORDER FORMS
  6 - PRINT SHIPPING FORMS

  X - EXIT SYSTEM
```

```
SET EXIT TO "N"
DISPLAY MENU SCREEN
DOWHILE EXIT = "N"
   READ OPTION
   CASE
      WHEN OPTION = 1 PERFORM "ADD ORDERS"
      WHEN OPTION = 2 PERFORM "CHANGE ORDER"
```

```
          WHEN OPTION = 3 PERFORM "REMOVE ORDER"
          WHEN OPTION = 4 PERFORM "DISPLAY ORDER"
          WHEN OPTION = 5 PERFORM "PRINT ORDER FORMS"
          WHEN OPTION = 6 PERFORM "PRINT SHIPPING FORMS"
          WHEN OPTION = X SET EXIT TO "Y"
          OTHERWISE WRITE "INVALID OPTION"
       ENDCASE
   ENDDO
```

The order system menu pseudocode.

The order additions preliminary screen.

```
 -------------------------------------------------
 !                                               !
 !           FRED'S FRIENDLY FISH MARKET         !
 !                ORDER ADDITIONS                !
 !                                               !
 !                                               !
 !       ORDER NUMBER:        ORDRN              !
 !                                               !
 !       CUSTOMER NUMBER:    CUSTN               !
 !                                               !
 --------------------------------------------------
```

The order additions screen.

```
 -------------------------------------------------
 !                                               !
 !           FRED'S FRIENDLY FISH MARKET         !
 !                ORDER ADDITIONS                !
 !                                               !
 !                                               !
 !       ORDER NUMBER:        ORDRN              !
 !                                               !
 !       CUSTOMER NUMBER:    CUSTN               !
 !                                               !
 !       COMPANY:      COMPANY------------X      !
 !       LAST  NAME: LNAME--------------X        !
 !       FIRST NAME: FNAME--------------X        !
 !                                               !
 !                                               !
 !       DATE ORDERED: MM/DD/YY                  !
 --------------------------------------------------
```

```
---------------------------------------------------
|                                                 |
|      FRED'S FRIENDLY FISH MARKET                |
|          ORDER ITEM ADDITIONS                   |
|   ORDER NUMBER:     ORDRN                        |
|                                                 |
|   COMPANY:      COMPANY--------------X           |
|   LAST  NAME: LNAME---------------X              |
|   FIRST NAME: FNAME--------------X               |
|                                                 |
|    #   QUANTITY   ITEM NUMBER                    |
|    1    QTY        ITEMN                         |
|    2    QTY        ITEMN                         |
|    3    QTY        ITEMN                         |
|   ...   QTY        ITEMN                         |
|    10   QTY        ITEMN                         |
|                                                 |
---------------------------------------------------
```

The order items additions screen.

```
ADD AN ORDER
    ACCESS ORDER FILE
    SET ORDER NUMBER TO NOT BLANK
    DO WHILE ORDER NUMBER NOT BLANK
       DISPLAY SCREEN
       ENTER ORDER NUMBER AND CUSTOMER NUMBER
       IF ORDER NUMBER NOT BLANK
          VERIFY ORDER NUMBER
          IF NEW NUMBER
             THEN
                 ACCESS CUSTOMER FILE
                 VERIFY CUSTOMER NUMBER
                 IF FOUND
                    THEN
                        DISPLAY CUSTOMER DATA
                        ENTER DATE FIELD
                        ADD TO ORDER FILE
                        PERFORM "ADD ITEMS"
                    ELSE
                        WRITE "CUSTOMER NUMBER NOT FOUND"
                 ENDIF
             ELSE
                 WRITE "ORDER NUMBER ALREADY ON FILE"
          ENDIF
       ENDIF
    ENDDO
```

The order additions pseudocode.

```
ADD ITEMS

    ACCESS ORDER FILE
    ACCESS ORDER ITEM FILE
    SET ITEMCOUNT TO 1
    SET QUANTITY TO NOT BLANK
    DO WHILE QUANTITY NOT BLANK
       DISPLAY SCREEN AND EXISTING ITEM NUMBERS
       ENTER QUANTITY AND ITEM NUMBER
       IF QUANTITY NOT BLANK
         VERIFY ITEM NUMBER
         IF FOUND
           THEN
              RETRIEVE PRICE
              WRITE RECORD TO ORDER ITEM FILE
              INCREMENT ITEMCOUNT BY 1
           ELSE
              WRITE "ITEM NUMBER NOT ON FILE"
         ENDIF
       ENDIF
       IF ITEMCOUNT IS A MULTIPLE OF 10
         THEN REDISPLAY ITEM SCREEN
       ENDIF
    ENDDO
```

The order item additions pseudocode.

The order changes preliminary screen.

```
-----------------------------------------------------
|                                                   |
|          FRED'S FRIENDLY FISH MARKET              |
|                 ORDER CHANGES                     |
|                                                   |
|                                                   |
|       ORDER NUMBER:        ORDRN                   |
|                                                   |
|                                                   |
-----------------------------------------------------
```

```
+-----------------------------------------------+
|                                               |
|      FRED'S FRIENDLY FISH MARKET              |
|            ORDER CHANGES                      |
|                                               |
|      CHANGE ITEMS? ===> __                    |
|    ENTER <cr> TO CONTINUE, X TO ABORT         |
|                                               |
|    ORDER NUMBER:      ORDRN                    |
|                                               |
|    CUSTOMER NUMBER:   CUSTN                    |
|                                               |
|    COMPANY:     COMPANY-------------X          |
|    LAST  NAME: LNAME----------------X          |
|    FIRST NAME: FNAME----------------X          |
|                                               |
|    DATE ORDERED: MM/DD/YY                     |
|                                               |
+-----------------------------------------------+
```

The order changes screen.

```
CHANGE AN ORDER

    ACCESS ORDER FILE
    SET ORDER NUMBER TO NOT BLANK
    DO WHILE ORDER NUMBER NOT BLANK
      DISPLAY SCREEN
      ENTER ORDER NUMBER
      IF ORDER NUMBER NOT BLANK
        VERIFY ORDER NUMBER
        IF FOUND
          THEN
            ACCESS CUSTOMER FILE
            RETRIEVE CUSTOMER INFORMATION
            DISPLAY "CHANGE ITEMS" MESSAGE
            READ CHOICE
            IF CHOICE NOT X
              THEN PERFORM "CHANGE ITEMS MENU"
            ENDIF
          ELSE WRITE "ORDER NUMBER NOT FOUND"
        ENDIF
      ENDIF
    ENDDO
```

The order changes pseudocode.

```
---------------------------------------------------
|                                                 |
|       FRED'S FRIENDLY FISH MARKET               |
|           ORDER ITEM CHANGES                    |
|                                                 |
|       ENTER SELECTION ===>  __                  |
|       C/CHANGE,S/SCROLL,X/EXIT                  |
|                                                 |
|    ORDER NUMBER:      ORDRN                      |
|                                                 |
|    COMPANY:      COMPANY-------------X           |
|    LAST   NAME:  LNAME---------------X           |
|    FIRST  NAME:  FNAME---------------X           |
|                                                 |
|       #   QUANTITY   ITEM NUMBER                 |
|                                                 |
|       1    QTY        ITEMN                      |
|       2    QTY        ITEMN                      |
|       3    QTY        ITEMN                      |
|      ...   QTY        ITEMN                      |
|      10    QTY        ITEMN                      |
|                                                 |
---------------------------------------------------
```

The first order items change screen.

The second order items change screen.

```
---------------------------------------------------
|                                                 |
|       FRED'S FRIENDLY FISH MARKET               |
|           ORDER ITEM CHANGES                    |
|                                                 |
|       RECORD NUMBER ==>  __                      |
|     ENTER RECORD NUMBER TO BE CHANGED           |
|                                                 |
|     ORDER NUMBER:      ORDRN                     |
|                                                 |
|     COMPANY:      COMPANY-------------X          |
|     LAST   NAME:  LNAME---------------X          |
|     FIRST  NAME:  FNAME---------------X          |
|                                                 |
|        #   QUANTITY   ITEM NUMBER               |
|                                                 |
|        1    QTY        ITEMN                     |
|        2    QTY        ITEMN                     |
|        3    QTY        ITEMN                     |
|       ...   QTY        ITEMN                     |
|       10    QTY        ITEMN                     |
|                                                 |
---------------------------------------------------
```

239

```
----------------------------------------------
|                                              |
|        FRED'S FRIENDLY FISH MARKET           |
|           ORDER ITEM CHANGES                 |
|                                              |
|    QUANTITY: QTY   ITEM NUMBER: ITEMN        |
|            ENTER CHANGES                      |
|                                              |
|    ORDER NUMBER:        ORDRN                 |
|                                              |
|    COMPANY:       COMPANY------------X        |
|    LAST   NAME: LNAME--------------X          |
|    FIRST  NAME: FNAME--------------X          |
|                                              |
|     #   QUANTITY   ITEM NUMBER               |
|                                              |
|     1    QTY         ITEMN                   |
|     2    QTY         ITEMN                   |
|     3    QTY         ITEMN                   |
|    ...   QTY         ITEMN                    |
|    10    QTY         ITEMN                    |
|                                              |
----------------------------------------------
```

The third order items change screen.

The order items scroll screen.

```
----------------------------------------------------
|                                                    |
|          FRED'S FRIENDLY FISH MARKET               |
|             ORDER ITEM CHANGES                     |
|                                                    |
|        RECORD NUMBER ==>  __                        |
|      ENTER RECORD NUMBER TO BE CHANGED             |
|                                                    |
|      ORDER NUMBER:        ORDRN                     |
|                                                    |
|      COMPANY:       COMPANY------------X            |
|      LAST   NAME: LNAME--------------X              |
|      FIRST  NAME: FNAME--------------X              |
|                                                    |
|       #   QUANTITY   ITEM NUMBER                   |
|                                                    |
|      11    QTY         ITEMN                       |
|      12    QTY         ITEMN                       |
|      13    QTY         ITEMN                       |
|     ...    QTY         ITEMN                        |
|      20    QTY         ITEMN                        |
|                                                    |
----------------------------------------------------
```

```
CHANGE ITEMS

 SET EXIT TO 'N'
 DISPLAY MENU SCREEN
 DOWHILE EXIT = 'N'
    DISPLAY ITEMS
    DISPLAY SELECTION
    READ SELECTION
    CASE
      WHEN SELECTION = 'X'
         SET EXIT TO 'Y'
      WHEN SELECTION = 'C'
         ACCESS ORDER ITEM FILE
         SET RECORD NUMBER TO NOT BLANK
         SET SCROLL COUNTER TO 10
         DO WHILE RECORD NUMBER NOT BLANK
            DISPLAY SCREEN
            ENTER RECORD NUMBER
            IF RECORD NUMBER NOT BLANK
              THEN
                 VERIFY RECORD NUMBER IN THE 10 DISPLAYED
                 IF IN THE 10
                   THEN
                      RETRIEVE RECORD
                      DISPLAY QTY AND ITEMN
                      IF BLANK
                        THEN
                           DISPLAY ADD MESSAGE
                      ENDIF
                      ENTER CHANGES
                      IF QTY AND ITEMN NOT BLANK
                        THEN                            /* ADD RECORD */
                           IF OLD QUANTITY BLANK
                             THEN
                                VERIFY ITEM NUMBER
                                IF FOUND
                                  THEN
                                     RETRIEVE PRICE
                                     WRITE RECORD TO ORDER ITEM FILE
                                  ELSE
                                     WRITE "ITEM NUMBER NOT ON FILE"
                                ENDIF
                           ENDIF
                           IF QTY OR ITEM NUMBER DIFFERENT THEN ORIGINAL
```

```
                    THEN                              /* DELETE RECORD */
                      IF QTY = O
                        THEN
                          REMOVE RECORD FROM ORDER ITEM FILE
                        ELSE                          /* CHANGE RECORD */
                          VERIFY ITEM NUMBER
                          IF FOUND
                            THEN
                              RETRIEVE PRICE
                              WRITE RECORD TO ORDER ITEM FILE
                            ELSE
                              WRITE "ITEM NUMBER NOT ON FILE"
                          ENDIF
                      ENDIF
                  ENDIF
                ENDIF
              ELSE
                WRITE "RECORD NUMBER NOT ON DISPLAY"
            ENDIF
      ENDIF
ENDDO

    WHEN SELECTION = 'S'
      ADD 10 TO SCROLL COUNTER
  ENDCASE
ENDDO
```

The order item changes pseudocode.

The preliminary order removal screen.

```
-------------------------------------------------------
:                                                     :
:           FRED'S FRIENDLY FISH MARKET               :
:               ORDER REMOVAL                         :
:                                                     :
:                                                     :
:        ORDER NUMBER:       ORDRN                    :
:                                                     :
:                                                     :
-------------------------------------------------------
```

```
 _____
|                                        |
|       FRED'S FRIENDLY FISH MARKET       |
|             ORDER REMOVAL               |
|                                        |
|   ENTER D TO CONFIRM DELETE ==> __      |
|                                        |
|    ORDER NUMBER:      ORDRN             |
|                                        |
|                                        |
|    COMPANY:      COMPANY------------X   |
|    LAST  NAME: LNAME--------------X     |
|    FIRST NAME: FNAME--------------X     |
|                                        |
|    DATE ORDERED: MM/DD/YY               |
|                                        |
|       #    QUANTITY   ITEM NUMBER       |
|       1      QTY         ITEMN          |
|       2      QTY         ITEMN          |
|       3      QTY         ITEMN          |
|      ...     QTY         ITEMN          |
|      10      QTY         ITEMN          |
|                                        |
|_____|
```

The order removal screen.

```
                REMOVE ORDERS

                    ACCESS ORDER FILE
                    SET ORDER NUMBER TO NOT BLANK
                    DO WHILE ORDER NUMBER NOT BLANK
                       DISPLAY SCREEN
                       ENTER ORDER NUMBER
                       IF ORDER NUMBER NOT BLANK
                         VERIFY ORDER NUMBER
                         IF FOUND
                           THEN
                               RETRIEVE ORDER
                               ACCESS CUSTOMER FILE
                               RETRIEVE CUSTOMER INFORMATION
                               DISPLAY ORDER
                               ACCESS ORDER ITEMS FILE
                               DISPLAY 1ST 10 ITEMS
                               ENTER DELETE CONFITMATION
                               IF CONFIRM = D
                                 THEN
                                     DELETE MAIN ORDER RECORD
                                     DELETE ALL ITEM RECORDS
                               ENDIF
                           ELSE
                               WRITE "ORDER NOT ON FILE"
                         ENDIF
                       ENDIF
                    ENDDO
```

The order removal pseudocode.

```
,-------------------------------------------.
:                                           :
:      FRED'S FRIENDLY FISH MARKET          :
:           ORDER DISPLAY                   :
:                                           :
:                                           :
:                                           :
:      ORDER NUMBER:      ORDRN             :
:                                           :
:                                           :
:                                           :
`-------------------------------------------'
```

The preliminary order display screen.

```
,---------------------------------------------------.
:                                                   :
:         FRED'S FRIENDLY FISH MARKET               :
:              ORDER DISPLAY                        :
:                                                   :
:           ENTER <cr> TO CONTINUE                  :
:                                                   :
:                                                   :
:      ORDER NUMBER:       ORDRN                    :
:                                                   :
:      CUSTOMER NUMBER:   CUSTN                     :
:                                                   :
:      COMPANY:       COMPANY-------------X         :
:      LAST   NAME: LNAME---------------X           :
:      FIRST NAME: FNAME----------------X           :
:                                                   :
:      DATE ORDERED: MM/DD/YY                        :
:                                                   :
:                                                   :
:         #   QUANTITY   ITEM NUMBER                :
:                                                   :
:         1     QTY         ITEMN                   :
:         2     QTY         ITEMN                   :
:         3     QTY         ITEMN                   :
:        ...    QTY         ITEMN                   :
:        10     QTY         ITEMN                   :
`---------------------------------------------------'
```

The order display screen.

244

```
DISPLAY ORDERS

    ACCESS ORDER FILE
    SET ORDER NUMBER TO NOT BLANK
    DO WHILE ORDER NUMBER NOT BLANK
       DISPLAY SCREEN
       ENTER ORDER NUMBER
       IF ORDER NUMBER NOT BLANK
          VERIFY ORDER NUMBER
          IF FOUND
             THEN
                RETRIEVE ORDER
                ACCESS CUSTOMER FILE
                RETRIEVE CUSTOMER INFORMATION
                DISPLAY ORDER
                ACCESS ITEM FILE
                DO WHILE MORE RECORDS
                   DISPLAY 10 ITEMS
                   ENTER CONTINUE CONFIRMATION
                ENDIF
             ELSE
                WRITE "ORDER NOT ON FILE"
          ENDIF
       ENDIF
    ENDDO
```

The order display pseudocode.

The print order forms screen.

```
---------------------------------------------
|                                           |
|          FRED'S FRIENDLY FISH MARKET       |
|             ORDER FORMS PRINT              |
|                                           |
|                                           |
|       ORDER NUMBER:      ORDRN             |
|                                           |
|                                           |
|                                           |
---------------------------------------------
```

```
            Order Number: ORDRN
            X------COMPANY------X
            X------FNAME--------X  X-------LNAME-------X

            Order Date: MM/DD/YY

ITEM #        QUANTITY        ITEM NUMBER           DESCRIPTION
   1            QTN              ITEMN        X-----------DESC----------X
   2            QTN              ITEMN        X-----------DESC----------X
   3            QTN              ITEMN        X-----------DESC----------X
   4            QTN              ITEMN        X-----------DESC----------X
   5            QTN              ITEMN        X-----------DESC----------X
   6            QTN              ITEMN        X-----------DESC----------X
   7            QTN              ITEMN        X-----------DESC----------X
   8            QTN              ITEMN        X-----------DESC----------X
```

The order form print layout.

```
        PRINT ORDER FORM
            STORE BLANK TO ORDER NUMBER
            DO WHILE ORDER NUMBER NOT BLANK
               DISPLAY SCREEN
               ENTER ORDER NUMBER
               IF ORDER NUMBER NOT BLANK
                  ACCESS ORDER FILE
                  VERIFY ORDER NUMBER
                  IF FOUND
                     THEN
                        PRINT HEADER OF ORDER
                        ACCESS CUSTOMER FILE
                        RETRIEVE CUSTOMER INFORMATION
                        DISPLAY ORDER INFORMATION
                        ACCESS ORDER ITEM FILE
                        DO WHILE MORE RECORDS
                           RETRIEVE QUANTITY AND ITEM NUMBER
                           ACCESS ITEM FILE
                           RETRIEVE DESCRIPTION
                           PRINT RECORD
                        ENDDO
                     ELSE
                        WRITE "ORDER NUMBER NOT ON FILE"
                  ENDIF
               ENDIF
            ENDDO
```

The order form print pseudocode.

246

```
+-------------------------------------------------+
|                                                 |
|      FRED'S FRIENDLY FISH MARKET                |
|         SHIPPING FORMS PRINT                    |
|                                                 |
|                                                 |    The print shipping forms screen.
|      ORDER NUMBER:      ORDRN                   |
|                                                 |
|                                                 |
+-------------------------------------------------+
```

```
+--------------------------------------------------------------------+
|                                                                    |
|                                                                    |
|       Order Number: ORDRN                                          |
|                                                                    |
|       X-------FNAME-------X  X-------LNAME-------X                  |
|       X------COMPANY------X                                        |
|       X--------ADDRESS--------X                                    |
|       X------CITY------X, ST                                       |
|       X--ZIP---X                                                   |
|                                                                    |
|       Order Date: MM/DD/YY                                         |
|                                                                    |
|  Quantity          Description          Price Each        Amount   |
|                                                                    |
|     QTN      X----------DESC----------X     999.99     $99,999.99  |
|     QTN      X----------DESC----------X     999.99     $99,999.99  |
|     QTN      X----------DESC----------X     999.99     $99,999.99  |
|     QTN      X----------DESC----------X     999.99     $99,999.99  |
|     QTN      X----------DESC----------X     999.99     $99,999.99  |
|     QTN      X----------DESC----------X     999.99     $99,999.99  |
|     QTN      X----------DESC----------X     999.99     $99,999.99  |
|     QTN      X----------DESC----------X     999.99     $99,999.99  |
|                                                        ----------  |
|                                   Total Amount:    $999,999.99     |
|                                                                    |
|                                   Discount: (xx%) ($ 99,999.99)    |
|                                                        ----------  |
|                                   Amount Due:      $999,999.99     |
|                                                   ==============   |
|                                                                    |
|                                                                    |
+--------------------------------------------------------------------+
```

The shipping form print layout.

```
PRINT SHIPPING FORM

        STORE BLANK TO ORDER NUMBER
        DO WHILE ORDER NUMBER NOT BLANK
           DISPLAY SCREEN
           ENTER ORDER NUMBER
           IF ORDER NUMBER NOT BLANK
              ACCESS ORDER FILE
              VERIFY ORDER NUMBER
              IF FOUND
                 THEN
                     PRINT HEADER OF ORDER
                     ACCESS CUSTOMER FILE
                     RETRIEVE CUSTOMER INFORMATION
                     PRINT ORDER INFORMATION
                     ACCESS ORDER ITEM FILE
                     SET TOTAL TO 0
                     DO WHILE MORE RECORDS
                        RETRIEVE QUANTITY AND ITEM NUMBER
                        ACCESS ITEM FILE
                        RETRIEVE DESCRIPTION AND PRICE
                        AMOUNT = QUANTITY X PRICE
                        ADD AMOUNT TO TOTAL
                        PRINT RECORD
                     ENDDO
                     WRITE TOTAL
                     DISCOUNT AMOUNT = DISCOUNT/100 X TOTAL
                     WRITE DISCOUNT
                     SUBTRACT DISCOUNT FROM TOTAL
                     WRITE AMOUNT DUE
                 ELSE
                     WRITE "ORDER NUMBER NOT ON FILE"
              ENDIF
           ENDIF
        ENDDO
```

The order shipping form print pseudocode.

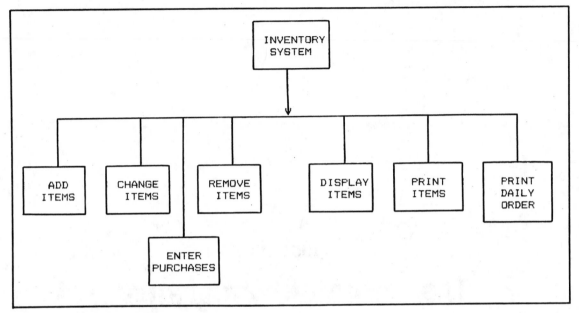

The inventory system hierarchy chart.

Appendix B
The Complete Programs

```
**************************************
*                                    *
*               MAIN                 *
*         FREDS FISH MARKET          *
*            MAIN MENU               *
*             MAIN.PRG               *
*                                    *
**************************************
SET ECHO OFF
SET EXACT ON
SET TALK OFF
SET BELL OFF
SET CONFIRM OFF
SET INTENSITY OFF
STORE 'F' TO EXIT
STORE ' ' TO OPTION
ERASE
DO WHILE EXIT = 'F'
   @  1,20 SAY 'FREDS FRIENDLY FISH MARKET'
   @  3,20 SAY '          MAIN MENU          '
   @  7,19 SAY '  ENTER SELECTION  ===>    ';
           GET OPTION
   @ 10,22 SAY ' 1 - CUSTOMER SYSTEM        '
```

```
   @ 11,22 SAY ' 2 - EMPLOYEE SYSTEM        '
   @ 12,22 SAY ' 3 - ORDER SYSTEM           '
   @ 13,22 SAY ' 4 - INVENTORY SYSTEM       '
   @ 15,22 SAY ' X - EXIT SYSTEM            '
   READ
   DO CASE
      CASE OPTION = '1'
         DO CUSTOMER
      CASE OPTION = '2'
         DO EMPLOYEE
      CASE OPTION = '3'
         DO ORDER
      CASE OPTION = '4'
         DO INVENTRY
      CASE !(OPTION) = 'X'
         QUIT
      OTHERWISE
         ? CHR(7)
         @ 5,18 SAY '*** INVALID ENTRY-TRY AGAIN ***'
   ENDCASE
   STORE ' ' TO OPTION
ENDDO




*************************************
*                                   *
*              1                    *
*         FREDS FISH MARKET         *
*          CUSTOMER MENU            *
*           CUSTOMER.PRG            *
*                                   *
*************************************
STORE 'F' TO CUSTEXIT
STORE ' ' TO OPTION
ERASE
DO WHILE CUSTEXIT = 'F'
   @  1,20 SAY 'FREDS FRIENDLY FISH MARKET'
   @  3,20 SAY '    CUSTOMER SYSTEM MENU    '
   @  7,19 SAY '   ENTER SELECTION  ===>    ';
           GET OPTION
   @ 10,21 SAY ' 1 - ADD CUSTOMER           '
   @ 11,21 SAY ' 2 - CHANGE CUSTOMER        '
   @ 12,21 SAY ' 3 - REMOVE CUSTOMER        '
   @ 13,21 SAY ' 4 - DISPLAY CUSTOMER       '
   @ 15,21 SAY ' 5 - PRINT MAILING LABELS   '
   @ 16,21 SAY ' 6 - PRINT DIRECTORY        '
```

```
    @ 18,21 SAY ' R - RETURN TO MAIN MENU  '
    @ 19,21 SAY ' X - EXIT SYSTEM            '
    READ
    DO CASE
      CASE OPTION = '1'
        DO CUSTADD
      CASE OPTION = '2'
        DO CUSTCHG
      CASE OPTION = '3'
        DO CUSTREM
      CASE OPTION = '4'
        DO CUSTDIS
      CASE OPTION = '5'
        DO CUSTLBL
      CASE OPTION = '6'
        DO CUSTDIR
      CASE !(OPTION) = 'R'
        ERASE
        RETURN
      CASE !(OPTION) = 'X'
        QUIT
      OTHERWISE
        ? CHR(7)
        @ 5,20 SAY '*** INVALID ENTRY -TRY AGAIN ***'
    ENDCASE
    STORE ' ' TO OPTION
ENDDO


*************************************
*                                   *
*              1.1                  *
*        FREDS FISH MARKET          *
*    CUSTOMER ADDITIONS PROGRAM     *
*          CUSTADD.PRG              *
*                                   *
*************************************
ERASE
USE CUSTOMER INDEX CUSTOMER
STORE T TO MORECUST
STORE '      ' TO CSN
STORE '                      ' TO CMP
STORE '                ' TO LNM
STORE '                ' TO FNM
STORE '                    ' TO ADR
STORE '              ' TO CTY
STORE '   ' TO STT
```

```
STORE '              ' TO ZP
STORE '                ' TO PHN
STORE 0 TO DS
DO WHILE MORECUST = 'T'
  @  1,20 SAY 'FREDS FRIENDLY FISH MARKET'
  @  3,20 SAY '  CUSTOMER ADDITIONS MENU  '
  @  7,18 SAY 'CUSTOMER NUMBER: ' GET CSN     PICTURE '#####'
  @  9,15 SAY 'COMPANY:       '    GET CMP
  @ 10,15 SAY 'LAST NAME:    '     GET LNM
  @ 11,15 SAY 'FIRST NAME: '       GET FNM
  @ 13,15 SAY 'ADDRESS: '          GET ADR
  @ 14,15 SAY 'CITY:       '       GET CTY
  @ 16,15 SAY 'STATE:     '        GET STT
  @ 16,30 SAY 'ZIP: '              GET ZP      PICTURE '#####-####'
  @ 18,15 SAY 'PHONE NUMBER: '     GET PHN     PICTURE '(###)###-####'
  @ 20,15 SAY 'DISCOUNT: '         GET DS      PICTURE '##'

  READ
  IF CSN = '        '
      USE
      ERASE
      RETURN
    ELSE
      FIND &CSN
      IF # = 0
          APPEND BLANK
          REPLACE CUSTN WITH VAL(CSN),COMP WITH CMP,LNAME WITH LNM;
            FNAME WITH FNM,ADDR WITH ADR,CITY WITH CTY,ST WITH STT;
            ZIP WITH ZP,PHONE WITH PHN,DIS WITH DS
          @ 5,1
          @ 5,15 SAY '       *** CUSTOMER ADDED  *** '
          STORE '       ' TO CSN
          STORE '                     ' TO CMP
          STORE '                     ' TO LNM
          STORE '                     ' TO FNM
          STORE '                         ' TO ADR
          STORE '                 ' TO CTY
          STORE '  ' TO STT
          STORE '            ' TO ZP
          STORE '              ' TO PHN
          STORE 0 TO DS
        ELSE
          ? CHR(7)
          @ 5,15 SAY '*** CUSTOMER NUMBER ALREADY ON FILE ***'
      ENDIF
  ENDIF
ENDDO
```

```
**********************************
*                                *
*              1.2               *
*        FREDS FISH MARKET       *
*    CUSTOMER CHANGE PROGRAM     *
*           CUSTCHG.PRG          *
*                                *
**********************************
USE CUSTOMER INDEX CUSTOMER
STORE 'T' TO MORECUST
STORE '     ' TO CSN
ERASE
DO WHILE MORECUST = 'T'
  @  1,20 SAY 'FREDS FRIENDLY FISH MARKET'
  @  3,20 SAY '    CUSTOMER CHANGES          '
  @  7,18 SAY 'CUSTOMER NUMBER: ' GET CSN PICTURE '#####'
  READ
  IF CSN = '       '
      USE
      ERASE
      RETURN
    ELSE
      FIND &CSN
      IF # # 0
          @  9,15 SAY 'COMPANY:     '   GET COMP
          @ 10,15 SAY 'LAST NAME: '     GET LNAME
          @ 11,15 SAY 'FIRST NAME: '    GET FNAME
          @ 13,15 SAY 'ADDRESS: '       GET ADDR
          @ 14,15 SAY 'CITY:       '    GET CITY
          @ 16,15 SAY 'STATE: '         GET ST
          @ 16,30 SAY 'ZIP: '           GET ZIP   PICTURE '#####-####'
          @ 18,15 SAY 'PHONE NUMBER: 'GET PHONE PICTURE '
                                      (###)###-####'
          @ 20,15 SAY 'DISCOUNT: '      GET DIS   PICTURE '##'
          READ
          ERASE
          @ 5,1
          @ 5,15 SAY '    *** CUSTOMER CHANGED   ***          '
          STORE '     ' TO CSN
        ELSE
          ? CHR(7)
          ERASE
          @ 5,15 SAY '*** CUSTOMER NUMBER NOT FOUND ***'
      ENDIF
  ENDIF
ENDDO
```

254

```
**************************************
*                                    *
*              1.3                   *
*        FREDS FISH MARKET           *
*    CUSTOMER REMOVAL PROGRAM        *
*           CUSTREM.PRG              *
*                                    *
**************************************
USE CUSTOMER INDEX CUSTOMER
STORE 'T' TO MORECUST
STORE '      ' TO CSN
ERASE
DO WHILE MORECUST = 'T'
   @  1,20 SAY 'FREDS FRIENDLY FISH MARKET'
   @  3,20 SAY '     CUSTOMER REMOVAL          '
   @  7,18 SAY 'CUSTOMER NUMBER: ' GET CSN PICTURE '#####'

   READ
   IF CSN = '        '
       PACK
       USE
       ERASE
       RETURN
     ELSE
       FIND &CSN
       IF # # 0
           @  9,15 SAY 'COMPANY:        '    GET COMP
           @ 10,15 SAY 'LAST NAME:      '    GET LNAME
           @ 11,15 SAY 'FIRST NAME:     '    GET FNAME
           @ 13,15 SAY 'ADDRESS:        '    GET ADDR
           @ 14,15 SAY 'CITY:           '    GET CITY
           @ 16,15 SAY 'STATE:          '    GET ST
           @ 16,35 SAY 'ZIP: '              GET ZIP
           @ 18,15 SAY 'PHONE NUMBER: '     GET PHONE
           @ 20,15 SAY 'DISCOUNT:       '    GET DIS
           CLEAR GETS
           STORE ' ' TO DELCON
           @ 5,15 SAY 'ENTER "D" TO CONFIRM DELETE ===> ' GET DELCON
           READ
           IF !(DELCON) = 'D'
               DELETE
               ERASE
               @ 5,15 SAY '     *** CUSTOMER DELETED ***          '
             ELSE
               ERASE
               @ 5,15 SAY '   *** CUSTOMER NOT DELETED ***        '
           ENDIF
```

```
          STORE '      ' TO CSN
       ELSE
          ? CHR(7)
          ERASE
          @ 5,15 SAY '*** CUSTOMER NUMBER NOT FOUND ***'
       ENDIF
   ENDIF
ENDDO


***********************************
*                                 *
*            1.4                  *
*      FREDS FISH MARKET          *
*   CUSTOMER DISPLAY PROGRAM      *
*          CUSTDIS.PRG            *
*                                 *
***********************************
USE CUSTOMER INDEX CUSTOMER
STORE 'T' TO MORECUST
STORE '      ' TO CSN
ERASE
DO WHILE MORECUST = 'T'
   @  1,20 SAY 'FREDS FRIENDLY FISH MARKET'
   @  3,20 SAY '    CUSTOMER DISPLAY        '
   @  7,18 SAY 'CUSTOMER NUMBER: ' GET CSN PICTURE '#####'
   READ
   @ 5,1
   IF CSN = '       '
       USE
       ERASE
       RETURN
    ELSE
      FIND &CSN
      IF # # 0
          SET COLON OFF
          @  9,15 SAY 'COMPANY:       '   GET COMP
          @ 10,15 SAY 'LAST NAME:     '   GET LNAME
          @ 11,15 SAY 'FIRST NAME:    '   GET FNAME
          @ 13,15 SAY 'ADDRESS:       '   GET ADDR
          @ 14,15 SAY 'CITY:          '   GET CITY
          @ 16,15 SAY 'STATE:         '   GET ST
          @ 16,35 SAY 'ZIP:  '            GET ZIP
          @ 18,15 SAY 'PHONE NUMBER: '    GET PHONE
          @ 20,15 SAY 'DISCOUNT:      '   GET DIS
          STORE ' ' TO RESP
          CLEAR GETS
```

256

```
            @ 5,20 SAY 'ENTER ANY KEY TO CONTINUE'  GET RESP
            READ
            SET COLON ON
            STORE '      '  TO CSN
            ERASE
          ELSE
            ? CHR(7)
            ERASE
            @ 5,15 SAY '*** CUSTOMER NUMBER NOT FOUND ***'
        ENDIF
    ENDIF
ENDDO


***********************************
*                                 *
*            1.5                  *
*        FREDS FISH MARKET        *
*    CUSTOMER MAILING LABEL PRINT *
*           CUSTLBL.PRG           *
*                                 *
***********************************
USE CUSTOMER INDEX CUSTOMER
STORE 'T' TO MOREANS
STORE ' ' TO OPTION
DO WHILE MOREANS = 'T'
  ERASE
  @  1,20 SAY 'FREDS FRIENDLY FISH MARKET'
  @  3,20 SAY ' CUSTOMER MAILING LABELS'
  @  7,18 SAY 'ENTER "A" FOR ALIGNMENT PRINT,'
  @  8,18 SAY '       "X" TO EXIT PRINT,'
  @  9,18 SAY '   OR <cr> TO BEGIN PRINT'
  @ 11,18 SAY '            ====> ' GET OPTION
  READ
  IF !(OPTION) = 'X'
    USE
    RELEASE A1,A2,A3,B1,B2,B3,C1,C2,C3,D1,D2,D3
    RETURN
  ENDIF
  IF !(OPTION) = 'A'
    DO CUSTLBLA
  ENDIF
  IF !(OPTION) # 'A' .AND. !(OPTION) # 'X'
    USE CUSTOMER INDEX CUSTOMER
    STORE 0 TO LBLCNT
    DO WHILE .NOT. EOF
      DO CUSTLBLF
```

```
      IF LBLCNT = 3
        SET PRINT ON
        ? A1,'          ',A2,'          ',A3
        ? B1,'     ',B2,'     ',B3
        ? C1,' ',C2,' ',C3
        ? D1,' ',D2,' ',D3
        ?
        STORE 0 TO LBLCNT
      ENDIF
      SKIP
    ENDDO
    IF LBLCNT = 1
      ? A1
      ? B1
      ? C1
      ? D1
      ?
    ENDIF
    IF LBLCNT = 2
      ? A1,'          ',A2
      ? B1,'     ',B2
      ? C1,' ',C2
      ? D1,' ',D2
      ?
    ENDIF
    SET PRINT OFF
  ENDIF
  STORE ' ' TO OPTION
ENDDO


***********************************
*                                 *
*         1.5.CUSTLBLA            *
*        FREDS FISH MARKET        *
*     CUSTOMER LABEL ALIGNMENT    *
*         CUSTLBLA.PRG            *
*                                 *
***********************************
    SET COLON OFF
    STORE ' ' TO ANS
    @ 7,13 SAY 'ALIGN PRINTER AND HIT ANY KEY TO CONTINUE' GET ANS
    @ 8,1
    @ 9,8  SAY 'THIS WILL PRINT THREE ROWS OF LABEL ALIGNMENT DATA'
    @ 11,1
    READ
    SET PRINT ON
```

```
      STORE 1 TO COUNT
      DO WHILE COUNT <= 3
        STORE COUNT + 1 TO COUNT
        ? 'XXXXXXXXXXXXXXXXXXXX        XXXXXXXXXXXXXXXXXXXX
          XXXXXXXXXXXXXXXXXXXXX'
        ? 'X. XXXXXXXXXXXXXXXXXXXX    X. XXXXXXXXXXXXXXXXXXXX
          X. XXXXXXXXXXXXXXXXXXXX
        ? 'XXXXXXXXXXXXXXXXXXXXXXXXX XXXXXXXXXXXXXXXXXXXXXXXXX
          XXXXXXXXXXXXXXXXXXXXXX
        ? 'XXXXXXXXXXXXXX, XX XXXXX XXXXXXXXXXXXXX, XX XXXXX
          XXXXXXXXXXXXXX, XX XX
        ? ' '
      ENDDO
      SET PRINT OFF
      RETURN




************************************
*                                  *
*         1.5.CUSTLBLF             *
*        FREDS FISH MARKET         *
*  CUSTOMER MAILING LABEL FORMAT   *
*         CUSTLBLF.PRG             *
*                                  *
************************************
STORE LBLCNT + 1 TO LBLCNT
IF LBLCNT = 1
  STORE COMP TO A1
  STORE $(FNAME,1,1)-'. '+LNAME TO B1
  STORE ADDR TO C1
  STORE CITY+' '+ST+' '+$(ZIP,1,5) TO D1
ENDIF
IF LBLCNT = 2
  STORE COMP TO A2
  STORE $(FNAME,1,1)-'. '+LNAME TO B2
  STORE ADDR TO C2
  STORE CITY+' '+ST+' '+$(ZIP,1,5) TO D2
ENDIF
IF LBLCNT = 3
  STORE COMP TO A3
  STORE $(FNAME,1,1)-'. '+LNAME TO B3
  STORE ADDR TO C3
  STORE CITY+' '+ST+' '+$(ZIP,1,5) TO D3
ENDIF
RETURN
```

```
**************************************
*                                    *
*              1.6                   *
*         FREDS FISH MARKET          *
*     CUSTOMER DIRECTORY PRINT       *
*            CUSTDIR.PRG             *
*                                    *
**************************************
USE CUSTOMER INDEX CUSTOMER
STORE 'T' TO MOREANS
STORE ' ' TO OPTION
DO WHILE MOREANS = 'T'
  ERASE
  @  1,20 SAY 'FREDS FRIENDLY FISH MARKET'
  @  3,20 SAY ' CUSTOMER DIRECTORY PRINT '
  @  7,20 SAY 'ENTER "X" TO EXIT PRINT,'
  @  8,18 SAY '   OR <cr> TO BEGIN PRINT'
  @ 10,18 SAY '         ====> ' GET OPTION
  READ
  IF !(OPTION) = 'X'
    USE
    STORE ' ' TO OPTION
    RETURN
  ENDIF
  USE CUSTOMER INDEX CUSTOMER
  STORE 1 TO LINECNT
  SET FORMAT TO PRINT
  DO WHILE .NOT. EOF
    IF LINECNT = 1 .OR. LINECNT = 56
      @ 1,30 SAY '   FREDS FISH MARKET'
      @ 2,30 SAY 'CUSTOMER DIRECTORY PRINT'
      STORE 4 TO LINECNT
    ENDIF
    STORE LINECNT + 4 TO LINECNT
    @ LINECNT,1 SAY 'Customer Number:'
    @ LINECNT,18 SAY CUSTN
    STORE LINECNT + 2 TO LINECNT
    @ LINECNT,1 SAY COMP
    STORE LINECNT + 1 TO LINECNT
    @ LINECNT,1 SAY TRIM(LNAME)+', '+FNAME
    STORE LINECNT + 1 TO LINECNT
    @ LINECNT,15 SAY ADDR
    STORE LINECNT + 1 TO LINECNT
    @ LINECNT,15 SAY TRIM(CITY)+', '+ST+' '+ZIP
    STORE LINECNT + 2 TO LINECNT
    @ LINECNT,15 SAY 'Phone: '+PHONE
```

```
       STORE LINECNT + 2 TO LINECNT
       @ LINECNT,15 SAY 'Discount: '
       @ LINECNT,25 SAY DIS
       @ LINECNT,27 SAY '%'
       SKIP
     ENDDO
     @ LINECNT+1,1
     SET FORMAT TO SCREEN
     STORE ' ' TO OPTION
   ENDDO


   ************************************
   *                                  *
   *                3                 *
   *         FREDS FISH MARKET        *
   *            ORDER MENU            *
   *            ORDER.PRG            *
   *                                  *
   ************************************
   STORE 'F' TO ORDREXIT
   STORE ' ' TO OPTION
   DO WHILE ORDREXIT = 'F'
     ERASE
     @  1,20 SAY 'FREDS FRIENDLY FISH MARKET'
     @  3,20 SAY '    ORDER SYSTEM MENU     '
     @  7,19 SAY '  ENTER SELECTION  ===>   ';
             GET OPTION
     @ 10,21 SAY ' 1 - ADD ORDERS          '
     @ 11,21 SAY ' 2 - CHANGE ORDERS       '
     @ 12,21 SAY ' 3 - REMOVE ORDERS       '
     @ 13,21 SAY ' 4 - DISPLAY ORDERS      '
     @ 15,21 SAY ' 5 - PRINT ORDER FORMS   '
     @ 16,21 SAY ' 6 - PRINT SHIPPING FORMS '
     @ 18,21 SAY ' R - RETURN TO MAIN MENU '
     @ 19,21 SAY ' X - EXIT SYSTEM         '
     READ
     @ 5,20
     DO CASE
       CASE OPTION = '1'
         DO ORDRADD
       CASE OPTION = '2'
         DO ORDRCHG
       CASE OPTION = '3'
         DO ORDRREM
       CASE OPTION = '4'
         DO ORDRDIS
```

```
      CASE OPTION = '5'
        DO ORDRFMS
      CASE OPTION = '6'
        DO ORDRSHP
      CASE OPTION = 'R'
        ERASE
        RETURN
      CASE !(OPTION) = 'X'
        QUIT
      OTHERWISE
        ? CHR(7)
        @ 5,20 SAY '*** INVALID ENTRY -TRY AGAIN ***'
    ENDCASE
    STORE ' ' TO OPTION
ENDDO


**************************************
*                                    *
*              3.1                   *
*        FREDS FISH MARKET           *
*     ORDER ADDITIONS PROGRAM        *
*          ORDRADD.PRG               *
*                                    *
**************************************
ERASE
USE ORDER INDEX ORDER
STORE T TO MOREORDR
STORE '      ' TO ORN
STORE '      ' TO CSN
STORE '         ' TO DTO
DO WHILE MOREORDR = 'T'
  @  1,20 SAY 'FREDS FRIENDLY FISH MARKET'
  @  3,20 SAY '  ORDER ADDITIONS MENU  '
  @  7,15 SAY 'ORDER NUMBER:     ' GET ORN    PICTURE '#####'
  @  9,15 SAY 'CUSTOMER NUMBER: ' GET CSN    PICTURE '#####'
  READ
  @ 5,1
  IF ORN = '      '
      SELECT PRIMARY
      USE
      SELECT SECONDARY
      USE
      ERASE
      RETURN
  ELSE
      SELECT PRIMARY
```

```
       FIND &ORN
       IF # = 0
           SELECT SECONDARY
           USE CUSTOMER INDEX CUSTOMER
           FIND &CSN
           IF # # 0
               @ 11,15 SAY 'COMPANY: '
               @ 11,32 SAY COMP
               @ 12,15 SAY 'LAST NAME:'
               @ 12,32 SAY LNAME
               @ 13,15 SAY 'FIRST NAME: '
               @ 13,32 SAY FNAME
               @ 15,15 SAY 'DATE ORDERED: 'GET DTO PICTURE '##/##/##'
               READ
               STORE COMP TO COMP
               STORE LNAME TO LNAME
               STORE FNAME TO FNAME
               SELECT PRIMARY
               APPEND BLANK
               REPLACE ORDRN WITH VAL(ORN),CUSTN WITH VAL(CSN),DATE
                WITH DTO
               DO ORDRADIT
               ERASE
               @ 5,20 SAY '  *** ORDER ADDED   *** '
               SELECT PRIMARY
               USE ORDER INDEX ORDER
               STORE '       ' TO ORN
               STORE '      ' TO CSN
               STORE '          ' TO DTO
           ELSE
               ? CHR(7)
               ERASE
               @ 5,15 SAY '  *** CUSTOMER NUMBER NOT ON FILE  ***'
           ENDIF
       ELSE
           ? CHR(7)
           ERASE
           @ 5,15 SAY '*** ORDER NUMBER ALREADY ON FILE ***'
       ENDIF
   ENDIF
ENDDO
```

```
**************************************
*                                    *
*          3.1.ORDRADIT              *
*         FREDS FISH MARKET          *
*   ORDER ITEM ADDITIONS PROGRAM     *
*           ORDRADIT.PRG             *
*                                    *
**************************************
SELECT PRIMARY
USE ORDERITM INDEX ORDERITM
SELECT SECONDARY
USE ITEM INDEX ITEM
STORE T TO MOREORDI
ERASE
@  1,20 SAY 'FREDS FRIENDLY FISH MARKET'
@  3,20 SAY 'ORDER ITEM ADDITIONS MENU'
@  7,20 SAY 'ORDER NUMBER:      '
@  7,37 SAY ORN
@  9,20 SAY 'COMPANY:'
@  9,37 SAY COMP
@ 10,20 SAY 'LAST NAME:'
@ 10,37 SAY LNAME
@ 11,20 SAY 'FIRST NAME:'
@ 11,37 SAY FNAME
@ 13,15 SAY '#'
@ 13,20 SAY 'QUANTITY'
@ 13,35 SAY 'ITEM NUMBER'
STORE 15 TO LINECNT
STORE 1 TO CNT
STORE '   ' TO QT
STORE '     ' TO ITN
DO WHILE MOREORDI = 'T'
   @ LINECNT,14 SAY CNT USING '99'
   @ LINECNT,22 GET QT PICTURE '###'
   @ LINECNT,38 GET ITN PICTURE '#####'
   READ
   @ 5,1
   IF QT = '   '
       RETURN
     ELSE
       SELECT SECONDARY
       FIND &ITN
       IF # # O
           STORE S.PRICE TO PRI
           SELECT PRIMARY
           APPEND BLANK
```

264

```
            REPLACE ORDRN WITH VAL(ORN),QTY WITH VAL(QT) ;
               ITEMN WITH VAL(ITN),PRICE WITH PRI
            @ 5,20 SAY '   *** ORDER ADDED  *** '
            STORE '     ' TO QT
            STORE '        ' TO ITN
            STORE CNT + 1 TO CNT
            STORE LINECNT + 1 TO LINECNT
            IF LINECNT = 25
               STORE 15 TO LINECNT
               STORE 15 TO ERASER
               DO WHILE ERASER < 25
                  @ ERASER,1
                  STORE ERASER + 1 TO ERASER
               ENDDO
            ENDIF
         ELSE
            ? CHR(7)
            @ 5,15 SAY '*** ITEM NUMBER NOT ON FILE ***'
         ENDIF
    ENDIF
ENDDO


***********************************
*                                 *
*            3.2                  *
*      FREDS FISH MARKET          *
*    ORDER CHANGES PROGRAM        *
*         ORDRCHG.PRG             *
*                                 *
***********************************
ERASE
USE ORDER INDEX ORDER
STORE T TO MOREORDR
STORE '     ' TO ORN
STORE '         ' TO DTO
DO WHILE MOREORDR = 'T'
   @ 1,20 SAY 'FREDS FRIENDLY FISH MARKET'
   @ 2,20 SAY '   ORDER CHANGES MENU  '
   @ 7,15 SAY 'ORDER NUMBER:    ' GET ORN     PICTURE '#####'
   READ
   @ 5,1
   IF ORN = '     '
       STORE 'F' TO MOREORDR
     ELSE
       SELECT PRIMARY
       FIND &ORN
```

```
       IF # # O
           @  9,15 SAY 'CUSTOMER NUMBER: '
           @  9,32 SAY CUSTN
           SELECT SECONDARY
           USE CUSTOMER INDEX CUSTOMER
           STORE STR(CUSTN,5) TO CSN
           FIND &CSN
           @ 11,15 SAY 'COMPANY: '
           @ 11,32 SAY COMP
           @ 12,15 SAY 'LAST NAME:'
           @ 12,32 SAY LNAME
           @ 13,15 SAY 'FIRST NAME: '
           @ 13,32 SAY FNAME
           SELECT PRIMARY
           @ 15,15 SAY 'DATE ORDERED: '
           @ 15,32 SAY DATE
           STORE COMP TO COMP
           STORE LNAME TO LNAME
           STORE FNAME TO FNAME
           STORE ' ' TO ANS
           @ 4,20 SAY 'CHANGE ITEMS? ===> ' GET ANS
           @ 5,15 SAY 'ENTER <cr> TO CONTINUE, X TO EXIT'
           READ
           IF !(ANS) # 'X'
              DO ORDRCHIT
           ENDIF
           ERASE
           @ 5,20 SAY '*** ORDER CHANGED *** '
           SELECT PRIMARY
           USE ORDER INDEX ORDER
           STORE '      ' TO ORN
           STORE '        ' TO DTO
         ELSE
           ? CHR(7)
           ERASE
           @ 5,15 SAY '*** ORDER NUMBER NOT FOUND ***'
       ENDIF
   ENDIF
ENDDO
SELECT SECONDARY
USE ORDERITM INDEX ORDERITM
PACK
USE
SELECT PRIMARY
USE
STORE ' ' TO OPTION
RETURN
```

```
*************************************
*                                   *
*        3.2.ORDRCHIT               *
*       FREDS FISH MARKET           *
*    ORDER ITEM CHANGES PROGRAM     *
*         ORDRCHIT.PRG              *
*                                   *
*************************************
SELECT PRIMARY
USE ORDERITM INDEX ORDERITM
SELECT SECONDARY
USE ITEM INDEX ITEM
STORE T TO MOREORDI
ERASE
@  1,20 SAY 'FREDS FRIENDLY FISH MARKET'
@  2,20 SAY ' ORDER ITEM CHANGES MENU'
@  7,20 SAY 'ORDER NUMBER:        '
@  7,37 SAY ORN
@  9,20 SAY 'COMPANY:'
@  9,37 SAY COMP
@ 10,20 SAY 'LAST NAME:'
@ 10,37 SAY LNAME
@ 11,20 SAY 'FIRST NAME:'
@ 11,37 SAY FNAME
@ 13,18 SAY '#'
@ 13,23 SAY 'QUANTITY'
@ 13,38 SAY 'ITEM NUMBER'
STORE 1 TO CNT
STORE '    ' TO QT
STORE '      ' TO ITN
STORE 10 TO SCRLCNT
DO WHILE MOREORDI = 'T'
  STORE 15 TO LINECNT
  SELECT PRIMARY
  FIND &ORN
  STORE 1 TO LOOPCNT
  DO WHILE LOOPCNT <= SCRLCNT-10 .AND. VAL(ORN)=P.ORDRN .AND. .NOT.
   EOF
    IF .NOT. *
      STORE LOOPCNT+1 TO LOOPCNT
    ENDIF
    SKIP
  ENDDO
  DO WHILE LOOPCNT<= SCRLCNT .AND. VAL(ORN)=P.ORDRN .AND. .NOT. EOF
    IF .NOT. *
```

267

```
           @ LINECNT,17 SAY LOOPCNT USING '99'
           @ LINECNT,25 SAY QTY USING '999'
           @ LINECNT,41 SAY ITEMN USING '99999'
           STORE LOOPCNT+1 TO LOOPCNT
           STORE LINECNT+1 TO LINECNT
        ENDIF
        SKIP
     ENDDO
     DO WHILE LINECNT < 25
        @ LINECNT,17 SAY LOOPCNT USING '99'
        @ LINECNT,25
        STORE LOOPCNT+1 TO LOOPCNT
        STORE LINECNT+1 TO LINECNT
     ENDDO
     STORE ' ' TO SEL
     @ 4,1
     @ 5,1
     @ 4,20 SAY 'ENTER SELECTION ===> ' GET SEL
     @ 5,20 SAY 'C/CHANGE,S/SCROLL,X/EXIT'
     @ 6,1
     READ
DO CASE
   CASE !(SEL) = 'X'
      RETURN
   CASE !(SEL) = 'C'
      STORE '    ' TO RN
      STORE 'T' TO MORERN
      DO WHILE MORERN = 'T'
         @ 4,1
         @ 5,1
         @ 4,20 SAY 'RECORD NUMBER ==>  ' GET RN
         @ 5,16 SAY 'ENTER RECORD NUMBER TO BE CHANGED'
         READ
         @ 6,1
         IF RN # '    '
             IF VAL(RN) <= SCRLCNT .AND VAL(RN) > SCRLCNT-10
                STORE 1 TO LOOPCNT
                FIND &ORN
                DO WHILE LOOPCNT < VAL(RN) .AND. VAL(ORN)=P.ORDRN
                   IF .NOT. *
                      STORE LOOPCNT+1 TO LOOPCNT
                   ENDIF
                   SKIP
                ENDDO
                IF *
                   SKIP
```

```
        ENDIF
        IF VAL(ORN) # P.ORDRN .OR. EOF
            STORE '   ' TO QT
            STORE '     ' TO ITN
            STORE 'T' TO ISW
            DO WHILE ISW = 'T'
              @ 4,1
              @ 4,14 SAY 'QUANTITY: ' GET QT PICTURE '###'
              @ 4,34 SAY 'ITEM NUMBER: ' GET ITN PICTURE '#####'
              @ 5,1
              READ
              @ 6,1
              IF QT = '   '
                    STORE 'F' TO ISW
                ELSE
                    SELECT SECONDARY
                    FIND &ITN
                    IF # # 0
                        STORE S.PRICE TO PRI
                        SELECT PRIMARY
                        APPEND BLANK
                        REPLACE P.ORDRN WITH VAL(ORN),QTY WITH VAL(QT) ;
                          P.ITEMN WITH VAL(ITN),P.PRICE WITH PRI
                        @ 6,20 SAY '  *** ITEM ADDED *** '
                        STORE 'F' TO ISW
                        STORE 'F' TO MORERN
                      ELSE
                        SELECT PRIMARY
                        ? CHR(7)
                        @ 5,15 SAY '*** ITEM NUMBER NOT ON FILE ***'
                    ENDIF
              ENDIF
            ENDDO
          ELSE
            STORE STR(QTY,3) TO QT
            STORE STR(ITEMN,5) TO ITN
            STORE 'T' TO ISW
            DO WHILE ISW = 'T'
              @ 4,1
              @ 4,14 SAY 'QUANTITY: ' GET QT PICTURE '999'
              @ 4,34 SAY 'ITEM NUMBER: ' GET ITN PICTURE '99999'
              @ 5,1
              READ
              @ 6,1
              IF VAL(QT) = 0
                    DELETE
```

```
                                    @ 6,20 SAY '   *** ITEM DELETED   *** '
                                    STORE 'F' TO ISW
                                    STORE 'F' TO MORERN
                              ELSE
                                 SELECT SECONDARY
                                 FIND &ITN
                                 IF # # 0
                                     STORE PRICE TO PRI
                                     SELECT PRIMARY
                                     REPLACE ORDRN WITH VAL(ORN),QTY WITH
                                      VAL(QT);
                                       ITEMN WITH VAL(ITN),PRICE WITH PRI
                                     @ 6,20 SAY '   *** ITEM CHANGED   *** '
                                     STORE 'F' TO ISW
                                     STORE 'F' TO MORERN
                                  ELSE
                                     ? CHR(7)
                                     @ 6,20 SAY '*** ITEM NUMBER NOT ON
                                         FILE ***'
                                 ENDIF
                             ENDIF
                          ENDDO
                      ENDIF
                  ELSE
                     ? CHR(7)
                     @ 6,15 SAY '*** RECORD NUMBER NOT ON SCREEN ***'
              ENDIF
          ELSE
              STORE 'F' TO MORERN
         ENDIF
       ENDDO
    CASE !(SEL) = 'S'
       STORE SCRLCNT+10 TO SCRLCNT
   ENDCASE
ENDDO
RETURN


**************************************
*                                    *
*               3.3                  *
*        FREDS FISH MARKET           *
*      ORDER REMOVAL PROGRAM         *
*          ORDRREM.PRG               *
*                                    *
**************************************
ERASE
```

270

```
USE ORDER INDEX ORDER
STORE T TO MOREORDR
STORE '      ' TO ORN
DO WHILE MOREORDR = 'T'
   @ 1,20 SAY 'FREDS FRIENDLY FISH MARKET'
   @ 2,20 SAY '   ORDER REMOVAL MENU  '
   @ 6,15 SAY 'ORDER NUMBER:    ' GET ORN     PICTURE '#####'
   READ
   @ 4,1
   IF ORN = '      '
       STORE 'F' TO MOREORDR
     ELSE
       SELECT PRIMARY
       FIND &ORN
       IF # # 0   .AND. .NOT. *
           SELECT SECONDARY
           USE CUSTOMER INDEX CUSTOMER
           STORE STR(CUSTN,5) TO CSN
           FIND &CSN
           @ 8,15 SAY 'COMPANY: '
           @ 8,32 SAY COMP
           @ 9,15 SAY 'LAST NAME:'
           @ 9,32 SAY LNAME
           @ 10,15 SAY 'FIRST NAME: '
           @ 10,32 SAY FNAME
           SELECT PRIMARY
           @ 12,15 SAY 'DATE ORDERED: '
           @ 12,32 SAY DATE
           @ 14,18 SAY '#'
           @ 14,23 SAY 'QUANTITY'
           @ 14,38 SAY 'ITEM NUMBER'
           STORE 1 TO LOOPCNT
           STORE 15 TO LINECNT
           SELECT SECONDARY
           USE ORDERITM INDEX ORDERITM
           FIND &ORN
           DO WHILE LOOPCNT <= 10 .AND. VAL(ORN)=S.ORDRN .AND. .NOT.
            EOF
              IF .NOT. *
                @ LINECNT,17 SAY LOOPCNT USING '99'
                @ LINECNT,25 SAY QTY USING '999'
                @ LINECNT,41 SAY ITEMN USING '99999'
                STORE LOOPCNT+1 TO LOOPCNT
                STORE LINECNT+1 TO LINECNT
              ENDIF
            SKIP
```

```
                    ENDDO
                    SELECT PRIMARY
                    STORE ' ' TO ANS
                    @ 4,1
                    @ 4,17 SAY 'ENTER D TO CONFIRM DELETE ==>  ' GET ANS
                    READ
                    IF !(ANS) = 'D'
                        DELETE
                        SELECT SECONDARY
                        USE ORDERITM INDEX ORDERITM
                        DELETE ALL FOR VAL(ORN) = S.ORDRN
                        SELECT PRIMARY
                        ERASE
                        @ 4,21 SAY '*** ORDER DELETED *** '
                    ELSE
                        ERASE
                        @ 4,19 SAY '*** ORDER NOT DELETED *** '
                    ENDIF
                    STORE '      ' TO ORN
                ELSE
                    ? CHR(7)
                    ERASE
                    @ 4,17 SAY '*** ORDER NUMBER NOT FOUND ***'
                ENDIF
        ENDIF
ENDDO
SELECT SECONDARY
USE ORDERITM INDEX ORDERITM
PACK
USE
SELECT PRIMARY
PACK
USE
STORE ' ' TO OPTION
RETURN




*************************************
*                                   *
*               3.4                 *
*        FREDS FISH MARKET          *
*      ORDER DISPLAY PROGRAM        *
*          ORDRDIS.PRG              *
*                                   *
*************************************
```

```
ERASE
USE ORDER INDEX ORDER
STORE T TO MOREORDR
STORE '     ' TO ORN
DO WHILE MOREORDR = 'T'
  @ 1,20 SAY 'FREDS FRIENDLY FISH MARKET'
  @ 2,20 SAY '   ORDER DISPLAY MENU  '
  @ 6,15 SAY 'ORDER NUMBER:    ' GET ORN     PICTURE '#####'
  READ
  @ 4,1
  IF ORN = '     '
      STORE 'F' TO MOREORDR
    ELSE
      SELECT PRIMARY
      FIND &ORN
      IF # # 0  .AND. .NOT. *
          SELECT SECONDARY
          USE CUSTOMER INDEX CUSTOMER
          STORE STR(CUSTN,5) TO CSN
          FIND &CSN
          @ 8,15 SAY 'COMPANY: '
          @ 8,32 SAY COMP
          @ 9,15 SAY 'LAST NAME:'
          @ 9,32 SAY LNAME
          @ 10,15 SAY 'FIRST NAME: '
          @ 10,32 SAY FNAME
          SELECT PRIMARY
          @ 12,15 SAY 'DATE ORDERED: '
          @ 12,32 SAY DATE
          @ 14,18 SAY '#'
          @ 14,23 SAY 'QUANTITY'
          @ 14,38 SAY 'ITEM NUMBER'
          STORE 1 TO LOOPCNT
          STORE 15 TO LINECNT
          SELECT SECONDARY
          USE ORDERITM INDEX ORDERITM
          FIND &ORN
          DO WHILE VAL(ORN)=S.ORDRN .AND. .NOT. EOF
             DO WHILE LINECNT <= 24 .AND. VAL(ORN)=S.ORDRN .AND.
               .NOT. EOF
               IF .NOT. *
                  @ LINECNT,17 SAY LOOPCNT USING '99'
                  @ LINECNT,25 SAY QTY USING '999'
                  @ LINECNT,41 SAY ITEMN USING '99999'
                  STORE LOOPCNT+1 TO LOOPCNT
                  STORE LINECNT+1 TO LINECNT
               ENDIF
```

```
               SKIP
            ENDDO
            IF LINECNT < 24
               DO WHILE LINECNT <= 24
                  @ LINECNT,1
                  STORE LINECNT + 1 TO LINECNT
               ENDDO
            ENDIF
            SELECT PRIMARY
            SET COLON OFF
            STORE ' ' TO ANS
            @ 4,1
            @ 4,21 SAY 'ENTER <cr> TO CONTINUE' GET ANS
            READ
            SET COLON ON
            STORE 15 TO LINECNT
         ENDDO
         ERASE
         STORE '      ' TO ORN
      ELSE
         ? CHR(7)
         ERASE
         @ 4,17 SAY '*** ORDER NUMBER NOT FOUND ***'
      ENDIF
   ENDIF
ENDDO
SELECT SECONDARY
USE
SELECT PRIMARY
USE
STORE ' ' TO OPTION
RETURN




*************************************
*                                   *
*               3.5                 *
*         FREDS FISH MARKET         *
*     ORDER FORMS PRINT PROGRAM     *
*           ORDRFMS.PRG             *
*                                   *
*************************************
ERASE
USE ORDER INDEX ORDER
STORE T TO MOREORDR
STORE '      ' TO ORN
```

```
DO WHILE MOREORDR = 'T'
   @  1,20 SAY 'FREDS FRIENDLY FISH MARKET'
   @  2,18 SAY '   ORDER FORMS PRINT MENU  '
   @  6,15 SAY 'ORDER NUMBER:    ' GET ORN    PICTURE '#####'
   READ
   @ 4,1
   IF ORN = '       '
      STORE 'F' TO MOREORDR
    ELSE
      SELECT PRIMARY
      FIND &ORN
      IF # # 0  .AND. .NOT. *
         SET COLON OFF
         STORE ' ' TO ANS
         @ 4,1
         @ 4,23 SAY 'ENTER <cr> TO PRINT' GET ANS
         READ
         SET COLON ON
         SET FORMAT TO PRINT
         SELECT SECONDARY
         USE CUSTOMER INDEX CUSTOMER
         STORE STR(CUSTN,5) TO CSN
         FIND &CSN
         @ 1,25 SAY 'FREDS FRIENDLY FISH MARKET'
         @ 3,25 SAY '   CUSTOMER ORDER FORM    '
         @ 6,15 SAY 'Order Number: '
         @ 6,29 SAY ORN PICTURE '99999'
         @ 8,15 SAY COMP
         @ 9,15 SAY TRIM(FNAME)+' '+LNAME
         SELECT PRIMARY
         @ 11,15 SAY 'Date Ordered: '
         @ 11,29 SAY DATE
         @ 14,15 SAY 'ITEM #'
         @ 14,26 SAY 'QUANTITY'
         @ 14,38 SAY 'ITEM NUMBER'
         @ 14,58 SAY 'DESCRIPTION'
         STORE 1 TO LOOPCNT
         STORE 17 TO LINECNT
         SELECT SECONDARY
         USE ORDERITM INDEX ORDERITM
         SELECT PRIMARY
         USE ITEM INDEX ITEM
         SELECT SECONDARY
         FIND &ORN
         DO WHILE VAL(ORN)=S.ORDRN .AND. .NOT. EOF
            IF .NOT. *
```

```
                    @ LINECNT,17 SAY LOOPCNT USING '99'
                    @ LINECNT,27 SAY S.QTY USING '999'
                    @ LINECNT,39 SAY S.ITEMN USING '99999'
                    STORE STR(S.ITEMN,5) TO ITN
                    SELECT PRIMARY
                    FIND &ITN
                    @ LINECNT,55 SAY DESC
                    STORE LOOPCNT+1 TO LOOPCNT
                    STORE LINECNT+1 TO LINECNT
                ENDIF
                SELECT SECONDARY
                SKIP
            ENDDO
            @ LINECNT+1,1
            SELECT PRIMARY
            USE ORDER INDEX ORDER
            SET FORMAT TO SCREEN
            ERASE
            STORE '        ' TO ORN
        ELSE
            ? CHR(7)
            ERASE
            @ 4,17 SAY '*** ORDER NUMBER NOT FOUND ***'
        ENDIF
    ENDIF
ENDDO
SELECT SECONDARY
USE
SELECT PRIMARY
USE
STORE ' ' TO OPTION
RETURN
```

Appendix C

dBASE II Database
Commands Used in This Book

DATABASE STRUCTURE COMMANDS

```
CREATE
USE
MODIFY STRUCTURE
SELECT
```

DATABASE RECORD COMMANDS

```
APPEND
COPY
EDIT
DELETE
PACK
RECALL
```

DATABASE SEARCH COMMANDS

```
LOCATE
FIND
SKIP
```

DATABASE DISPLAY COMMANDS

```
DISPLAY
LIST
REPORT
```

DATABASE MANIPULATION COMMANDS

```
JOIN
SORT
INDEX
```

Appendix D

dBASE II Programming
Commands Used in This Book

HOUSEKEEPING COMMANDS

```
SET ECHO OFF
SET TALK OFF
SET EXACT ON
SET BELL OFF
SET CONFIRM OFF
SET INTENSITY OFF
```

INPUT COMMANDS

```
@ line,column GET PICTURE
READ
CLEAR GETS
```

OUTPUT COMMANDS

```
SET PRINT ON
SET PRINT OFF
?
SET FORMAT TO PRINT
```

```
EJECT
SET FORMAT TO SCREEN
ERASE
@ line,column SAY USING
```

CHARACTER, STRING, AND NUMERIC COMMANDS

```
STR
VAL
TRIM
$
INT
!
```

CONNECTORS

```
.AND.
.OR.
.NOT.
```

LOGICAL CONSTRUCTS

STORE

IF
  THEN
  ELSE
ENDIF

DO WHILE
ENDDO

LOOP

SKIP

DO
RETURN

QUIT

DO CASE
  CASE
  OTHERWISE
ENDCASE

DATA MANAGEMENT COMMANDS

APPEND BLANK
REPLACE
FIND
#
EOF
DELETE
PACK
*
RELEASE

Index

A

Adding records, 95
Add order function, 61
APPEND, 95
APPEND BLANK, 160
Assignment statements, 3, 20, 149
@ GET, 152
@ SAY, 151

B

Boolean operators, 24
Businesses, small, 35

C

Calculations, 220
CASE, 26
Change order function, 65
Changing records, 99, 191
Changing records, coding, 182
Changing the database structure, 92, 131, 146
Character data, 2
CLEAR GETS, 154
Commands, database, 277
Commands, programming, 278

Comment statements, 31
Common key, 85
Comparison operators, 157
Comparisons, 24
Connectors, 106, 157
Control keys, 94
Corporations, large, 34
Correctness edit, 17
CREATE, 90
Customer list, 37

D

Data, 2
Data, arrangement of, 33
Data, calculated, 33
Data, designing, 32
Data, test, 31
Data, types, 32
Database, 84
Database, designing, 89
Database commands, 277
Database definition, 135
Database design, 134
Database manager, 85
Database programming, 2

Database structure, 87
Databases, creating, 143
Databases, multiple, 117
Data dictionary, 87
Data entry screens, 16
Data entry screens, coding, 173
Data redundancy, 116
Data validation, 18
Decimal places, 90
Decision statements, 4, 22
Defining the input, 7, 41
Defining the output, 6, 39
Defining the problem, 6
Defining the process, 7
Definition of databases, 135
DELETE, 162
Deleting records, 100, 186
Design, 6
Design for the system, 224
Designing processes, 13
Designing screens, 43
Dictionary, data, 87
Directory, customer, 41
Directory program, 199
DISPLAY, 97
Displaying records, 96, 107, 186

Display order function, 76
DISPLAY STRUCTURE, 92
DO CASE...ENDCASE, 159
Documentation, 6, 30
DO WHILE, 25, 64
DO WHILE...ENDDO, 158

E

Edit mask, 151
EJECT, 152
Environment, setting, 163
EOF, 161
ERASE, 152
Error messages, 18
Errors, 31

F

Fields, 86, 87
Files, 84
Files, splitting, 128
FIND, 111, 161
Flow, tracing the, 28
Flowcharting, 8-13
Flowerboxing, 18
Function charting, 13
Function hierarchy, 42, 59
Functions, 50
Functions:add, change, delete, display, 50

G

Generality, 14

H

Hierarchy of functions, 14, 42

I

IF-THEN-ELSE, 22
IF-THEN-ELSE...ENDIF, 157
Indexes, using, 104
Indexing, 85
Indexing databases, 146
Information, 2
Input definition, 41
Input/output statements, 4
Inputting records, 95
INT, 156
Interactive programs, 15, 35
Invalid data, 14
Inventory system, 81, 138

J

JOIN, 119
Joining multiple databases, 119

K

Key, common, 85
Keys, control, 94

L

Labels, mailing, 40
LIST, 96
Literals, 3
LOCATE, 110
Logical connectors, 157
Logical constructs, 11, 21-24, 157
Logical data, 32
LOOP, 158
Loop statements, 4

M

Mailing label program, 194
Main file, 206
Maintenance of databases, 130
Menu program, 50
Menus, 17, 18, 36
Menus, coding, 164
Menu system, 48
Microcomputers, 35
Modification of the database, 146
MODIFY STRUCTURE, 92
Modularity, 14
Module, 14
Multiple databases, 117
Multiple databases, designing with, 127
Multiple files, 216

N

Names, database, 86
Names, field, 86
Numeric data, 2

O

OPEN, 91
Opening file, 91
Operators, 157
Operators, boolean, 24
Ordering system, 51
Output, 5
Output commands, 150
Output definition, 39

P

PACK, 100, 162
Passive programs, 15
Printing reports, 216
Printing routines, 204
Print order form function, 77
Print shipping label function, 79
Problem definition, 6, 38

Q

Query, 88
QUIT, 159

R

Range edit, 17
READ, 152
RECALL, 100
Records, 3, 85
Records, changing, 182
Records, identification of, 32
Records, inputting, 95
Redundancy, data, 115
Relational database management system, 85
Relational databases, 58
RELEASE, 162
Remove order function, 75
Removing records, 186
REPLACE, 160
REPORT, 113, 125
Ripple effect, 130
Rules, field, 88

S

Screens, data entry, 173
Screens, designing, 43
Search, generic, 19
Search criteria, 110
Searching the database, 106
SELECT, 135, 206
Selected records, displaying, 107
Sequence logical construct, 22
Set commands, 163
SET PRINT ON, 150
SKIP, 161
Sorting the database, 102
Source code, 31
Speed, 127
Speed, determining, 129
Splitting files, 128
Statements, 3
Statements, assignment, 149
Storage, 127, 139
STORE, 149
STR, 155
Stubs, program, 17

Problem solving steps, 5
Process definition, 42
Program listings, 250
Programming commands, 278
Program stubs, 15
Prompt, 47
Pseudocoding, 9-12

Subfunctions, 51
Subroutine, 14
Subroutine call, 21
Subroutines, calling, 21
Subsidiary records, 210
Symbols, flowchart, 8, 9
System design, 224

T

Testing programs, 31
Totalling, 220
Totals, 19
TRIM, 155
Two-file system, 205
Two file system, 58

U

USE, 91

V

VAL, 155
Validity checking, 17
Variables, 3

Edited by Marilyn L. Johnson